By the Way

also by John Toren

Mountain Upside Down
The Seven States of Minnesota
Vacation Days

By the Way

essays on books and life,
music, birds, gardening, food,
firewood, and the great outdoors

John Toren

Copyright © 2013 John Toren, all rights reserved. No portion of this book may be reproduced in any form without the written consent of Nodin Press except for review purposes.

Cover art copyright © Bryan Iwamoto, all rights reserved. View more of Bryan's work at http://bryaniwamoto.tumblr.com.

ACKNOWLEDGEMENTS

Portions of the essays on Evan S. Connell and Javiar Marias originally appeared in *Rain Taxi Review*. Portions of the essay on pre-Columbian astronomy originally appeared in *The History Channel Magazine*. Longer versions of several essays first appeared in *Macaroni*.

It occurs to me that in this vaguely book-oriented collection, it might be appropriate for me to acknowledge a few friends and colleagues from the production side of the industry who have offered insight, support, and comaraderie over the years. Norton Stillman, with whom I've worked for more than three decades, would be on the top of that list. Others that come to mind, aside from those mentioned in the text, include Terry Monahan, Eric Lorberer, Marly Rusoff, Jim Tarbox, Margaret Hasse, Judith Palmatier, Jen Weverling, Dave Wood, Kate Thompson, Kathy Borkowski, Joni Sussman, Kay Brausen, Milt Adams, Joe Riley, Emilio DeGrazia, Barb Haselbeck, Craig Cox, Cary Griffith, Richard Sennott, Nicole Baxter, and Rachel Holscher.

Library of Congress Cataloging-in-Publication Data
Toren, John.
[Essays. Selections]
By the way : essays on life, literature, work, music, birds, rivers, food, firewood, and the great outdoors / John Toren.
pages cm
ISBN 978-1-935666-47-9
I. Title.
PS3620.O587476B9 2013
814'.6--dc23
2013005163

Nodin Press
530 North Third Street
Suite 120
Minneapolis, MN
55401

for Hilary

He who has made a thousand things and he who has made none, both feel the same desire: to make something.

– Antonio Porchia

If literature generally dares to speak, it is not at all because it is certain of its truth, but only because it is certain of its delight.

– Witold Gombrowicz

CONTENTS

PREFACE	9
ON BEING MOVED	13
ART SHANTY VILLAGE	22
MONTAIGNE: THE FIRST BLOGGER?	24
CLOSER TO HOME	28
WAS CONFUCIUS HAPPY?	30
INTERNET BIRDING	34
LATE MARCH	36
EVAN S. CONNELL	38
PINE NUTS	43
A GREAT THIRST	46
WISCONSIN FISH FRY	50
RED RIVER FRENCH CANADIANS	53
WAREHOUSE WORK	58
CRAVING FOR KALE	78
DENIS DIDEROT: VIBRATING STRINGS	80
CANZONIERE GRECANICO SALENTINO	91
ON THE ADVISABILITY OF ACCUMULATING BOOKS	95
GABRIEL MARCEL: E. M. CIORAN	114
POETRY – UNCERTAIN	125
LOVE SONGS AT THE WOMANS' CLUB	131
BEEHIVE CLUSTER	135
WORLD PRESS INSTITUTE	139

Kundera and Handke	146
Art Books and Book Arts	149
James Carter at the Dakota	153
The Thoreau You Don't Know	157
New Orleans Way	159
The Garden Gate	167
Scandinavians in Nisswa	172
Seventeen Miles on the Rum River	177
Steiner and Croce at Leech Lake	181
Tettegouche Backcountry	185
Bly at Blue Mound	187
Naturalist for a Day	193
Heartland Fall Forum	197
Running After Antelope	202
Twin Cities Book Festival	207
Culture Week: Frazier, Alexie, Dyer	210
The Absurd and the Impossible	218
Ford Madox Ford	221
November : Powerless	238
Javier Marias / Penelope Fitzgerald	240
Quest for Firewood	248
Madame Buffalo	255
The Master Class: Angela Hewitt	269
Advent Reflections	282

PREFACE

Though it may be naïve to admit it, I am repeatedly struck by how darned *interesting* life is. In the inconsequential events that make up a day or a week, the turn of the seasons, and the slow accumulation of more noteworthy stuff to which we eventually give the name "history," life presents itself as a churning flood (or a murmuring brook, at the very least) of novelties. Nowadays it's easier than ever to delve into a well-written history of saffron, deep-sea fishing, or the music of Dufay. Meanwhile, outside my window I just now spot a pileated woodpecker hammering away at the flank of a maple tree that was exposed when a *derecho* ripped off a large limb a few years ago. The trimmer who removed the limb from the roof of our house, with the aid of ropes the size of my wrist, told me, "The rest of this tree might not have more than ten years to live."

The essays collected in this book are records of a few incidental encounters I've had in that span of time—with books, rivers, friends and neighbors and food. A word of warning may be in order, however. You won't be able to make it through more than one or two before meeting up with some thinker from the past, vaunted or obscure as the case may be. That's also something that happens to interest me: how ideas percolate through the tissue of life.

For example, just now, as I was writing this little preface, I got to thinking of Leibniz's theory of monads. The great German polymath, in his idle hours, envisioned a world made up of countless metaphysical "points," as it were. In Leibniz's view, these self-organized points (or monads, as he called them) vary considerably in complexity, but each obeys an inner logic all its own. This might be a good way to describe life as we know it—a humming mix of creatures and substances, each pursuing its own agenda, each guided by the melody of its soul.

Perhaps I don't understand the theory very well, but it seems to me that Leibniz made two big mistakes. He imagined, first of all, that the actions of any given monad were utterly predetermined by its organizational logic. He further supposed that monads had no means of interacting with one another.

It seems to me, on the contrary, that the many and varied beings with which the universe is teeming exhibit a good deal of freedom in their actions—a point that should be obvious to anyone who's watched gulls or cormorants flying this way and that along the coast. By the same token, much of life's interest derives from how things—from how we—interact.

Few today put Leibniz's *Monodology* near the top of their reading list, I suspect. Nevertheless, his theories of emanative and reflective harmony do have an attractive ring. As for the most famous of his theories—that this is the best of all possible worlds—I'm not so sure. Maybe we should call it the best of all possible worlds, *so far*, and leave it at that.

A character in one of Diderot's dialogues remarks:

...the important thing is that you and I are, and that we are you and I...The best order of things, to my mind, is the one I am in, and a fig for the best of worlds if I form no part of it...

Italo Calvino was making a similar point, I think, when he began one of his essays:

A general explanation of the world and of history must first of all take into account the way our house was situated, in an area once known as "French Point"...

We find ourselves the midst of a pretty good world, I think. In the following essays I've attempted to describe some of the qualities and currents on display just outside our house.

By the Way

ON BEING MOVED

The minimum is the measuring unit in the realm of quantity. In the realm of values, the highest values are the measuring unit. Things can only be correctly evaluated by comparing them with the most valuable.

– José Ortega y Gasset

The scarlet elderberry, *sambucus pubens* (also known as the red-berried elderberry, the red elderberry, and the American red elderberry), is considered a weed by many gardeners. I noticed long ago, however, that it grows well under the spruce trees in my back yard. And so, as the lower branches of that once-beautiful line of evergreens began to die off, I made it a point to dig up the volunteer elderberries that sprouted up here and there and replant them strategically throughout the underbrush. The branches of the spruce trees have long since been lopped off to a height of twenty feet or more by our neighbor Derek, who owns the trees, but little matter—there is now a well-established bank of elderberry bushes filling in the lower reaches of the space those branches once occupied. It would be an exaggeration to call it a hedge. The shrubs shoot out willy-nilly, and the effect is more one of lofty mounds of leaves than of anything rigorous or formal. That's all the better, as far as I'm concerned. As an added bonus, the elderberry is covered in late spring by racemes of creamy white flowers, which are followed a few weeks later by clumps of tiny red berries that are equally dazzling in the shadows of our otherwise rather monochromatic backyard.

I can see why some people consider the plant a weed. It spreads seedlings liberally, and the soft, almost hollow branches quickly sprout to ungainly heights. When you break apart the

pruned branches you get some insight into its common name—
stinkbush. On the other hand, the time it takes to keep those
branches and seedlings under control amounts to only a few
minutes a year.

The elderberry is the first plant in our backyard to produce
leaves in the spring. I'd like to say that I'm moved at the sight
of this inaugural splash of green, but the truth is I'm seldom
much moved by anything in the early springtime. Yes, the winter
months can drag on, with too little snow for skiing and no vegetation to mask the increasingly harsh glare of the sun off the dry
brown dirt and naked underbrush; and yes, it's great fun to spot
the first returning bluebird, or hear the first coo of the mourning
dove, which enters the consciousness surreptitiously, subliminally,
like a half-remembered dream. But such experiences tend to be
short-lived and unduly intellectual. For me, early spring brings
with it neither the joy of rebirth nor the melancholy disappointment of unfulfilled promises, but simply a muteness of spirit. It's
a physiological thing, like a vitamin deficiency or a cold, and it
invariably passes.

Before long the fox sparrows are passing through the back
yard, scratching furiously amid the dead leaves with their talons,
as if to say, "This would be a lot easier if I had hands!" And then
it's the ruby-crowned kinglets with their nervous flitting and
their striking and exuberant songs. The brilliant color patch for
which this little bird is named is seldom visible, even at very
close range, but during the spring mating season you can often
see it from across the yard.

A few warm days, and although it's still very dry, that faint
haze of new color appears in the branches of the willows, the red
flowers of the maple trees, and the fuzzy catkins of the poplars.
Honeysuckles begin to leaf out. It's the time when we bring
the furniture back out onto the deck, when grilling once again
becomes a natural evening activity.

I was out a few days ago cutting down a few trees the size of
my forearm from the margin of our miniature forest, in the hope

that letting more light into the interior would help it to fill in. My neighbor Charles came out to grill a chicken, and we had our annual back-fence conversation.

Hilary and I carry our bikes up from the basement and take the first of those wonderful rides down the parkway, past the bridge construction north of Cedar Lake, and finally along the Twenty-Ninth Street Greenway, wending our way east past gardens and studios that remind us of Amsterdam. A visit to the Art Institute, a chat with friends who live nearby on their very urban porch, lunch at the Fuji-Ya, then back home along the fine new paths that circle the lakes, with spring clouds blustering past, followed by blasts of uncomfortably hot sunlight. We stop to watch the red-breasted mergansers, who are still doing their aquatic neck-dance out on Cedar Lake—in fact, everything is coming alive.

And then the thunderstorms. Gray clouds, distant rumbling, wind, calmness. The rain comes down as we emerge in late afternoon light from the Oak Street Theater, having watched yet one more of the intriguing foreign films that have been brought in for the local festival.

The other day, I selected a book off the shelf almost at random—*The Liar*, by Martin Hansen. I soon found myself immersed in a beautiful tale of the spring thaw on a tiny Danish island, as told by an observant and eccentric bachelor school-teacher from the mainland—a birdwatcher, a hunter, a naturalist, a parish clerk—about whom it might almost be said, a little grandiosely, "He saved others. Himself he could not save."

Yes, the world is coming alive, and so am I. Do you realize how long it's been since I've read an actual novel? Too many long and well-reasoned analyses of the debacle in Iraq, too many essays about cattle-rustling in Nevada, and life in the deserts of southern California, where we spent some time a few months ago. Too much George Perec! And too much Bach!

II

The world you have a presentiment of, when you are full of a new sorrow, or when you are moved by great music, or when you are struck by the beauty of a verse, or when you see a miracle in the misty dawn, tells you that you are a stranger on this earth.

—Martin Hansen: *The Liar*

And yet I was moved to ask myself, during that sluggish, somnambulant interval, What does it mean, then, to be moved? And I came to a number of conclusions, which, following the current fashion, I thought I might as well make into a list.

1) Being moved is a good thing, rather than a bad thing. Of course we're sometimes moved in a bad way, but when such an event takes place we refer to it differently, saying, for example, that we're "appalled" or "disgusted."

2) Being moved implies a degree of depth. It never happens that we're "superficially" moved. When such cases do arise we say, rather, that we've been surprised or manipulated.

3) Being moved entails a degree of passivity. We can't will ourselves to be moved. It's something that happens to us, rather than something we do. On the other hand, the experience has nothing of the indignity associated with being re-moved, as, for example, when the drunken baseball fan is forcibly removed from the stadium. The difference lies in the fact that although being moved suggests a degree of passivity, we also willfully enter into it, because the experience engages and quickens important parts of us.

4) The experience of being moved is self-contained. In this it differs from the experience of being inspired, for example, which impels us to attempt some remarkable creative act.

5) When we're moved, we're always moved by *something*. In this way being moved distinguishes itself from, say, being in a good mood.

6) The experience of being moved is by nature intuitive, rather than conceptual. We may be moved by the sight of a mother and daughter riding together on a bus, but we will never be moved by the logical elegance of an economic treatise. Inspired? Possibly. Exhilarated? Perhaps. Moved? Not really.

7) The experience of being moved is fleeting. It's too bad, I suppose. On the other hand, being moved often shifts our perspective, so that for a time everything we experience is given added luster, like the countryside after a rain, and in any case—

8) One's capacity for being moved is limited. Repeated exposure to a particular thing that moves us will result in a jaded disconnect, which is undesirable and distressing.

9) Being moved elevates us. Aristotle defines tragedy as "an imitation of an action that is serious and also complete in itself... with incidents arousing pity and fear, wherewith to accomplish its catharsis of such emotions." It seems to me, however, that when we're actually moved by something, we're not merely cleaned or purged or wrung out—we're also brought to a new level of awareness, or fitness.

It isn't an awareness that we can readily describe: "Now I see what I never saw before, namely...." but the effect is real nonetheless, and it differs dramatically from the one we get during a roller-coaster ride, for example, or while watching a scary movie.

10) Being moved grounds us. Strange but true.

◆

Attempts have been made, over the centuries, to create a more or less standard process by which we can effectively induce the experience of being moved, priming the pump of human emotion, as it were. I'm not referring only to drugs or alcohol. This is also what the passion of Christ is all about. During the period of Lent we're enjoined to deprive ourselves of things, and also to burrow inside ourselves in a continuing act of self-examination and contrition. The Lenten ceremonies, and especially the last few days, further intensify this period of harshness, negativity, and self-laceration. On Easter Sunday we return to light, to colored eggs, bunnies, green grass, and a risen Christ. Our spirits have been challenged, stirred, moved, and refreshed, in pace with the season. Whether, in fact, we'll live forever remains a matter of conjecture, but it would seem that at least we've learned how to live again—for now.

The word "passion" is itself somewhat curious. Although in common speech it has come, in our day, to mean "intensity of feeling" it derives from the same root as the words "passive" and "patient." Christ's passion is the story not of the things he did, but of what he allowed other to do to him. On the other hand, perhaps no amount of beatific sloganeering, no catalog of miracle cures can equal the power of a good and noble story of undeserved suffering that each of us can enter into emotionally—we've all been wrongly judged and punished for things we didn't do. And there is little harm, I think, in observing that the most moving parts of the story—the eleventh hour cry, for example—are also the most human ones.

This combination of passivity and of "entering into" experience lies at the heart of being moved, I think. One common experience that might help us to clarify how the process actually works is that of being picked up at the airport. We know our friends are coming to meet us, and we know very well what they look like—and yet, when we actually see their faces, standing amid a throng of strangers, our world lights up a little. The mood, the slant changes. To everything that we see in our mind's eye has been added the presence of living beings with whom we can interact. There is an engagement, a rapport, and it moves and also elevates us.

This spontaneous wringing out of the heart can be elicited by all sorts of experiences, of course. As Heraclitus remarked some six centuries before the birth of Christ, "He who would be wise must acquaint himself with a great many particulars." The great advantage of becoming familiar with things is that it allows us greater opportunities to interact and enter into them—to be moved.

I occasionally find that I'm moved simply by the sight of a shelf of books. I may have been in their presence daily for weeks or months, preoccupied by this or that literary project or computer game. I'm familiar with the books, of course, the titles, the authors—I bought them, after all—but they might as well be wallpaper, until that moment when I look again, as if for the first time, with what might be called "loving interest" and am surprised and moved by the delightful opportunities that are presenting themselves to me. I have once again become "available" to them. *Modern Hungarian Poets, Spain at the Dawn of History*, Handke's *A Moment of True Feeling, A Maigret Trio, Verdi with a Vengeance.* The heart aches with the desire to pull them all down at once and consume with the appetite of a Titan.

Our most moving experiences are often accompanied by a sharpening of inner vision, to a point that seems to encompass all of experience—both inner and outer—and this feeling has the virtue of being not in the least bit withdrawn or mystical. But whatever the intensity involved, being moved seems invariably to involve elements of both discovery and recollection. Perhaps the experience isn't that far removed from the "transport" that Plato associates with the experience of making contact with the Ideal.

◆

Plato's philosophy of Forms is not one to be entering into on a whim, I suppose, but it seems to me that it's rooted in experiences similar to the one we're exploring. In the *Phaedo*, for example, Socrates, in conversation with two Pythagoreans, asks the following question:

> *And must we not allow, that when I or anyone, looking at any object, observe that the thing he sees aims at being some other thing, but falls short of and cannot be that other thing, but is inferior, he who makes this observation must have had a previous knowledge of that to which the other, although similar, was inferior?*

The intuition Socrates describes here is negatively couched, but it's similar to the one I've just been describing. If we're disappointed by something, it can only be because we already have a vague idea of something else that's superior to it. If a work of art moves us, it expands our vision but at the same time it reminds us of things we'd forgotten; and if we feel outrage when witnessing an act of injustice, it's because we have some knowledge of what justice is, of how people *ought* to behave toward one another. We carry ideas around with us, in other words, and they guide our judgment.

The most important issue that Plato examines in his work is this: Where do such ideas come from? The obvious answer is that our ideas come from past experience. Once we've seen several trees, for example, we begin to understand what a tree is; if we come upon a tree with a broken limb, the fact will be evident to us based on our experience of trees. Yet this obvious theory, which goes by the name "induction," can't explain why it is that we occasionally feel the deficiency or absence of something we've never actually experienced fully. We don't come to know love or beauty, for example, by blasély encountering it time and again, and then developing a category to encompass it. On the contrary, impressions of this kind sneak up on us, seize us violently in ways that surprise, excite, and occasionally transform us. It's not induction but intuition at work here. Similarly, moral indignation rises unbidden when we come face to face with cruelty or injustice. We can be taught to ignore such feelings, but they arise spontaneously, and this simple fact lies at the root of all attempts to explain, describe, or defend the existence of the soul.

A little later in the *Phaedo* Socrates amplifies the sense of the remark I've quoted above, extending it beyond the specific issue he was discussing with his friends—it happened to be the notion of equality—to other aspects of experience that also involve us, not with empirical categories—tree, fish, supermarket—but with values:

...we are not speaking only of equality, but of beauty, goodness, justice, holiness, and of all which we stamp with the name of essence....

In the course of his work Plato suggests repeatedly that we have been endowed with a knowledge of values that comes to us from a source other than practical experience. At times he argues that we remember such things from a former life; at other times he suggests that the Forms themselves tangibly exist somewhere, and that we can occasionally make contact by means of either reasoning or eros. Both of these theories present difficulties, but the impulse upon which they're based is sound—it's the desire to objectify our values. Plato wants to give mass and concreteness to the essences that animate the experiences that move us. He wants to place value on a reasonable, rather than an emotional footing, so that we can continue to believe in beauty, truth, and goodness, at those times when we don't actually feel their reality and power.

Although this impulse is natural and understandable, I'm afraid it may be a little misguided. After all, it's a part of both the beauty and the mystery of living (and also the challenge and danger) that although we can sense, experience, and embody value, we can never actually possess it, the way we possess a tackle-box full of lures or a collection of Roman coins. We can't actually possess value because value is an attribute of actions, not of things. Or perhaps it might be more accurate, in light of the preceding remarks, to say that value is an attribute of interactions. I suppose it would not be too far off the beam to suggest that we can be moved only when we put ourselves in a position to spontaneously experience, suffer along with, enter into, and interact with people and things.

Art Shanty Village

On a gray and gloomy Sunday morning, we toddled over to Medicine Lake to see the Art Shanty village. The brightly colored buildings cheered us up. The spirit of "let's build a fort" is clearly alive and well, regardless of the electronic devices that clutter our lives, and the idea of gathering "forts" together into a little community on the ephemeral real estate of lake ice is brilliant. A spirit of child-like fun pervades the place, though the word "fort" isn't quite accurate to describe the various buildings set out at random along the east side of Medicine Lake, fifty or a hundred feet off shore.

At the center of the community is a Nordic Village Bridge, a project created by the staff of Concordia Language Villages. From the top of the bridge you can look down on the other structures below, though a troll sometimes lurks under the span, jabbing people who cross the bridge with his walking stick. The bridge's stated purpose is "to challenge visitors' assumptions about what it means to bridge cultures in our global community." Weddings are held in the vicinity regularly, though I suspect most of them are of the "renewing vows" variety. In any case, if you want to tie the knot, Sami- or Sicilian-style, this is definitely the place to come.

The Sashay Shanty is so full of vintage clothes you can hardly get inside the door. (They hold runway-style fashion shows from bygone eras periodically throughout the season.) The Dance Shanty is an empty building facing out toward the big lake where people can dance, often jiving to music from headphones provided at the shanty. (Don't want to upset the neighbors.)

The more contemplative Reflection Shanty is lined with mirrors but open on one end, so you can step inside and ogle the beauty of Medicine Lake in "infinite reflection." The Robo Shanty is a giant tin man—maybe twelve feet tall—that can accommodate

up to eight people within its limbs and torso. It's mounted on runners and can be pushed back and forth across the ice.

The Solar Ark Shanty has a wall tipped at an angle and designed to take in the sun's rays through tiny slits. If you lay in the hammock strung across the interior and look up you'll see a marvelous array of glittering lights—I'm sure it's even more impressive when the sun is out.

One shanty, fashioned from an old aluminum Airstream trailer, contains a functioning two-room sauna. (We'd neglected to bring our suits.) Another has a letter-press on which the village newspaper, the *Shantiquarian*, is printed. It gives new shades of meaning to the concept of cold-type printing.

The village also has a one-room schoolhouse where lectures are given, and a "capitol" building with a Wall of Dreams inside. Among the many dreams posted there on scraps of paper, two that Hilary noticed were "I want to marry James and have three beautiful children" and "NO PUBLIC FUNDING FOR THE STADIUM!"

We wandered the ice for an hour at least, though things had not really gotten started by the time we left. The dance hall remained closed, and just as we were leaving we passed the members of a jug band heading out onto the ice with their instruments.

Though T-shirts and hotdogs were on sale at the Social Shanty, the spirit of the village was largely uncommercial. Most of the shanties hold only a few guests at a time; the acrid smell of smoke from the wood-burning stoves (which I love) drifted by, and everything was pretty casual. A few adults were shooting baskets, others pedalled by on ice-bicycles in the shape of fish and foxes.

Out in the center of the village, near the bridge, an old-fashioned boom box sent music wafting—James Taylor or Hardanger fiddling—whenever anyone took the time to pedal the stationary bicycle that powered the contraption.

We took a whirl in an egg-shaped Sit-and-Spin, but skipped the big black Monsters-Under-the Bed Shanty, which you reach through a low-hung sliding door. It looked far too crowded for grown-ups to enter.

Next year we'll come later in the day. I wouldn't want to miss the production of *Waiting for Godot* performed on skates!

Montaigne: the First Blogger?

Even for those of us who are self-employed, and sometimes practically idle, the day after Thanksgiving seems more like a holiday than a work day. The morning sky was clear and sunny, though at this time of year even sunny days can be distinctly wan. A trip to the gym to run my obligatory three miles—the locker room is almost like a temple, with lots of people fiddling with their togs, zipping up gym bags, heading to the shower… and no one saying a word.

Back home, I begin to sift through a pile of old *New Yorkers* and come upon Jane Kramer's essay, "Me Myself, and I: What made Michel de Montaigne the first modern man?" It's an interesting subject, though I don't much like the subtitle. It seems to me that "modern man" is often fanatical, opinionated, pig-headed, all of which Montaigne especially hated and railed against in his essays. He was ever-fascinated by the things we don't know, but only think we know or feign knowing, and returned to that subject again and again. At one point he complained, with respect to the need felt by many to choose sides amid the religious strife of his day: "We are not allowed not to know what we do not know."

But if Montaigne were nothing more than a skeptic, endlessly reiterating how little we can really know about anything, his writings would not have endured as long as they have. His essays are often about things, not merely about our ignorance of things. Just take a glance at the table of contents: "Of sadness," "Of liars," "How the soul discharges its passions on false objects when true ones are wanting," "Of solitude," "Of warhorses," "We taste nothing pure," "Of smells," "Of honorary awards," and so on. At one point he writes:

> *I could wish that every one would write what he knows and as much as he knows, not about one subject alone, but about all others; for one may have some special knowledge or experience as to the nature of a river or a fountain, who about other things knows what everyone knows. He will undertake, however, in order to give currency to that little scrap of knowledge, to write on the whole science of physics. From this fault may spring grave disadvantages.*

Montaigne has a point here, though I'm not sure he always followed his own advice. It's not that he went overboard in padding his observations to make them sound more authoritative, but that he knew about a great many things which he kept to himself. Kramer's mini-bio makes it clear that Montaigne was a man of the world, serving as mayor of Bordeaux, head of an estate a day's ride east of the city, and sometime counselor to Henry IV, the future king of France. Yet to a large degree, his essays consist of references to classical authors such as Horace and Livy, well-turned nuggets of philosophic wisdom, things he's read about the customs of other nations, and generalizations about "human nature"—a thing that he felt did not exist. There is not much that brings us into direct contact with sixteenth-century Aquitaine to be found in them.

Similarly, we might approve when he remarks, "All our efforts can not so much as reproduce the nest of the tiniest birdling, its contexture, its beauty, and its usefulness; nay, nor the web of the little spider." But that being the case, why does Montaigne spent so little time describing such beautiful creations? Perhaps it's because he took an overriding interest in the "inner" aspect of things human—and himself above all else. Details of politics, husbandry, clothing, cuisine, and his natural surroundings often fell by the wayside, too mundane to relieve his persistent melancholy.

We may be thankful that Montaigne had both the leisure and the talent to bring a Gallic *joie de vivre* to those habits and foibles of human conduct that we exhibit repeatedly without reflecting much on them. (The first modern man? Maybe Kramer is right.) He considered conversation to be the supreme art, and turned his ruminations into internal dialogues, challenging his own assertions, wandering hither and yon, holding the "chain" of thought (such as it is) together by a supple prose style that remains umatched even today, and makes Francis Bacon, to take an example from among his contemporaries, sound like an utter blockhead. You can open the essays to almost any page with profit and amusement. To read more than two or three essays in a row is sometimes difficult.

Montaigne reworked his essays again and again; in the Modern Library edition translated by Donald Frame, superscript markings indicate which sentences date from which revisions. In this respect Montaigne doesn't much resemble modern bloggers, who seldom rewrite anything. The comparison is apt only in so far as Montaigne's focus on personal and often inconsequential reflections anticipates his modern confreres.

Montaigne might have benefited from the advice of an editor. (Couldn't we all!) His reiterations of exemplary events and cautionary tales from classical history are often dull. And readers may soon tire of his repeated assertion that both his character and his views change as easily and as often as the wind.

> *I cannot fix my subject. He is always restless, and reels with natural intoxication…I do not portray his being; I portray his passage…from day to day, from minute to minute…*

How are we to reconcile this remark with the one that follows a few pages later?

> *Habitually, I do what I do with all my being, and keep step with myself; I seldom do anything that hides from and escapes my reason, and that is not guided more or less by the concurrence of all my faculties, without division and without internal rebellion. My judgment takes all the blame, and keeps it for good; for it has been the same almost since birth, with the same character, the same inclinations, the same strength.*

The Italian savant Benedetto Croce once wrote a book called *Shakespeare: Corneille: Ariosto*. That strikes me as an odd trio, though perhaps the thrust of the book was to highlight differences rather than similarities. To my mind the trio that calls out for simultaneous analysis is *Shakespeare: Montaigne: Cervantes*. These writers differ in temperament but are equal in stature, and they stand at the peak of their respective genres. (If it were necessary to include an Italian in the group, my candidate would be Castiglione rather than Ariosto, though his chapter would be a short one.) In the introduction to one recent edition of the *Essays*, Stuart Hampshire offers a different trio for consideration—Montaigne, Diderot, Stendhal—whom he describes as "the three great monuments of secular French sensibility."

CLOSER TO HOME

In a recent travel piece in the *New York Times*, novelist Nicholas Delbanco described a trip he and his wife made to Provence, a region they first explored on an extended honeymoon forty years ago. Hilary and I have been to Provence several times but not recently, and I was curious to see how the return visit struck him. (Many years ago I read and was impressed by one of Delbanco's early novels, *Small Rain*, which is set in the south of France.)

For Delbanco, there were not many surprises. Things have changed, he says, but there is still plenty of beauty and culture to be enjoyed, especially if you move further up into the hills with bigger wads of cash in your pocket. Even the Luberon Valley, he tells us, has not been utterly ruined by the outlandish popularity of Peter Mayle's books—which inspired one of our visits years ago.

What *did* surprise me was the digression Delbanco made, early on in the piece, to ponder the issues associated with seeing things anew that you already think you know pretty well:

> *It's difficult to know, in the wake of Heisenberg and Einstein, what is absolute, what relative, and why. Do we change as witnesses, or does that which we witness change, or both; does it alter because of the viewing, and is our estimate altered by the consciousness of sight? Think of a train track and moving train; does the world pass by while we sit still, or is it the reverse? These problems of philosophy and mathematics are personal riddles also; was it always just like this, and did we fail to notice? For we have changed more than the landscape, no matter how the locals complain that the landscape has changed.*

What I find odd about this passage is that Delbanco is presenting as "philosophical riddles" questions that most of us know the answers to intuitively. More understandable, but also more distressing, are the references to physicists whose opinions have little to do with the issue. Most of us realize that when we look out the window of a train, the train is moving, while the earth is pretty much staying put. We note that when the engineer builds up a head of steam, we lurch ahead; when he puts on the brakes, we stop.

Delbanco's real concern is to ponder the conundrum of a seemingly static personal point of view in the midst of an ever-changing world. No matter how old we get or how radically we change, we seem to remain, in some basic sense, "ourselves." When we return to a place (or run into an old friend) this change/no change is thrown into relief as distant memories collide with the immediacy of new experiences.  The event can be rich with pleasant nostalgia or tinged with a dreadful sense of loss or disparagement. It all depends.

What does all this have to do with Heisenberg and Einstein? Nothing. Centuries before anyone had examined an electron, Heraclitus and other philosophers were telling us that we can never really be certain of anything. After all, we've all been certain of things that have turned out *not to be true*. It follows that certainty is a feeling, rather than an attribute of truth.

In any case, there is no use protesting the fact that with time, *everything* changes. We change, the landscape changes, the people change, the prices change. You never step into the same river twice, and if you remain standing on shore, reluctant to take the plunge, the winds of time flutter by just the same. You continue to change in spite of yourself. In the end, nothing is stable, nothing is absolute, and the sooner we get used to it the better off we'll be.

Delbanco's description of Provence, a region that has retained much of its appeal through time, carries, among other things, an unspoken message of maturation, I think. The things we respond to remain the same—food, wine, lavender, rosemary, history, comfort; he speaks nostalgically of "the insouciance of youth" but the rooms the couple stay in cost $600 per night. The question is: As we age, do these "romantic" aspects of travel sink in further, resonate more deeply? I would agree with Delbanco (though he doesn't come right out and say so) that they do. But we also begin to learn, as we age, that you don't have to travel as far as you thought to meet up with them.

❦

WAS CONFUCIUS HAPPY?

In *The Happiness Equation*, an economist at the University of York (Nick Powdthavee) examines the relationship between various economic indicators and human happiness. The results could be encapsulated in a single time-worn cliché: "Money can't buy happiness."

It's remarkable, when you come to think about it, that the author was probably well-paid to reconfirm this far-from-startling conclusion. I'm reminded of a slightly less-well-known adage, "Money isn't everything...but it sure beats the heck out of whatever comes in second."

I don't have a lot of money, and I haven't read the book in question, but I consider myself a fairly happy chap. The relevant adage here might be: Happy is the man who's found his work. In my case the work consists of playing around with ideas like these.

Here are a few other things I've noticed that may bear on the issue:

30   *BY THE WAY*

– People who have read a good novel cherish it as if it were a god.
– People who've just returned from a vacation sometimes reach a pitch of excitement when describing a noisy motel room they slept in or the lackluster food they were served at a restaurant in the Travestere.

There is a passage in one of Willa Cather's novels, maybe *My Antonia*, that made an impression on me. I looked it up just now on-line:

> "*I was something that lay under the sun and felt it, like the pumpkins, and I did not want to be anything more. I was entirely happy. Perhaps we feel like that when we die and become a part of something entire, whether it is sun and air, or goodness and knowledge. At any rate, that is happiness; to be dissolved into something complete and great...*"

An interesting notion, though perhaps an even better thing would be to become immersed in something great and *incomplete*. It would give you something to do.

Fernando Pessoa touches on a similar theme a little more obliquely in a poem about a shepherd:

> *And if sometimes, in my imagination,*
> *I desire to be a small lamb*
> *(Or to be the whole flock*
> *So as to be scattered across the hillside*
> *As many happy things at the same time),*
> *It's only because I feel what I write when the sun sets*
> *Or when a cloud passes its hand over the light*
> *And a silence sweeps through the grass.*

Politics can be a noble pursuit, but talking about politics is sometimes dull. Too often it boils down to reiterating things we read in the newspaper and expressing our exasperation that everyone in Alabama doesn't think just like us.

So, what should people talk about?

The other day, Hilary and I were sitting on the deck. We were enjoying a glass of wine, we had a candle burning in our dragonfly candleholder. The crickets were chirping from every corner of the darkness. I brought up the disconnect between happiness and money that I mentioned just now, and Hilary began to tell me about what Karen Armstrong has to say about Confucius in her recent book, *Twelve Steps to a Compassionate Life*. At that point I leapt from my chair and said, "I've got an idea, let's see what Confucius himself has to say."

I ducked back into the house and returned a few minutes later with three translations of *The Analects*: the groundbreaking Arthur Waley translation (1924); the Penguin edition translated by D. C. Lau (1979); and the recent David Hinton translation (1998).

We began to read out loud, back and forth, the same passage in different translations. And then we would discuss which we preferred. Let me give you an example:

> *The Master said: "Of villages, Humanity is the most beautiful. If you choose to dwell anywhere else, how can you be called wise?" (Hinton)*

> *The Master said, "Of neighborhoods, benevolence is the most beautiful. How can a man be considered wise who, when he has the choice, does not settle for benevolence?" (Lau)*

> *The Master said, "It is Goodness that gives to a neighborhood its beauty. One who is free to choose, yet does not prefer to dwell among the Good—how can he be accorded the name of wise?" (Waley)*

In the example above, we agreed that Hinton's falls short, due to a somewhat chilly translation of that essential Confucian concept, Jen, as Humanity. Other scholars have proposed love, altruism, kindness, charity, humaneness, compassion, magnanimity, human-heartedness, perfect virtue, and true manhood. Waley's version is probably the best here, though we didn't invariably find that to be the case. Nor did we always agree on which translation we preferred. Consider this example, one of my favorites:

The Master said: 'At fifteen I devoted myself to learning, and at thirty stood firm. At forty I had no doubts, and at fifty understood the mandate of Heaven. At sixty I listened in effortless accord. And at seventy I followed the mind's passing fancies without overstepping any bounds.' (Hinton)

The Master said, 'At fifteen I set my heart upon learning. At thirty, I had planted my feet firm upon the ground. At forty, I no longer suffered from perplexities. At fifty, I knew what were the biddings of Heaven. At sixty, I heard them with docile ear. At seventy, I could follow the dictates of my own heart; for what I desired no longer overstepped the boundaries of right.' (Waley)

The Master said, 'At fifteen I set my heart on learning; at thirty I took my stand; at forty I came to be free from doubts; at fifty I understood the Decree of Heaven; at sixty my ear was atuned; at seventy I followed my heart's desire without overstepping the line.' (Lau)

Here, I think Lau has the edge, especially in the phrase, "At sixty my ear was atuned."

Mr. Powdthavee observes in his book about happiness that the rich are slightly more anxious than the poor; his findings also suggest that many people are concerned not only about the size of their paychecks, but also about how their pay compares to that of their neighbors.

This strikes me as a bit odd.

In Book Six of *The Analects* Confucius remarks:

The Master said, "To be fond of something is better than merely to know it, and to find joy in it is better than merely to be fond of it."

Internet Birding

There is no way to go birding on the internet, because birds can't survive for long in the ether. You can look at photos of birds online, or play Angry Birds, and you can find all sorts of information online about what birds people have seen, and where.

The other day, a friend of mine passed along the web link to the Great Backyard Bird Count. Between February 17 and 20, we were all supposed to keep an eye on the feeder or head out into the field, keeping track of our sightings and tallying the results at the official web site. This has been going on for years, though it always struck me as odd that such an event would take place in the winter, when there aren't many birds around.

On President's Day Hilary and I left town on a field trip and ended up at Spring Lake Regional Park, a few miles west of Hastings. This under-used park occupies a bluff overlooking Gray Cloud Island and the Mississippi. It's one of the most spectacular panoramas in the Twin Cities, and the drama is enhanced by the contrast between the strips of white ice, the blue open water, and the gray leafless island trees that drape themselves across the river landscape.

We hiked along the edge of Scharr's Bluff, where Indians camped eight thousand years ago as the raging torrents of Glacial River Warren flooded past below them. Then we drove down into a hardwood forest in a lower section of the park and took a hike past a succession of archery stands to the banks of the Mississippi.

As we emerged from the woods we spotted a cluster of ducks—scores of mallards, a few golden eye, and four mergansers that I took to be the red-breasted sort, due to the distinctive top-notch on the female. A few minutes later a genuine birding party arrived and one of the men asked us what we'd seen.

"Were they common mergansers or red-breasted mergansers?" he wanted to know.

"My understanding is that the female red-breasted has that distinctive top-notch. Isn't that so?"

"Actually, the common can have that, too," he corrected me politely. "A better sign in the female is whether the head coloring ends abruptly or in a blurred muddle."

"Yeah, I think they were red-breasted," I held to my story.

We made our way back to the car, leaving the group to rue the fact that the birds they'd come to see had been spooked by novices who didn't know their winter ducks!

The best sighting we had was on the way out, when we spotted a pair of red-tailed hawks sitting one behind the other on two branches at eye level, maybe five feet apart, as if they were posing for a fiftieth wedding anniversary photo. Sweet.

Back home, I took a look online at the merganser issue and came across such remarks as

> ...*One point that's not usually mentioned is the extension of maxillary feathering on the side of the bill. It forms a wedge or triangle on red-breasted. On common the feathering comes straight down and doesn't project into a point. However, this only works in North American populations.*

Somewhere along the way, I was reminded of the link to the Great Backyard Bird Count, and though we hadn't been tallying anything, I filled out a report, including a few species we'd seen in the back yard: Canada Goose (80), Mallard (60), Common Goldeneye (4), Red-Breasted Merganser (4), Wild Turkey (6), Bald Eagle (1), Red-Tailed Hawk (2), Red-bellied Woodpecker (1), Downy Woodpecker (1), Black-capped Chickadee (20)...and so on.

Here's where the internet begins to strut its stuff. Once I'd submitted my list, I took a look at what other Minnesotans had seen. (You can reference the data by species.) Only a single birder had seen red-breasted mergansers—in Duluth. On the other hand, observers in Hastings, Rosemount, Fridley, Burnsville,

Internet Birding 35

Minneapolis, South St. Paul, and Bloomington (all Mississippi towns) had seen common mergansers. The handwriting was on the wall.

I resubmitted my tally, changing red-breasted to common… and downgraded my skill level from "excellent" to "good."

Late March

It's been a typical spring…it just came a month too early. This has made everyone uneasy, including me. Then again, a year ago I was writing in my journal:

It's a miserable gray cold rainy day, windy, the river's rising. They'll be out sandbagging in Stillwater, Hastings, and Saint Paul. Maybe they already are.

A few days later I noted:

We got some icy slush last week, topped in the evening by maybe six new inches of snow. Horrendous driving.

Last year I made my inaugural bike tour down the parkway and around Cedar Lake on April 11. This year it was March 12.

So who's complaining?

The birds returned early, following the bugs north, I guess. I spotted a fox sparrow rummaging through the leaves behind the house on March 15. Four days later I drove up to Cold Spring to give a travel talk and came upon my first red-winged blackbirds and bluebirds along the way. They'd probably been in the neighborhood

36   *By the Way*

for a week. The robins have long since returned in large numbers. And now the ratchet-trill of the chipping sparrow begins to fill the morning air.

On a cool and sunny spring afternoon, I find myself sitting on the deck, ruing the disappearance of the tiny, pale green leaves, which have given way to the yellow-green leaves, soon to be followed by the dark green leaves. The seed pods on the silver maple are bright red, though hardly visible without the help of binoculars.

Ohio buckeye trees are sprouting here and there across the yard. I know they won't do well in those shady places but find it difficult to pull them up. I did succeed in removing some of the ferns that have been inching their way across the terraced garden under the bedroom window for years.

Cardinals and goldfinches arrive and depart, but the juncos are also still among us. There are more juncos than people in North America. Soon they'll be fanning out across the pine woods of Canada—a fitting subject for a children's book by Margaret Wise Brown, don't you think?

On such an afternoon, I find it difficult to focus on Tony Judt's *Thinking the Twentieth Century*, which I've been doing a pretty good job of making my way through.

> *To be a revolutionary Marxist was to make a virtue of your rootlessness, not least the absence of religious roots, while clinging—even if half-knowingly—to a style of reasoning which would have been very familiar to every Hebrew school student.*

Or how about this one?

> *For Hayek, in short, the lesson of Austria and indeed the disaster of interwar Europe at large boiled down to this: don't intervene, and don't plan. Planning hands the initiative to those who would, in the end, destroy society (and the economy) to the benefit of the state. Three quarters of a century later, this remains for many people (especially here in the U.S.) the salient moral lesson of the twentieth century.*

I'm more inclined to return to a potted essay on Plato's theory of ideals that I'm forever revising:

And the soul is like the eye: when resting upon that on which truth and being shine, the soul perceives and understands, and is radiant with intelligence; but when turned towards the twilight of becoming and perishing, then she has opinion only, and goes blinking about, and is first of one opinion and then of another, and seems to have no intelligence.

In my view, "becoming and perishing" is a part of truth and being. These days we stand in daily awe of the "becoming" part. Consider the serviceberry over there at the edge of the woods, just now creeping into bloom. My mother, who died in 1980, loved this humble, spindly shrub that does its best to look like a tree. So do I. What to do, what to do?

❧

EVAN S. CONNELL

When the novelist and poet Evan S. Connell died in the winter of 2013, American letters lost a true original. From the beginning, Connell viewed the dolorous aspects of modern life with a mordant glee that was more European than American. Yet his touch was usually humane—more Chekovian that Kafkaesque. For example, his depiction of the bourgeois milieu of post-war Kansas City in *Mrs. Bridge* is pitiless, but also affectionate; and his Pulitzer Prize winning study of Custer, *Son of the Morning Star*, maintains a literary standard we seldom meet up with in books about the West.

38   BY THE WAY

Connell's early essays, recently reprinted in the volume *The Aztec Treasure House*, exhibit a boyish fascination with the arcana of lost cultures, death-defying exploration, and other Gee-Whiz! subjects. Meanwhile, his book-length poem *Points for a Compass Rose* (which appeared during the Vietnam War) makes use of similar material to weave a subtle critique of the vanity and fruitlessness of imperialist pretensions.

Connell had a few misfires—*The Alchymist's Journal* comes to mind—but the quality of his work was almost invariably high, and the musicality of his prose kept readers moving ahead during those patches when the references were truly obscure.

The works mentioned above would provide any reader with a few months of engaging reading. Also noteworthy among Connell's early works is the short novel *The Connoisseur*, which describes in the simplest terms how a casual interest in pre-Columbian antiquities can become a sanity-threatening obsession.

In the short biography, *Francisco Goya* (2005), Connell once again chose a subject well-suited to his predilections. Of peasant stock and vaguely liberal ideals, Goya rose within the ranks of painters and eventually distinguished himself to a degree that brought him to the attention of the Spanish court. By early middle age, Goya was the most famous painter in Spain, receiving generous commissions from wealthy patrons while also serving the king's family. Yet Goya depicted the superstition and violence of the times no less effectively than the fragile beauty of its gilded upper crust—sometimes within the scope of a single canvas. His renderings of the irrationality and fanaticism of the masses have never been surpassed. His shaky position in the art pantheon—a few critics of every age have found his technique shoddy and his subject-matter disgusting—further enhances his appeal as an object of the kind of extended meditation at which Connell was adept.

Yet Connell's brief biography isn't a book for everyone. In the first place, it lacks illustrations. Readers without an appropriate coffee-table book near at hand may, at times, find Connell's descriptions of the paintings and lithographs more frustrating than insightful. Then again, the economy of Connell's prose, and the obvious pleasure he takes in unanswered questions, may leave some readers with the unpleasant sense that he's failed to bring the "real" Goya fully to life. To those who are familiar with his style, on the other hand, the book offers all the pleasures we've come to expect from the master story-teller and literary high-priest of history's curiosities and conundrums.

Connell begins with characteristic obliqueness, introducing us to the vastly wealthy and irresistibly beautiful Duchess of Alba, whom Goya not only painted several times but lived with for seven months. Connell doesn't describe the duchess, however, so much as he relates what others have said about her, and we've read no more than a page before we come upon the following passage:

As good students of female nature may have guessed by now, the Duchess was cruel, an essential trait of mankillers rich or poor. Certain biographers assert the opposite, that she was kindness itself. No doubt this could be just as true; after all, a woman isn't a bolt of cloth, identical in texture from thread to thread.

Connell relishes this clutch of evident contradictions, and he's clearly fascinated by the woman who possesses them. In the space of a few pages he passes that interest on to us, establishing an emotional anchor for the unconventional story that follows.

In the course of tracing the trajectory of Goya's own life, Connell examines the man's paintings, discusses his friends and court appointments, speculates on the sources and significance of his imagery, and analyses his correspondence. He also sifts through the comments of other biographers and art-historians, weighing opinion against opinion, while only occasionally offering one himself. "One critic thinks the composition stilted, satirical, family members anemic...Another critic thinks it an affectionate family portrait." What does Connell think? He doesn't say.

Connell recognizes that in order to provide an effective portrait of the artist who executed *The Caprichos*, *The Disasters of War*, the famously equivocal portrait of King Charles and his family, and "The Third of May," he'll have to make the historical background comprehensible to those of us who know little of Spanish history. It's not an easy task. The protagonists in that story are mediocre and the moral valences are anything but clear. Napoleon, his brother Joseph, the Duke of Wellington, and various other foreigners offer striking personalities, and they're all liberal in one way or another...but they're intruders. Meanwhile Charles III, Charles IV, Godoy, and Queen Maria Teresa are distinguished largely by their venality, lack of vision, superstitious religiosity, and vice. Connell's story-telling skills come fully into play here, and his rendering of the times is vivid. In fact, Goya drops from sight repeatedly as we follow one or another thread of the Peninsular Campaigns, only to reappear a few pages later, moving in lofty social circles or in service to the king.

Although Connell has steeped himself in his subject, his tone remains light rather than scholarly throughout, and he doesn't hesitate to get personal from time to time. He compares Goya's wife, who seemed to care about nothing but frilly clothes, to the housekeeper Connell's parents employed when he was a child; and in his efforts to explain why many Spaniards seem so sympathetic to authoritarian institutions, he offers an affectionate portrait of some members of the Guardia Civil with whom he travelled on a train during his student days, their machine-guns stacked casually on the seats beside them.

In his analysis of the return of repression to Spain following the downfall of the Napoleonic regime, Connell relates matter-of-factly:

I remember one afternoon in a Barcelona cafe talking to a Canadian who said that on a narrow street of the Gothic quarter he had been robbed. He reported this to the police and the next day he got his wallet back. Secret police were everywhere and just about everywhere you looked there stood the Guardia Civil with those guns. Barcelona during the early 1950s was not contaminated by error, law and order prevailed; from which you may conclude that a fascism government is best. Some people think so. It's a matter of opinion. It depends on your values. You might conclude that Ferdinand acted on behalf of Spain in the name of national security when he restored the Inquisition. The garotte, he quite rightly thought, was an effective way to stifle dissent. He announced that every heretic would have his tongue bored through with a red hot iron.

"Some people think so...It depends on your values." It's not entirely obvious, once again, what Connell's view is. In any case, he's intrigued by the fanaticism of those dark times and he admires Goya's ability to enter into it and convey its force. Yet he's chosen his subject, I suspect, because Goya's depiction of that fanaticism is also a rejection of its cruelty and blindness. In the pages of this marvelous book Connell, too, has summoned dark forces and given them their due. He's given us the opportunity to look squarely at the irrationality and violence—a grim reality of those times, and of our own—while also convincing us that from the midst of such a mire, both then and now, works of beauty and significance do occasionally emerge.

I MET CONNELL once. I ran into him in the plaza in Santa Fe one morning at dawn, and though he was polite, he seemed eager to be off. At the time he was hard at work on a book about the Crusades, or so he told me. This would be *Deus Lo Volt!*, which stares down on me to this day from the top shelf of the bookcase. I've never read it.

I was hoping Connell would invite us over for coffee that morning. Evidently he had better things to do. He did agree to sign a postcard I'd bought a few minutes earlier in the lobby of La Fonda, and when I went back to buy another one, I said, "Hey! I just ran into Evan S. Connell in the plaza!"

The elderly lady behind the counter replied, in a purring voice, "He comes in here quite often. Isn't he a *nice* man."

PINE NUTS

The price per pound was roughly half what they charge at a discount supermarket. And a few big clumps of basil happened to be sitting on the kitchen counter back home, waiting to be chopped into pesto and frozen for the winter. So I bought the great big bag of pine nuts at Costco at $11 dollars a pound, little considering that due to their high oil content, pine nuts go bad quickly, and a pound and a half of those tasty little nuts will take you a long ways into the autumn.

We made the pesto—though a friend later reminded me that it's better to toast the pine nuts in a frying pan and sprinkle them on top just before serving. And we gave some to my mother-in-law for her birthday. At that point I began to dig out a few tried and true recipes…

Why are pine nuts so expensive? Because they take eighteen months to mature (which seems like a very odd life-cycle to me) and must be harvested by hand. I can remember driving north from Pie Town to Fence Lake, New Mexico, through several monotonous hours of miniature hills covered with juniper and piñon pine—a Georgia O'Keefe nightmare. There were pick-up trucks parked in the ditches here and there, and we finally figured out that folks were out gathering pine nuts. We stopped at a café—it may have been in Quemado—and I was pleased to listen in on the conversation of two chunky young Indian men in the booth next door. It seems that one absent member of the party wasn't pulling his weight. I heard one of them say, "Next year, I think it should be just you, me…and grandma."

Pine nuts grow best at elevations between six and eight thousand feet. That's the zone at which the snowpack is likely to linger, providing run-off well into the summer. But there's no telling if a crop of nuts will mature or wither in any given year.

Harvesting pine nuts doesn't have to be a drag, however. The Spanish composer Enrique Granados published a set of *canciones amatorias* in 1915 that includes a number called "They Went into the Pine Woods."

> *Country girls from Cuenca go up into the pine-woods,*
> *Some for the pine nuts, some for the dancing.*
> *As they dance and shell the pine nuts*
> *The pretty country girls enjoy*
> *Throwing the darts of love at one another.*
> *Between the branches—when blind Cupid*
> *Asks the sun for his eyes to see them better—*
> *You can see them treading on the eyes of the sun.*
> *Some go for the pine-nuts, some go for the dancing.*

I'm not sure what's going on up there in the woods, but it sounds a little more interesting than "You, me, and grandma."

Quite a few species of pine trees produce edible nuts. The pine nuts they sell at roadside stands in the American Southwest are very different from the ones we buy at the store, being larger and less delicate in flavor. (Maybe they'd taste better if I shelled them.) The bag I bought at Costco came from China, where, it's said, they mercilessly denude the trees of branches to make the job of harvesting easier, and then move on. In any case, these Chinese nuts are as good as any I've tasted. In fact, the pesto we made the other day was almost too rich.

I also recently made a salad of fresh beets, Gorgonzola, pine nuts, and vinaigrette—you can't miss with that combination.

But the best of the dishes I cooked up is an orzo salad that I rank among the most pleasing concoctions in the world. What's interesting about this salad is that when you take a bite, you don't taste much of anything. Little bits of flavor pull you this way and that, and only gradually does the full impact hit home.

I once made a batch of this stuff and something seemed wrong. I finally figured out that the raisins were sticking to each other in little clumps. You need every little touch, in the right proportion, or the thing won't go.

Orzo Salad with
Lemon, Feta, and Pine Nuts

¼ cup olive oil
2 tablespoons fresh lemon juice
1½ teaspoons minced garlic
½ teaspoon dried oregano
½ teaspoon kosher salt, plus more as needed
⅛ teaspoon freshly ground pepper, plus more as needed
½ teaspoon sugar
1 cup orzo
¼ cup pine nuts
¼ cup golden raisins
3 tablespoons finely chopped black olives
3 tablespoons finely chopped red onion
¼ cup thinly sliced fresh basil
2 oz. feta cheese, crumbled

Combine the olive oil, lemon juice, garlic, oregano, salt, pepper, and sugar in a jar. Shake and set aside.

Cook orzo according to package directions. Meanwhile, toast the pine nuts in a dry skillet over medium-low heat. Pay attention, they burn easily. They're done when they start to turn golden and you can smell them.

Drain the orzo and transfer it to a bowl. Add the dressing to the hot pasta and toss to coat. Let cool to room temperature.

Add the pine nuts, raisins, olives, red onion, and basil and stir to combine. (Separate the raisins by hand if they clump.) Add the feta and toss lightly. Taste and adjust the seasonings to your liking.

A GREAT THIRST

All the great philosophical ideas of the past century—the philosophies of Marx and Nietzsche, phenomenology, German existentialism, and psycho-analysis—had their beginning in Hegel; it was he who started the attempt to explore the irrational and integrate it into an expanded reason which remains the task of our century. He is the inventor of that Reason, broader than the understanding, which can respect the variety and singularity of individual consciousnesses, civilizations, ways of thinking, and historical contingency but which nevertheless does not give up the attempt to master them in order to guide them to their own truth.

— Merleau-Ponty: *Sense & Non-Sense*

I came across this passage the other day; it struck me as worth pondering. A bit later in the essay, Merleau-Ponty describes the movement of consciousness as one from a subjective "certainty" to action, which (according to Hegel) always has unexpected consequences. These consequences are an objective truth of sorts, in the light of which man modifies his project, acts with somewhat greater discernment, until at last man in his subjectivity finally brings himself into line with objective truth and "he becomes fully what he already obscurely was."

What makes this little essay interesting is the odd mixture of accurate depiction of certain aspects of Hegel's phenomenology (rare enough) and bogus French existential terminology (common enough). What seems to be altogether missing from Merleau-Ponty's analysis is any understanding of the impetus behind the dialectical process Hegel is describing.

At one point he remarks, astutely, with regard to Hegel's phenomenology, "Absolute knowledge, the final stage in the evolution of the spirit as phenomenon wherein consciousness at last becomes equal to its spontaneous life and regains its self-possession, is perhaps not a philosophy but a way of life."

But the weakness of his analysis here, and of the French existentialist analysis generally, lies in the mistaken notion that the end to be achieved is some sort of personal peace as a result of elevated consciousness. On the contrary, Hegel's evolution of spirit is driven by a dim awareness of the ideal—which is not the same thing as knowing oneself. (Though the two are related in an interesting way.) The end result of "the evolution of spirit" is the creation of an environment within which that spirit can continue to flourish. It is not Nirvana. It's not the Kingdom of Heaven—though that phrase brings us nearer to the truth. No, it's civilization.

Everyone has a different notion of "the ideal." Some are simple and narrow in focus; others are far-reaching and complex. And in fact, we all have far more ideals than we commonly recognize. It isn't a matter of the Ideal, as if there were a single thing toward which all our energies were directed. Whatever moves us to act is, in some sense, an ideal. Individuals are often motivated by a really good meal, sex, athletic competition, moments of solitude, natural beauty, art, the administration of justice, lively conversation, handyman projects, the passing countryside, religious awe, the challenge of raising a family, teaching, and even the satisfactions of physical labor.

We tend to equate "the ideal" with the ultimate, but that equation is misleading. There is not, and never will be, an "ultimate" novel, crème brûlée, or scientific discovery. And what would the ultimate benevolent act be?

George Steiner may have been referring to something of the sort when he wrote:

> *The intuition—is it something deeper than even that?—* *the conjecture, so strangely resistant to falsification, that there is "otherness" out of reach, gives to our elemental existence its pulse of unfulfllment. We are the creatures of a*

A GREAT THIRST 47

great thirst. Bent on coming home to a place we have never known. The "irrationality" of the transcendental intuition dignifies reason. The will to ascension is founded not on any "because it is there" but on a "because it is not there."

In the course of a few sentences, Steiner identifies this "thirst" first with an otherness, then with a home, and finally with a transcendental intuition that we aspire to, however irrational it may seem.

This conglomeration of notions may be bound by an inner logic, but something's missing—the force of dialectic through which the "otherness" of the ideal can be approachable, a force which, to take the argument a step further, is already within us. For how could we recognize a just act or a beautiful work of art if justice and beauty were not already a part of our kit-bag? And why would we care to do so, except that we dimly recognize these values—beauty, justice—to be the most precious and authentic aspects of our being? Steiner himself acknowledges as much when he associates the ideal with "coming home."

It might be suggested that underlying the impulses I've mentioned here is the simple desire to exert ourselves, to put ourselves forward, egotistically, as it were—to rise above the rest. And few would deny that there is pleasure to be got by excelling. A classic case in our times involves the scientist who works nobly to discover a cure for a virulent disease—while at the same time tenaciously insisting that the discovery be associated with his name alone, and no one else's. Such impulses can come into conflict with one another, no doubt, but the presence of the one doesn't vitiate or undermine the other.

In short, the opposition between selfish and selfless actions doesn't illuminate much. Perhaps we truly come to know ourselves only in the act of showering the world with our gifts. In that restless, anxious progress of spirit, we discover simultaneously who we are and what the world needs.

An awareness of this fact is likely to alter the way we look at our world and the people around us. It may give us pleasure to differentiate ourselves from those who sport a more primitive or "fundamentalist" view of life, but there is often a degree of congruence between our ideals and those of others very unlike ourselves—it's only that we define them differently, with greater or lesser subtlety and nuance.

Can anything be said about the root ideal of which all personal ideals are but imperfect copies. History teaches that this is a dangerous avenue to traverse. Proponents of Roman Catholic orthodoxy, Aryan supremacy, the classless state, and democracy, American-style, have all the confidence they've found it, and had no qualms about enforcing it on others.

No, if there is a universal ideal, it can only be described in the simplest terms—to promote life. But am I to promote my life, the lives of my children, the homeless, the Party? Or "life" in general? It all depends. Although the ideal is always the same, the situation changes, as do the talents and potentialities of the agents involved. That's what makes life difficult and keeps the agonists— you and me—in a state of anxiety.

Yet the force of aspirant energy is everywhere at work, and not only in those arenas—science, the arts, politics—where remarkable individuals excel.

This may be what Novalis was referring to when he wrote: "Novels arise out of the shortcomings of history." And it's most certainly what the French philosopher Gabriel Marcel had in mind when he wrote:

> ...the knowledge of an individual being cannot be separated from the act of love or charity by which this being is accepted in all which makes of him a unique creature or, if you like, the image of God.

As we ate our pot roast and vegetables, we watched a flying squirrel on the bird-feeder, and later five very fat raccoons waddled into view from the shadows beyond the yard light.

WISCONSIN FISH FRY

It being Friday, and Lent, we piled into a car with our friends Don and Sherry and headed out of town, down the Mississippi and across the bridge to Prescott, Wisconsin. Once across the bridge we cut a hard left and continued east along Highway 10 across the rolling hills of western Wisconsin toward Ellsworth. It was a drizzly day and the snow had vanished entirely from the fields—a melancholy spring afternoon, you might say, and melancholy is of the essence of spring. But we were in high spirits, and we asked ourselves once again why it is that once you cross the border into Wisconsin suddenly everything seems different?

The hills were lovely, and the trunks of the trees in the distant woodlots were almost black in the gray air, but it seemed we were headed for nowhere—not a town, not a building, and nary a car in sight. Finally a building appeared at the top of a hill, with a string of trucks and SUVs parked alongside it. It was on the wrong side of the road, however. A place called Jimmy's Supper Club.

At the bottom of the next hill the Valley Bar and Grill came into view, with trucks and cars jammed in every which way and some oozing out onto the edges of the highway. It was clear we had come to the right place. A line stretched out the front door and alongside the building under an awning, and we joined it. We asked the tall slim man standing in front of us if he'd eaten here before, and he said, "I come here all the time. I live four miles away." And he gestured to the north with a half-crooked finger. "This place is good; but have you been to the Bluffs, down by Red Wing? Also very good." Clearly he was a connoisseur.

He told us he owed fifty-seven acres, and I asked him if he was a farmer. "No, I work at Anderson Windows."

50   *By the Way*

"My brother used to work there," I replied, as if that would establish some sort of bond between us. "What do you do with the land?"

"Nothing. I just like the space," he replied. "Forty acres are woods, and some is in a government set-aside program."

He explained how that worked. You put in a bid, and if they accept it then that's what they pay you not to work the land. "This year I put in 65 dollars an acre and they took it. If they won't take it you go lower. But what I don't like are the taxes. I paid $8,500 last year."

"That doesn't sound that bad to me," I said. "for all that land."

"But all I have on it is a house, a garage, and a shed!"

His wife, a petite, middle-aged woman whom we later learned was a grandma twice over, was only half-listening to the conversation, but she perked up when another man came up with a boisterous Hello.

"You remember the Hergesheimers," she said to her husband. "Their daughter used to baby-sit for us years ago." The man pulled a stack of snapshots from his pocket and soon they were all engrossed in a private world of "catching up."

Once inside the low-sling building, we saw that we still had a ways to go to reach the food. The line snaked around the pool table and along a lengthy bar, then turned the corner and continued down the other side to a cash register, where you paid your $11.25. Beyond that was the buffet. We ordered a beer as we inched along and pondered whether to snag a table.

"You could do that. Nothing wrong with that," our new farmer friend said, a little dubiously. "But there's always somewhere to sit."

In the end, we did claim a few places at the end of a long community table just before we reached the register—so we could set down our beer. Then, finally, we began to work our way through the food.

The woman at the cash register told us that there were only two people working in the kitchen, plus a dishwasher. Then she

WISCONSIN FISH FRY   51

showed us the long list of take-out orders that people would be coming by for soon. "They must be doing a good job back there," Hilary said. "And you're doing a good job, too."

"I know I am," the woman smiled.

The odd thing about a buffet is that even if the offerings are uniformly good the desire to sample everything leads to some very strange combinations. Undaunted by this consideration, I filled my plate with dollops of baked beans, herring, au gratin potatoes, three-bean salad, and a potato-flour roll before arriving at the fried fish and ham. I applied a generous slathering of tartar sauce to my crispy fish chunks, ignored the marshmallow salad and French fries, and reserved the celery, coleslaw, and macaroni salad for a return trip—wondering all the while what happened to the pickled beets!

The $64 dollar question at any fish fry is this: How greasy are the fish? These fish were light, flaky, and very hot. The chunks were the size of a thick wallet, and the supply was replenished every few minutes by an adolescent boy from the kitchen who would dump an oversized plate of the compact fillets into the stainless steel bin and then retrieve any that had missed the mark with his bare hands and return them to the pile.

Yes, the fish were good. The ham was also good. The beans were surprisingly firm and free of that overly-sweet bacony flavor, and even the tartar sauce, though straight out of an industrial-sized plastic jar, was (refreshingly) less sweet than is often the case. The potatoes? Cheesy and good. In fact, everything was good.

Two women wearing baseball caps and carrying very small glasses of thin red wine sat down at the other end of our table.

"We won't bite," I said.

"And we won't spill," one of them replied, with somewhat greater wit. But they spotted a free table elsewhere and moved off without further comment. A middle-aged couple arrived a few minutes later, and we soon established that they lived four blocks from our friends in the Mac-Groveland neighborhood of St. Paul. But I doubt whether many of the people enjoying the fish had come all the way from the Twin Cities. River Falls, Prescott, Hastings, Hudson, and Red Wing are a lot closer, not to mention Martell, El Paso, and Hager City. And then there are all the genuine country folk roundabout.

As we were finishing up, the wife of the man we'd been talking to earlier appeared out of the blue at our table. "Are you enjoying the food?" she asked pleasantly. Indeed we were.

"You should come back in the summer," she said, "when it's less crowded."

·❦·

Red River French Canadians

Virgil Benoit, professor of French at the University of North Dakota, Grand Forks, and president of l'Association des Francais du Nord of the Red River Valley, talks like a Frenchman. By that I mean, he shapes his remarks into humorous or mildly caustic anecdotes that seldom have a punch line other than: "Life is like that. Eh? What more can you say?" The kind you come across in a book by the film-maker Jean Renoir or the picture dealer Ambroise Vollard. His beard is gray but his cheeks are rosy, and there's an anxious, pestering, and gleeful sparkle in his eye.

I heard Virgil speak a while back at a Sylvestre-Mercil family reunion at the legion Hall in Crookston. His ostensible subject was Gentilly (pronounced *GENT-ly*), a miniscule farm community established by French immigrants a hundred years ago and more.

Virgil himself was raised on a farm just north of there. His presentation—once again "typically French"—was vague but suggestive. His research into the village appeared to have been focused on a) those immigrants who came, failed, and left without leaving a trace; b) the values that those who succeeded stressed in the testimonials they sent home urging others to join them from Canada; c) the attitudes about property, religion, and community solidarity that remain for us to see in backyard shrines and in Gentilly's church-operated cheese factory (no longer functioning, alas) and in the massive Catholic church that still dominates the village.

St. Peter's Catholic Church, built in 1914, received a certain notoriety in 1984 due to an peculiar incident that bears repeating. I may not have the story straight but it seems a newly appointed priest took it into his head, following the fashion (and the bishop's request) to remove the communion rail. The parishioners chased him out of town and across the fields, pitchforks in hand. The bishop then gave the parish two options: they could abide by the council's decision to remove the rail and stay a active parish, or keep the rail and let the church become a museum. They chose to drop the rail. (I'm not sure if the poor priest ever came back.)

Virgil takes this incident as yet another example of the region's heart-felt, if vaguely defined, sense of a religio-cultural identity reflecting the values of an earlier age.

After the presentation I cornered Virgil by the Mercil family tree. The man who had introduced him, Lowell Mercil (my great uncle by marriage, once removed, in case you're wondering) had mentioned that Virgil was building a Quebec-style house for himself out in the sticks near Red Lake Falls. I thought it might be interesting to see it. I wasn't given an opportunity to ask, however. As soon as I brought up the subject, Virgil said, "Would you like to come out and take a look around?"

Fortunately I knew the road. Hilary and I had driven out that way before on visits to a nearby wildlife preserve. I knew where the Treaty Crossing Park was, I knew where the bridge across the river was, I knew where the hamlet of Huet was, I knew where the cemetery was, and so on. So as Virgil described the route to his house I merely repeated "yes, yes, yes," which somehow made me feel less awkward about the imposition.

The following morning we set out early—we were due at Mass at the Gentilly church at ten. The sun was shining, and the summer-long drought notwithstanding, some of the fields were glowing green. Potatoes, soybeans, sugar beets.

We found the house. A snug blue cottage tucked in amongst a grove of spruce trees. The structure was dwarfed by the metal hay-barn standing behind it. Virgil was out in the front yard; he smiled and greeted us as we clamored out of the car. "*Bonjour. Bonjour. Comme ca va?*" as if we were old friends. We shook hands and the tour began.

"Now this is an oven," Virgil said, pointing to a square slab of concrete sitting in the front yard just outside the fence. "Or it's *going* to be an oven. You see the doors there, I got them in Quebec. Those are the old-style oven doors, not so easy to find these days. And here," he pointed to a pile of bricks. "You line the oven with these bricks, you build a fire to heat the bricks, you sweep out the fire, and you can bake all day! Your bread, your beans," and he twirled his hand in the air, as if to say "And on and on, you get it?"

Virgil's enthusiasm was infectious, his self-deprecation endearing. It was obvious at a glance the place was bristling with homespun intelligence and taste. And yet in describing it he would look you challengingly in the eye, to see if you were actually listening, before he spoke. After all, this was his love, his life.

"See that shrine," he said, pointing to an enormous rockpile in the woods off to the north of the house. "My parents built that. They live there," he gestured vaguely toward a farmhouse out near the highway. "I could tell you a story about that crazy shrine, but it would take too long."

And so we turned away from the smooth, white arms and the gentle gaze of Mary, half-seen through the shadows amid the trees, and went through the gate toward the house.

RED RIVER FRENCH CANADIANS   55

"I'm building an addition. I'm not really a carpenter, you know. Right here I had to shape each board to fit." He grinned sheepishly, pointing up at the rafters. "The roof bends."

We stepped inside the porch-like room, which smelled of cedar and wet earth. Tools and open studs were everywhere. "I got the wood from an old granary. This door I got from my great-grandparents' house. It's not that I'm sentimental. I never knew my great grandparents. It happened to be a nice door."

We passed through it into the darkness of the interior.

"I'm sorry to say that my wife isn't home today. She sells wool." He gestured toward a row of baskets overflowing with billows of white and brown and gray. "A house this size should be neat, but we have no place to put things!" Virgil laughed. "And no real plumbing, as you can see. The bathroom, when we have a bathroom, will be over here."

Although Virgil apologized for the clutter, the room we were standing in struck me as marvelously alive with things of interest—books, photographs, works of art, raw wool, weavings, baskets. The north wall, through which we had entered the room, was lined with books. A couch had been set against it. The east wall had windows. In the southeast corner a spiral staircase led to the sleeping loft. A desk stood against the south wall. More books. And beyond them the dining-room table. Fresh fruit in a wooden bowl. Kitchen cupboards. A refrigerator and an old-fashioned sink. And up through the center of it all, dividing one side of the house from the other, an unusually large, squat, and solid-looking granite chimney decorated with a single, wrought-iron *fleur de lis*. The stove itself, no larger than a large television set and altogether dwarfed by the immensity of the stonework supporting it, sat on a ledge pointing out toward the east wall.

"These granite slabs I got from the railroad. They were building a bridge not far from here. They had no use for them. I went down there in the winter and hauled them into a pile on shore. Then in the spring I loaded them all into the truck and brought them over here. That was work!"

In fact Virgil scavenged much of the material that went into the making of his house from derilect buildings in the neighborhood. The foot-wide beams that run up either side of the front door, for example, were originally part of a pig barn, while the floorboards of the second story were removed one by one from an old granary.

"That was when I was working at the sugar-beet factory," Virgil said. "I would work all day and then go and get a few boards. They were all different sizes. I would bring them here and cut notches in the cross-beam to match the different widths. These strips keep the light from shining through between the boards." The work involved was painstaking and meticulous, but the resultant effect, an irregular pattern of dark and light strips, some raised above the others, could not have been more pleasing.

The most incongruous thing in the room was the television set that stood near the door on a chrome-plated plastic stand. "We never watch that." Virgil said dismissively.

From the rack under the set he drew something closer to his heart—a coffee-table book titled *The Barns of Western Canada*. He passed it around. "I was teaching school in Vermont, going to Quebec on weekends, touring old homes, exploring junk shops, and looking at books like that, and I said to myself, 'They're so beautiful! I've got to have one.'"

I suppose most of us have said something like that at one time or another. But Virgil really *did* have to have one. And so, between the teaching, the researches into local history, the long hours at the sugar-beet factory (I'm not quite sure where that fits in), the writing and editing, and the organizational efforts on behalf of AFRAN, he built himself a house. He's been working on it for ten years. They just drilled a new well. He hopes to get the bathroom in soon.

Back out in the open air, he took us around behind the house to see his wife's sheep. Holding up a bucket of feed in his hand he shouted out something in French that I didn't catch, although the sheep did. They came running. Some were white, some tan, some chocolate, and some had a coppery sheen. They scrambled for position, and Virgil laughed again.

WAREHOUSE WORK

The pastoral tradition is no longer with us much, but for more than two thousand years city-dwellers took the rustic life of the lonely shepherd as a model of simple, dignified, and even "poetic" living. Perhaps few who read and enjoyed the works of Theocritus or Longus made much of an attempt to emulate that rustic way of life. Then again, the actual *work* associated with sheep-herding was never central to its appeal. Rather, it was the solitude and the rhapsodizing about gurgling brooks and rustling leaves (occasionally capped by an encounter with a nymph or a guileless and beautiful shepherdess).

As city life declined following the collapse of the Roman Empire, so did the pastoral tradition—the realities of the countryside trumped the poetic convention, though Christ the shepherd remained a popular icon. But as urban life began to re-assert itself, literary pastoralism also experienced a revival. Both Petrarch and Boccaccio sang the praises of the shepherd's lowly life, and Sannazaro's *Arcadia* (1502) was popular throughout the sixteenth century. (I've never been able to get through it). We come upon similar conceits in Sir Phillip Sydney's all but unreadable *Arcadia* and Shakespeare's far more engaging *As You Like It*, among many other examples.

During the Enlightenment a new perspective developed alongside the poetic fancies of pastoralism, focusing less on the rhapsodies and more on the *work* not only of shepherds but of other lowly folk. Skilled labor in *all* its forms was held up as an object of praise. This was a daring position to advance at a time when, among the aristocracy in France, it was *déclassé* to engage in business of any kind. In the famous *Encyclopedia* Diderot and his cohorts celebrated the trades and published several volumes of dazzling engravings to illustrate the intricacies involved in such crafts as metal-working, glass-blowing, textile production, masonry, printing, leatherwork, husbandry, carpentry, fashion-design, baking, distilling, candlemaking, shipbuilding, saddlery, basket-making, brewing, and soap-making. Yet the thrust of such efforts was practical and moral rather than literary, for the most part. The dignity of honest work was at stake, not the romance of pondering life and love in the midst of a flock of sheep.

In his entry on craft Diderot himself gives us the following comments:

> *CRAFT. This name is given to any profession that requires the use of the hands, and is limited to a certain number of mechanical operations to produce the same piece of work, made over and over again. I do not know why people have a low opinion of what this word implies; for we depend on the crafts for all the necessary things of life. Anyone who has taken the trouble to visit casually the workshops will see in all places utility allied with the greatest evidence of intelligence: antiquity made gods of those who invented the crafts; the following centuries threw into the mud those who perfected the same work. I leave to those who have some principle of equity to judge if it is reason or prejudice that makes us look with such a disdainful eye on such indispensable men. The poet, the philosopher, the orator, the minister, the warrior, the hero would all be nude, and lack bread without this craftsman, the object of their cruel scorn.*

Here Diderot identifies a number of professions that were considered dignified in his day—poet, minister, warrior. Lurking in the mist behind these exalted activities we may detect the tri-partate division of society—the sword, the plow, and the book—that anthropologists have traced back to the earliest days of Indo-European culture. The sword and the book are there, at any rate: Mitra and Varuna. Let's give a little credit to the plow as well, Diderot is saying. And not merely the farmer, but all those ingenious working people who contribute to our well-being.

In the early years of the twentieth century the English essayist G. K. Chesterton remarked, "… I genuinely regret that the shepherd is the only democratic calling that has ever been raised to the level of the heroic callings conceived by an aristocratic age. So far from objecting to the Ideal shepherd, I wish there were an Ideal postman, and Ideal grocer, and an Ideal plumber."

THE WORK

As I write these words I'm looking out my window at three young men who are shoving the severed limbs of my neighbor's beautiful white pine into a wood-chipper. Now *there* is an ideal occupation: arborist. And all day today I've been listening to the unfamiliar sounds of KQRS. The radio belongs to a handyman who's been pounding the decrepit tiles out of the shower-surround in the bathroom down the hall. The plan is to set new concrete wallboard in place, then redo the tiles and grout. That isn't a job I'd be comfortable taking on, but I admire those who can do it right.

And how about warehouse work as a democratic ideal? I'm not much for nostalgia, but I occasionally feel a twang of it when I pass the loading dock of a warehouse—any warehouse—and see the sign Shipping/Receiving hanging above the door. It's a job I did for more than twenty years, mostly on the receiving end.

If you haven't actually done it (and I doubt if you have), then you'd probably be hard-pressed to imagine how much fun warehouse work can be. Yet it's difficult to convey the virtues of such work in a few words. During my years as a warehouse worker, I would occasionally make the attempt to do so, at a family gathering or a cocktail party, though I met very few people who were able to listen for more than a few seconds to even a cursory description of what the process entails. My interlocutor's eyes would glaze over, or begin scouring the room to locate the punch-bowl or a newly-arrived guest, with a hasty exit in mind. At times I could almost see the thought surface, "Poor fellow... Such dolor, such tedium, such mindless effort!!! And yet, he *seems* fairly bright." And in all fairness, I have to admit that the world of freight bills and pallet jacks, two-wheelers and shrink wrap, bin locations and routing slips, is hardly glamorous.

Once, however, at a friend's wedding, I described my line of work to a stranger who was just finishing up a Ph.D. on a minor aspect of one of Kierkegaard's pseudonyms. "Working with your hands? Working with books? Boy, that's something I would really enjoy," he said. I could tell he was serious. I think he understood.

At its best, warehouse work offers a marvelous blend of physical exertion, intellectual challenge, and sociability. A lot depends on the product being warehoused, I suppose. Managing an inventory of spark plugs or party favors might get old fairly quickly. Groceries or even shoes would be better, I think.

I worked at a book distributor. The product itself was both interesting and ever-changing (unlike spark plugs or soda) and the product itself drew a wide range of interesting women and men through the warehouse doors, many of whom had recently completed a liberal arts education and were casting about for steady work while they figured out what they *really* wanted to do.

A company's management style also has an important role to play in any work environment, no doubt, and it's fair to say, I think, that the management style at the Bookmen, where I worked, was fairly laid-back.

In fact, in its day the Bookmen was an institution in the regional book world, and since its demise it's become a legend. Not long ago I was chatting with a senior editor of a prestigious local monthly magazine. When I mentioned that I'd worked for many years at Bookmen he replied, "I applied there—they wouldn't hire me." The bitterness and disappointment of the experience were still plainly to be seen on the man's face.

WAREHOUSE WORK   61

The building itself, which has recently been converted into lavish half-million dollar lofts, is actually two buildings standing side by side. In the early years we were located in the more narrow of the two, and even in that building there were other tenants on some of the upper floors. (There are even older stories, from earlier times in other buildings, but I don't know them.)

The adjoining building was occupied at one time by a plumbing wholesaler. I can remember the Saturday morning we broke through the wall from one building to the other using jackhammers to pound through the brick and plaster and chicken wire. Ever since that day the geography of the Bookmen included an "old" building and a "new" building, though with the passage of time this distinction was lost on a growing number of newer employees, who had known only a single unified space with a few irregular openings in the walls.

Bookmen did draw an interesting crowd. Among the folks with whom I worked I can recall former bartenders, horse trainers, lawyers, sommeliers, actors, installation artists, pyrotechnicians, dance drummers, Sumerian scholars, professional bicyclists, auto mechanics, professors, potters, and DJs. Colleagues went on from Bookmen to become X-ray technicians, journalists, lawyers, preachers, housewives, bookstore managers, buyers, and real estate agents. The turnover was high, and a worker that had stuck around for a year was considered a veteran. Yet surprising as it may seem, one distinctive thing about the Bookmen was how many of the old-timers continued to hang around. When the operation finally folded, nearly every one of the floor managers was from the same generation of employees who had come on board in the mid-to-late seventies.

A colleague once remarked to me that the department I'd wound up with—receiving—was the best. Why? Because I had no contact with customers! On the other hand, I was also largely isolated from contact with the vaguely prestigious world of sales reps, free lunches, free books, sneak-preview movie tickets, author

visits, book conventions, and all the rest of that. Yet unlike shipping, which bore the burden of daily deadlines, workers in the receiving department could simply drop a less important order if a hotter one arrived. And unlike Target and Returns, both of which were located in the basement, the receiving department was on a floor with high ceilings, large south-facing windows, and fresh air blowing in through the loading dock doors for many months of the year.

Standing thirty feet from the open dock door, at the crest of an almost imperceptible upward slope, you could look with pleasure down the length of the interior toward the accounting offices, the elevator, and the customer service department in its glass booth on the opposite corner of the building. Nearer at hand were the packers, most of whom had their backs to you (later they were moved into the "old" building), and the back-order department, tucked behind a row of tall tables and shelves which made it difficult to tell precisely what they were doing—if anything.

On some afternoons thunderstorms would roll in from the west; we could smell the dust rising from the asphalt parking lot as the first drops of rain hit. We would stand in the dock door, (the one that was behind a wall of plastic sheeting out of sight of the offices), as the lightning streaked across the sky and the rain came down. The water would stream across the parking lot and gather in large pools in the low spots along the railroad tracks.

My professional contact with the outside world in those days was largely limited to the North Loop truck drivers who brought in our freight. The same men showed up day after day, of course, and we got to know them quite well. We knew some of them by their nick-names—Froggy, Hammer, Cowboy, Herman the German, Red—but with most of them it was first names only. In the early years, before de-regulation, there were more carriers and therefore more drivers stopping by. I'm thinking of Admiral Merchants, Crouse Cartage, McCleans, Smith, Witte, Werner, Murphy, Neuendorf, Hyman, Freightmasters, PIE, Roadway, CFWY, Yellow, and K&R.

In the early years the shipping department was on the fourth floor, and as a truck pulled up to the dock we would call up the carrier's name on the intercom, then wait by the elevator for the freight to descend. The UPS cart—part green, part orange—would come rolling down at around 3:30, piled high with boxes, and when the truck arrived we'd toss the packages one by one into the back of it. Two decades later we were using that same long six-wheeled cart. The only difference was that by 3:30 the UPS driver had already been by several times to load a pallet or two of shrink-wrapped packages into his "straight job." During the holiday season UPS spotted a semi-trailer at one of our dock doors every night and we'd roll the pallets in ourselves as they accumulated on the dock.

In the course of chewing the fat after a freight delivery we'd learn about a driver's pheasant-hunting trip to South Dakota, his remodeling schemes for the rec room, the latest Teamsters meetings, the kids' homework assignments, the trips to Vegas, and the snowmobile accidents. Some of the drivers later became sales reps for their companies, or for other ones. Among the veterans were Larry Fyten (PIE); George Wohls (Halls) who owned several apartment buildings and was considered "rich" by his colleagues; Orville (Hyman) whose wife ran off with a dispatcher, catching him completely by surprise; Dennie (Smith) who had a glass eye and thought he was a really good softball player; Paul (K&R) who looked a lot like the lead-guitarist for a local band called the Groove Merchants; Roadway Bob; Lee (Yellow); and Clem (CFWY), who stopped in daily for many years simply to use the phone.

UPS and RPS also made twice-daily visits, though the personnel tended to change every few years, as a driver hurt his back and was fired or forced to quit. In Bookmen's final years we were blessed with two very fine and durable drivers, Steve (RPS) who often took time off to go kayaking in Central America, and Wayne (UPS.) I still see Wayne driving his brown truck when I'm in the old neighborhood, and we discuss how his retirement date is receding into the future at the same time that his pension plan is being sabotaged by the company.

One of the great pleasures of working in receiving was that you never knew what the day would bring. It might be a few pallets of the monthly releases from Bantam or Pinnacle or Warner. It might be the Silhouettes or the Harlequins, which came in three batches every month. Some of the most interesting titles came via UPS in small shipments. And in August every year the huge Random House "dating" order arrived. It typically ran from twelve to sixteen pallets and took more than a week to check in. (The "dating" order was the one you didn't have to pay for until after Christmas. The bill was post-dated, which encouraged you to order more.)

Our UPS deliveries ran upward of several hundred pieces daily, and it was a challenge to sort out the individual multi-box orders, many of which looked exactly alike except for small computer-generated markings on the labels. On a given day we might get four or five Warner shipments via UPS, some complete, others not, several of which were of the same number of cartons, so that it wasn't sufficient merely to separate the shipments by carton count. And if it happened that we got behind in

WAREHOUSE WORK   65

the sorting process, the difficulty of catching up again increased exponentially as each day passed.

On the other hand, shipments would often roll off the trucks neatly stacked and shrink-wrapped. You could determine the "block" at a glance—that is, the number of books on a layer—and arrive at the carton count before the pallet-jack had come to a stop. Many mass-market shipments came in fourteen-blocks, Health Communications had long thin boxes well suited to a ten-block. Chimney blocks—eight on a layer, hollow in the center—were popular, and seven-blocks were often used for large squarish boxes.

But there were also palletized orders containing boxes of many sizes and shapes piled willy-nilly and wrapped tightly to prevent them from collapsing. Bantam children's orders were the worst. You'd have to take them apart, stack them in piles on the floor, and count the boxes one by one. You might end up counting 704, though the freight bill said 705. So you started all over again.

Other drivers might be waiting in line to unload, and there was always the temptation, on busy days, to *presume* that everything was there and sign off on a shipment without counting it. I frequently reminded my staff on the dock that we were counting hundred-dollar bills, and the extra time required to "get it right" was always well-spent.

Once a given order had been counted and signed for, it was ready to be "received." In other words, we had to determine if we'd gotten everything we'd been billed for. At the same time, we had to make sure we'd actually *ordered* the things that had been shipped to us. Publishers invariable combined several of our POs on their invoices, and they often combined more than one invoice in a shipment. Untangling this skein of ISBN numbers, PO numbers, and invoices was often a complicated enterprise. At the same time, just counting the books correctly was an operation fraught with potential for error. The task was so simple, and yet so monotonous, that the mind invariably tended to wander. In the end it was harder than weeding a Japanese moss-garden, and headphones were a genuine blessing. By distracting and occupying four or five levels of thought, this convenient contraption (called the Walkman in those days) left a slice of intelligence free that was just thick enough to perform the task at hand properly.

Once an order had been received, the formidable task remained of entering the information into our proprietary computer system, which had plenty of idiosyncrasies of its own to accommodate.

Once we'd determined precisely what we'd received and entered it into the system (the numbers went off in two entirely different directions: our inventory and financial systems were never integrated) the task remained of routing the books themselves to the correct departments.

It all may sound deadly dull, but it was a lot like doing an elaborate Chinese puzzle, and I found it very satisfying to bring the receiving count into line with the invoice count, see the dollar figures match up, make the necessary adjustments for ISBN changes, books sent in error, missing books, price changes, and various other curious anomalies, and then deliver the books to the departments that had ordered them.

The act of delivering the books to the various floors of the warehouse gave the receiving personnel the opportunity to move about and see what was going on in other parts of the building. Ah, freedom! After bringing a completed shipment up to the second floor, for example, I would more than occasionally stick my head through the door of the central office there to chat with the buyer's assistant who was positioned at a desk just on the other side—Ann Penaz or Jane Boers or Kate Gustaveson or Ardie Eckard, depending on the era. On the third floor there was always the likelihood of striking up a conversation with Louis Allgeyer or Jim Henderson, who ran the remainder department. I would sometimes arrive in the basemen to find Mike Weiss (grizzled beard and Harley Davidson T-shirt) discussing boutique Napa Valley wines with his colleagues.

By the same token, people were often passing by the receiving department on one errand or another. During the daily garbage pick-up, for example, each floor sent someone down pushing a big blue two-yard dumpster, and we'd all stand around as they were tipped one by one into the hopper on the back of the truck. Members of the stock department would show up periodically to see what was coming down the pipe for them, and the buyers would occasionally cruise through looking for titles they'd been waiting for. Rick Johnston of the computer department would stop by almost daily to discuss movies or exchange CDs. Over the years he introduced me to Sun Volt, Charlie Haden's Quartet West, Karin Allyson, Lucinda Williams, Jimmy Dale Gilmore, and Allison Krause, among many others.

I would occasionally bring a waffle iron in to work and we'd have a little breakfast get-together in the receiving area. The smell of toasting waffles would soon be circulating up the elevator shaft and off into every corner of the building.

SPECIAL OCCASIONS

The Bookmen year, like the medieval calendar of saints-days, was punctuated by a number of special events. On the first spring day that the temperature reached 70° everyone got out at three. Inventory was a three-day escape from routine. And for many years we had a hat contest on Halloween. The shippers, packers, stockers, and pickers would be hard at work for days (during their down-times, of course) devising creative headgear using posters, card-board boxes, and whatever lay close at hand. (Bringing material from home was against the rules.) After the entries had been properly paraded around the floor, three judges would confer and choose a winner. Many of the entries were takeoffs on currently popular mass-market titles like *Flowers in the Attic* and *The Things They Carried*, and Wayne Dwyer, Elvis, and other personalities showed their faces every now and again. The most imaginative hat I can recall—or at any rate the most kinetic—was put together by Terry Sanborn of the shipping department. He rigged up a vacuum cleaner to a cardboard box, set it on "blow" and paraded around the room blowing packing peanuts all over the room.

Our yearly Open House was held every year on the first Sunday in December, and it was as memorable for the employees as it was for the customers, though for different reasons. The Christmas party, held a few weeks later, was perhaps the only time when most Bookmen employees were gathered together in the same room at the same time. The meal consisted of Norton's pesto, smoked salmon from Morey's Fish House, corned beef and cole slaw left over from the Open House, and an assortment of other delicacies. Someone invariably made a speech—the best that I can remember were delivered by Dana Rhodes, Glenn Schmidt, John Dole, and Jim Henderson. Every employee was given a Dayton's catalog from which to choose a gift, and there was heated controversy aroused by the question of whether the clock radio in my catalog measured up to the DVD player in your catalog, and why so-and-so, who did almost *nothing* all day, got the catalog with the motorcycle in it.

In the receiving department the unexpected arrival of a shipment of Brimax Books marked an entirely different type of event. Brimax Books were cheap board books printed in China with titles like "1-2-3," "God Loves Me," and "Dogs and Cats." They arrived in containers, some of them forty-feet long, and the pallets were invariably double-stacked. Because we didn't have a fork-lift, this meant we had to unload at least half of the shipment case by case. And more often than not, the flimsy plastic bands holding the pallets together had popped during the rough passage across the Pacific Ocean, and the entire trailer would be a chaos of loose books with the titles intermixed Unloading and sorting forty tons of books case by case could take all afternoon.

Yet there was something almost fun about shouldering such a task, breathing in the paper-dust that had collected in the trailer as the cases rubbed against one another during the long ocean voyage, restacking the pallets and hauling them off one after the other. This was work. This was real. And when we were finished we feel like we'de actually *done* something.

I myself was privy to relatively few of the after-hours social activities that went on around the building, but from time to time an organization would spring up that was hard to miss. A Brewers Guild developed for a few years on the third floor, spearheaded by Tom Vetter and Gil Wahl. To be a genuine member, you had to be a home-brewer, though from time to time they'd bring in their latest batches and invite others up to the third floor for a late afternoon sampling party—an event that the owners, Norton Stillman, Ned Waldman, andNed's son Brett, indulgently sanctioned. Tom Vetter was a sort of Encyclopedia Brown mechanical tinkerer, most famous for having fashioned a Barbie Doll that drank beer from a tiny plastic mug. Tom would bring this doll to each gathering. When Barbie raised her glass, however, holding it in both her hands, she invariably spilled all of the beer down her ample chest—an event that never failed to amuse the assembled crowd. Tom later developed a bungy-jumping Barbie Doll, and at gatherings on the first floor we'd all watch in mild amazement as she leapt from the rafters, bobbed up and down a few times, and than dangled lifelessly in the air at the end of her bungy chord.

Jan Leigh was also a vigorous presence on the third floor in those days. She was an actress, and several of us made the journey

one evening to St. Paul to see her in a staging of Steven Sondheim's *Assassins*, in which she played a hysterical murderer brilliantly. Jan was also the moving force behind a theatrical performance of Shakespeare's *Julius Caesar* that we staged in the packing department one afternoon after work. Jan had cut the play to a twenty-minute length, and the production was filled with many unusual warehouse touches. For example, at one point the dead body of Julius Caesar was brought out from backstage lying lifeless on the green-and-orange UPS cart. The entire performance was taped, along with a number of interviews that capture quite a bit of the inventiveness and wit that was circulating around the building in those days. Big Jim Frame, who worked with me in receiving at the time, hosted a very stimulating party on his backyard deck after the show.

In an earlier era, the attempt was made to bring the collective insight of the warehouse together by means of a weekly lunchroom gathering called Remnant Thoughts. The short-lived but lively group was organized by Bob Villani and Tim Danz, as I recall. We would meet in the lunchroom and discuss poems, or a short-story, or women's rights. Bill Mockler attended regularly, along with Chuck Viren, Gretchen Bratvolt, and Linda Belmont.

The longest surviving group that I was a part of, however, was a nameless Bookmen writer's group. We would meet once a month at the Bassett Creek Saloon to discuss a story or poem that one of the members had written. The discussions were preceded every month by at least an hour of semi-humorous repartee based on curious phrases we spotted on the menu. The Bassett Creek Cod came in for unusually rough treatment. Once the serious discussion finally got underway, it almost invariably consisted of ripping apart the month's offering, regardless of who had submitted it. Either the details were irrelevant, or there were too many details. Either the events were incomprehensible, or too obvious to be described in such great detail. By the end of the evening the scope of discussion had broadened, and we found ourselves considering such issues as whether communism had ever done *anyone* any good. (One of our members, Jim Henderson, was a self-proclaimed Communist—under the influence of his wife Athena, I suspect, a very nice woman who had spent some time in a Greek prison.) Another favorite topic was whether the martial art of Akido could be considered "peaceful," (one of our members, Chuck Viren, was working his way through its various levels of rank.) Along with Jim and Chuck, the group consisted of Rod Richards, Rick Johnston, Brett Laidlaw, Gil Wahl, and John Steininger.

Brett was undoubtedly the star of the group, insofar as he had studied with Annie Dillard and also had a novel coming out soon from Farrar-Straus-Giroux. The group eventually fell apart, but we revived it a year or so later when Brett, who had quit the Bookmen, published his book, won a prize, gone on a promotional tour, and taught English in China, stopped by to say hi to his old friends. The revival was brief, but Brett moved on to a career as a baker, and recently penned an award-winning cookbook, *Trout Cavier*. What next?

FOOTBALL

There can be little doubt that the most durable of all Bookmen institutions was the lunch-hour touch football game. The first games that I participated in took place before 1980, when we were still in the *old* building, and the teams were huge—six or seven on a side, including a number of old-timers I hardly knew. We would all pile into a few cars and head out Highway 55 to Harrison Field a mile or two away. An hour or more later we'd come straggling back to the building, aching and bruised, and stand around discussing the great interceptions we'd almost made, and how so-and-so hadn't counted to "three-football" before rushing in on that critical third down.

As the years went by there were many revivals of lunch-hour football as new-comers joined the staff who seemed willing and able to throw and catch the ball. Jim Henderson was the most avid participant and seldom mised a game. His enthusiasm was so great that he carried a set of orange cones in his car, and would go out early before every game to chalk the field. Mild-mannered to the point of lethargy at work, he would spring to life on the playing field, where he was an accurate passer and deceptively fast while running routes. Other regulars during the early years included Rod Richards, Chuck Viren, and John Dole. In later years the cadre of devoted players included Guy Neske, our controller Paul Sykora (who lived for sports and later became controller for the Minnesota North Stars hockey team), and Bill Kaufmann, who had been a cornerback at St. John's before he ruined his knees.

It was only in the last few years that Jim and I found it impossible to generate enthusiasm for a game among the younger employees. Something had happened to the youth of America. They'd become sissies and wimps. Or maybe it was just that they didn't want to hang around with a couple of washed-up warehouse workers who had never really grown up.

REMAINDER SALES

Then there were the remainder sales. Our remainder department was a bust, when considered in terms of revenue per square foot. But Norton liked to sticker remainders. And the theory was that the sales brought customers into the warehouse that we might not otherwise see. We'd often receive large cardboard shrouds full of books that were pristine except for a little red or black dot on the bottom edge identifying them as a "remainder." Most of the titles were commonplace and some were dreadful. One shipment contained an entire pallet of Merv Griffin's biography. But there were almost invariably a few gems scattered here and there—art books, cookbooks, poetry, fiction, first editions of John Berryman and little novels by Milan Kundera and Peter Handke and Julian Barnes. We'd occasionally get pallets of Penguin classics that would be marked at $1.98 apiece.

In the course of these remarks it may have become clear that aside from the stimulating work, the extra-curricular activities, and the great deals on books, it was the camaraderie that made working at the Bookmen so gratifying. I realize that this is not a pastoral virtue, but it was nonetheless real, and I think I ought to mention it. Over the years I had the pleasure of working with a number of great people, many of whom I've already mentioned. Rod Richards was my stalwart assistant for many years, and I learned a lot about both music and literature from him. He introduced me to Los Lobos, for example, and also spoke highly of the Surrealists. Rod later got married, had a son, ran a small-press book warehouse in St. Paul called Bookslinger, and moved to Arizona. The last I heard, he was serving as a Unitarian minister in Paso Robles, California.

Among other co-workers who passed through the receiving department I might mention James Lindbloom, a jazz enthusiast with a heavy leaning toward what we used to call "free jazz"; he may have had the world's biggest collection of bootleg Sun Ra recordings. I am eternally in his debt for reviving my moribund interest in Pharaoh Sanders. His aunt had once been married to soprano saxophonist Steve Lacy, and he would occasionally bring in a *New Yorker* with a poem that his mother, Nancy Willard, had written about him, or a children's book dedicated to him and a girlfriend he'd long since broken up with by the time it went to press. Brooding Anne Penaz, a talented installation artist and poet, brought an edgy artiness to the daily grind; John Steininger always seemed to be nursing an exotic enthusiasm, be it Pre-Raphaelite painting or Alexander Dumas.

The artistic proclivities of our personnel were made evident on those occasions when the third floor staff would host an after-hours art show. From bowling-ball sculptures to naked Jesuses, from Goth metalwork to amateur photography, the shows were full of interest—though I suppose that wasn't really the point. It was at one of those after-hours events that I first read some of the work of Kate DiCamillo. She'd framed one of her very short stories and hung it on the endcap of the Young Adult aisle.

Occasionally authors that had *already* become famous dropped by the warehouse as part of their promotional tour. Joseph Heller, Frederick Manfred, Annie Leibovitz, Margaret Atwood, James Salter, Bill Moyers, and Rosalyn Carter were among the most notable. On one occasion it was rumored that Isaac Singer might make it down. He never showed. And it was also rumored that George Harrison would come in to sign copies of *I, Me, Mine...*

During my last few years on the dock, I was put in charge of a few more departments—shipping, packing, and customer care—and the daily routine got a little more challenging. Even building maintenance eventually fell under my purview. It was my good fortune to have knowledgeable colleagues already in place at various parts of the building, including Jim Lavigne, Clark Gould, Judy Nelson, and Richard Stegal. Richard was a master at dealing with "walk-in" customers—often teachers or librarians with fifty dollars to spend. You could sometimes see the steam rising out of the back of his head. He's also the only person I've ever met who could read a book of poetry from cover to cover. I saw him do it many times!

My life at Bookmen definitely improved when John Steininger, whom I've already mentioned several times, came over and lend a hand with receiving. This gave me greater freedom to attend to things in other parts of the building. It was also a great boon that John had for many years done all sorts of building maintenance. He alone knew where the re-set buttons were on the freight elevators, for example, and he initiated me into the methods of reviving our largest elevator by applying pressure to the contacts in the penthouse motor shaft from the far side of the room using two-by-fours. The sparks would fly and the noise was horrendous, though the technique worked. (Considered in retrospect, I doubt whether it was a sensible thing to do.)

Because the elevators were old, the repairmen we brought in from time to time to fix them would often underscore how difficult it was to find replacements for the contacts that kept them running. I followed a few friendly leads and eventually found suppliers that would make both the copper and the carbon parts of these contacts, and I ordered what I considered to be a ten-year supply. Within a few years the repairmen were asking me where I'd gotten the contacts and offering to buy them from *me*.

Among the other responsibilities that went with building maintenance were to patrol the parking lot for unwanted cars, realign the elevator doors when they went off-track, hire and fire janitorial services, deal with requests from the fire marshal to see that the fire doors and fire extinguishers worked, arrange leases for the postage and copying machines, and so on. In my role as shipping manager I was responsible for negotiating freight rates with the various truck lines and also for keeping huge stacks of cardboard boxes on hand at all times.

But don't get me wrong. During its heyday the Bookmen had a staff of well over a hundred people, and there were plenty of things going on in the building about which I knew absolutely nothing. In its final years, meeting after meeting was held up in the offices on the second floor at which the newly-christened Leadership Team (CFO, HR, Controller, IT, etc) plotted strategies to escape the dismal fate that Gordon's, Pacific Pipeline, and other mid-sized wholesalers had already met with in other parts of the country. That stuff was way over my head. What I'm talking about here is work. Warehouse work. I'm merely trying to suggest how varied and interesting it can sometimes be. And I hardly need to add that there were more than a few dull moments along the way, too. Often during the month of January, for example,

76   BY THE WAY

which tended to be slow, we would spend hours opening box sets of Beverly Cleary and Choose Your Own Adventure titles. After removing and sorting the books, to be resold as individual titles, we would see who was best at tossing the empty boxes into a dumpster positioned half-way across the floor.

In the spring of 2002 the Bookmen closed its doors. Ingram, the country's largest book wholesaler, had bought it, and Ingram had no need for our warehouse operation. All they were interested in was developing relations with a few of our corporate accounts. The doors closed in May. During the summer months the returns drifted back from our customers. By early September this accumulated inventory had been sent back to the publishers and the building was empty. (It was later converted into high-end lofts.)

Many regional publishers lamented Bookmen's demise, because it had offered them a convenient channel of distribution to the major chains. Local independent booksellers also shed a tear, though they had never bought much from us, preferring to order from bigger wholesalers out east who had more extensive inventories. Teachers and librarians also felt the loss.

But the Bookmen had always been more that just a business, both to the Twin Cities book community and to the men who owned it—Norton, Ned, Brett. These three men believed in the community of books and the creative spirit associated with it. This belief was widely appreciated, I think, by the local literary community, and I, for one, can testify to the impact it had on many of the individuals who drifted through the Bookmen on their way to other, perhaps even *more* stimulating, careers.

CRAVING FOR KALE

It came over me all of a sudden, one sunny March afternoon, like the flu. I really wanted to have some kale. I found a recipe on the Epicurious website for Kale and White Bean Soup, and a few minutes later I was at the local grocery store loading my cart.

When I tried to weigh my bag of kale at the self-serve checkout I attracted the attention of the supervisor, a tall, middle-aged black woman with a long pony tail. She came over to investigate.

"How many bunches you got in there?" she asked, not exactly accusatorily but looking at me askance.

"Two," I replied. "Two and a half, in fact. I thought they sold it by weight."

She pushed a few buttons, clearing the screen, then flashed the ID card that was hanging by a cord around her neck across the scanner. Then she pushed a few more buttons and entered the code for kale, which she evidently knew by heart. When the quantity field came up she pushed "3."

"Wait a second," I said as good-humoredly as I could. "Let's take a look."

She pulled out one, then two. There were some loose fronds in there, too. That was the "half" I was talking about. But I had to admit, when you grouped them together, those stragglers also made up a pretty robust bunch.

"You're getting a lot of kale for $1.95," she said. "What are you going to do with it?"

"Eat it." That sounded a little obvious, so I added, "I'm making a soup." That also sounded a little lame, so I said, "They say it's good for you."

"Tell me about it," she replied, cracking a smile for the first time, "We've been eating it for centuries."

Back home, I got the onions sautéing and put a rarely-

78   BY THE WAY

played Johnny Cash CD on the stereo. As usual, I didn't make it past the second number. Better suited to the occasion was *Jazz Jumps In: Swing This*, an anthology of classics from the early Big Band era that included "East St. Louis Troodle-oo" and "Doggin' Around," performed by the likes of Jimmie Lunceford, Lionel Hampton, and the famous Andy Kirk and His Twelve Clouds of Joy (never heard of 'em).

I dropped in the beans, sliced the kielbasa, and then browned it in a cast iron pan. (Andouille sausage also works well.) As I chopped up the kale, so crinkling and seemingly indestructable, I said to myself, "I could see a brontosaurus eating this."

The author of the recipe I was using suggests that "lacinato" kale is the best. I've never seen that in any produce department, nor the other names it goes by: Tuscan kale, black cabbage, cavolo nero, dinosaur kale, and flat black cabbage. Then again, I haven't been looking very hard.

White Bean Soup with Kale and Sausage

3 cans cannellini or Great Northern beans
2 onions, coarsely chopped
2 tablespoons olive oil
4 cloves garlic, finely chopped
5 cups chicken broth
1 teaspoon salt
½ teaspoon black pepper
1 bay leaf
1 teaspoon dried rosemary
1 lb smoked sausage sliced crosswise into ¼-inch pieces
8 carrots, halved and cut crosswise into ½-inch pieces
1 lb kale (stems and ribs discarded) coarsely chopped

Cook onions in oil in an 8-quart pot over moderately low heat, stirring occasionally, until softened, 4 to 5 minutes. Add garlic and cook, stirring, 1 minute. Add broth, salt, pepper, bay leaf, and rosemary and simmer, uncovered, for a while.

While soup is simmering, brown the sausage in batches in a heavy skillet over moderate heat, turning once, then transfer to paper towels. Stir carrots into soup and simmer 5 minutes. Stir in kale, sausage, beans, and more water and simmer, uncovered, stirring occasionally, until kale is reasonably tender, 12 to 15 minutes. Season with salt and pepper.

DENIS DIDEROT: VIBRATING STRINGS

The eighteenth century is the last in which thinkers commonly took it upon themselves to address any and every issue that intrigued them in language most of us can understand. Among the most attractive of such thinkers is Denis Diderot.

It may seem odd that I've used the word "attractive" to describe a thinker, and stranger still that I've applied it to someone not associated with any famous theoretical work or philosophical school. But the turn of Diderot's mind, the figure he cut in conversational circles, and the diversity of subjects he examined, is remarkable. If you study the early history of art criticism you'll come upon Diderot's *Salons* before long; if your interest is in the theatre, you can hardly avoid his treatise "The Paradox of the Actor." His *Letter on the Blind* and *Letter on the Deaf* figure prominently in the materialist/sensationalist philosophy of the time—he was the Oliver Sacks of pre-Revolutionary Paris. His indefatigable efforts as editor of the first major encyclopedia in France occupied him for twenty years. This litany of slightly obscure achievements may give you the impression that Diderot never quite "got it all together." He lacked Hume's dogged persistence in exploring a line of argument, Richardson's patience in developing a plot, Voltaire's spleen, Rousseau's extravagant irrationality. But there are two literary works, at the very least, in which the qualities for which Diderot distinguished himself in conversation stand out. Both are relatively brief. Neither was published in his lifetime.

> *Rain or shine, it is my custom toward five o'clock in the afternoon to walk in the Palais-Royal. There I may be observed, always alone, musing on the bench by the Hotel d'Argenson. I am my own interlocutor, and discuss politics, love, taste, and philosophy. I give my mind full fling: I let it follow the first notion...*

Rameau's Nephew opens with these inconsequential words, followed immediately by more of the same.

> *If the weather be too cold or two rainy, I seek shelter in the Café de la Régence. There I amuse myself watching the chess-players. Paris is the corner of the world, and the Café de la Régence the corner of Paris where the best chess is played: here, at Rey's, the profound Légal, the subtle Philidor, the solid Mayot do battle...*

On one of these breezy afternoon walks, the narrator, identified later in the text as Diderot himself, comes upon a ne'er-do-well with whom he's had occasion to chat with in the past. A music teacher by profession, this fellow has wormed his way into several good homes "where there was a place laid for him on the condition that he did not speak unless permission had been given." A talented mime and an outrageous fool and scandal-monger, his conversation and his services are valued by the idle rich, who find him amusing, though he's a mediocre teacher at best and displays no aptitude whatever for composition—notwithstanding the fact that he's the nephew of the pre-eminent composer of the day, Jean-Phillipe Rameau.

Young Rameau's experiences as a swindler, sycophant, and hanger-on in high places have given him a view of life considerably different from the one Diderot himself professes. Rameau possesses glaring honesty but he's entirely lacking in "moral sense." At a number of points in their conversation our narrator finds himself outraged—but at the same time highly amused—by his interlocutor's observations, judgments, and pantomimes.

> *As I was listening to him acting the scene of the pimp and the maiden he was procuring, I was torn between opposite impulses and did not know whether to give in to laughter or furious indignation. I felt embarrassed. A score of times a burst of laughter prevented a burst of rage, and a score of times the anger rising from the depths of my heart ended in a burst of laughter. I was dumbfounded by such sagacity and such baseness, such alternately true and false notions, such absolute perversion of feeling and utter turpitude, and yet such uncommon candor...*

At the time Diderot was writing *Rameau's Nephew*, a literary genre was in full bloom—the moral tale. Writers were making every effort to produce narratives that put exemplary ethical conduct on display without recourse to Biblical traditions, attempting to illuminate the fact that virtue was a natural human quality and not a gift from God with all sorts of strings attached. Samuel Johnson made the attempt in *Rassalas*, and Voltaire plowed the same field repeated in *Zadig*, *The Child of Nature*, and other works.

With *Rameaew's Nephew*, Didedot is giving us something a little different, and a lot more interesting. Rameau is not a paragon of virtue. On the contrary, he's a scalawag, a rascal, a fast-talker who's only in it for himself. One night he'll be dining with aristocrats, the next he'll be sleeping in a barn amid the cattle. We might call him the first anti-hero, except that Diderot isn't setting him up as a hero at all.

Yet Diderot must admit that there's something not only entertaining but challenging about the fellow. Rameau stirs his "moral sense" by setting it at odds with two other vital instincts: the

82   By the Way

aesthetic and the practical. With regard to his hypocritical and sychophantic behavior, Rameau, who is unemployed and often short of cash, puts the matter simply: "The voice of conscience and honor is very hard to hear when your guts are crying out." And he challenges what he takes to be Diderot's smugness in the following terms:

> ...you think that happiness is the same for all. What a strange illusion! Your own brand presupposes a certain romantic turn of mind that we don't all possess, an unusual type of soul, a peculiar taste. You dignify this oddity with the name of virtue and you call it philosophy. But are virtue and philosophy made for everybody? Some can acquire them, some can keep them. Imagine the universe good and philosophical, and admit that it would be devilishly dull.

Diderot counters this argument with an appeal first to the impulse of patriotism, then to friendship, then to social duty and family obligation. Rameau parries each thrust with an argument reducing it to a disguised form of vanity. He's on thin ice here, however—after all, he's no philosopher. He refers to himself on one occasion as an "ignoramus, a fool, a lunatic, rude, lazy and what we in Burgundy call an out and out shirker..." Diderot often siezes the high ground, at one point defending his way of life in the following terms:

> I'm not above the pleasures of the senses myself. I have a palate too, and it is tickled by a delicate dish or a rare wine... I am not averse to a night out with my men friends sometimes, and even a pretty rowdy one. But I won't hide the fact that it is infinitely more pleasurable for me to have helped the unfortunate, successfully concluded some tricky bit of business, given some good advice, read something pleasant, taken a walk with a man or woman I am fond of, spent a few instructional hours with my children...

And he continues with a story of a man who, having been scorned and rejected by his parents, spends the better part of his adult life restoring them to health and security after they've been hoodwinked and driven from their home by his elder brother. The years he spent laboring on his parent's behalf were, Diderot reports, (with joy stirring in his heart) the happiest in his life.

Rameau responds drolly: "What funny people you are!"

Diderot was familiar with Shaftesbury's theory of moral sense; his first publication was a translation of a part of Shaftesbury's work. But in *Rameau's Nephew* he draws our attention to a wider field of inquiry by suggesting that if our understanding of good and evil rests on such a sense, there are other senses to be considered as well—other realms of value, other activities, which have nothing to do with morality at all.

We associate this line of argument with British thinkers such as Hobbes and Mandeville, but I'm also reminded of the assertion of the Neapolitan philosopher Giambattista Vico's that there are three phases of any culture, each of which has values and activities peculiar to it. Vico pointed out, for example, that it would be a mistake for us to evaluate the heroism of an Achilles from the point of view of a later and less poetic age. After all, he points out, Achilles would rather see all his countrymen die to a man than to suffer a personal humiliation at the hands of Agamemnon. And when Priam visits him alone in his tent in an effort to ransom the body of his son, Achilles flies into a rage as a result of "a little phrase that does not please him":

> *Forgetting the sacred laws of hospitality, unmindful of the simple faith in which Priam has come all alone to him because he trusts completely in him alone, unmoved by the many great misfortunes of such a king or by pity for such a father or by veneration due to so old a man, heedless of the common lot which avails more than anything else to arouse compassion, he allows his bestial wrath to reach such a point as to thunder at Priam that he "will cut off his head."*

Vico condemns Achilles' bizarre behavior from the loftier plane of reason, describing it as "crude, coarse, wild, savage, volatile, unreasonable…obstinate, frivolous, and foolish," just as Diderot censures Rameau's cockeyed ideas, but both men acknowledge that honesty, poetic richness, and sheer vitality also have their place in life. Odd creatures like Rameau interest Diderot, he remarks, because "their characters contrast sharply with other people's and break the tedious uniformity that our social conventions and set politenesses have brought about. If one of them appears in a company of people he is the speck of yeast that leavens the whole and restores to each of us a portion of his natural individuality."

I might point out here that although the composer Rameau did have a nephew, he didn't much resemble the man who appears in Diderot's sketch. On the other hand, Diderot himself spent more than a decade in Paris scrambling to make ends meet before he made a name for himself. There is certainly something of the young Diderot in the elder Diderot's portrait of Rameau. Having known poverty, having experienced firsthand the often cruel disparity between effort and reward, having lived by his wits, committed crimes or at any rate acts of questionable morality, Diderot was in a good position to reflect on these things with insight, conscience, and also, perhaps, contrition. Hence the complex and even-handed tenor of his portrait of the young Rameau.

One commentator describes *Rameau's Nephew* as a fascinating piece of literary art—"a masterpiece alone of its kind." But is it philosophy? Well, if short fragments of pre-Socratic insight and long-winded flights of transcendental German idealism are to be considered as such—and I think they should be—then it would be nothing short of perverse to deny that label to a work that's consistently readable and more than occasionally profound. Meanwhile, the parallels Diderot explores between concord and discord in music, and those same elements as they appear in life, have more to commend them, I think, than the mathematicisms which we've grown accustomed to accept as "philosophy" since the time of Descartes.

DENIS DIDEROT   85

Diderot wrote a second work, equally brief, fresh, and light, that takes us deeper into that musico/logical/conceptual realm which is philosophy's natural home.

D'Alembert's Dream is a distillation of Diderot's mature position on a number of issues, conveyed in the course of three dialogues. The first, between Diderot and his old friend the mathematician D'Alembert, outlines Diderot's very simple (yet even today widely misconstrued) ideas about the relations between form and matter. The third dialogue is a toss-off focused (in so far as any of these lively encounters can be said to be focused) on morality, sex, and society. The second and most meaty exchange involves the mistress of a salon (Mademoiselle de L'Espinasse) who has called in a local physician by the name of Bordeu to attend to the famous mathematician. She's worried because D'Alembert has been mumbling some very strange ideas in his sleep. The physician finds little to criticize in D'Alembert's disconnected remarks, however. In the course of fleshing out the man's oneiric theories and explaining them to Mademoiselle de L'Espinasse, Bordeu also conveys Diderot's views on a variety of subjects to us.

Diderot is sometimes described as a materialist, by which it is presumably meant that in his view, everything is "made of" something. Materialism is not a philosophy, however. At best it can only be a part of a philosophy. To say that everything is 'made of' something is not to say much; the more serious question remains unanswered—"What makes a thing a thing?" Even more to the point is the question, "What makes a thing better or worse than another thing?" It can't be the matter itself, because there is only one matter. It must be the way the matter is organized. Yet the minute we begin to consider *forms* or *types* of matter, we leave the world of matter itself behind. And when we begin to make judgments about the things we've differentiated, we enter the realm of axiology—the philosophy of value, which is about as far removed from materialism as we can get.

Questions of value lie at the crux of *D'Alembert's Dream,* and the notions Diderot comes up to explain why it is that things differ are sophisticated. In his view two qualities—form and sensitivity—lie at the heart of the issue.

Diderot sets the stage for his inquiry with a passage that might almost be a parody of Leibniz or Spinoza.

D'Alembert: *I grant you that a Being who exists somewhere but corresponds to no one point in space, a Being with no dimensions yet occupying space, who is complete in himself at every point in this space, who differs in essence from matter but is one with matter, who is moved by matter and moves matter but never moves himself, who acts upon matter yet undergoes all its changes, a Being of whom I have no conception whatever, so contradictory is he by nature—I grant you that such a being is difficult to accept. But other difficulties lie in wait for anyone who rejects him, for after all, if this sensitivity that you substitute for him is a general and essential property of nature, then stone must feel.*

Diderot: *Why not?*

Diderot is identifying a single concept—not matter, not God's essence, but sensitivity—as integral to reality. Some things have more sensitivity than others, no doubt, but everything feels, at least potentially. He counters D'Alembert's objection that stones can't feel by observing that minerals are an essential part of our organic make-up.

In our day it has become more widely recognized that on a low level of senticnce, stones do "feel" on their own behalf. But Diderot is interested less in this curious aspect of his theory than in painting a more general outline of life based on a single indwelling quality that waxes and wanes in force as life-forms develop and then fall into decline.

In the second part of the dialogue, Diderot describes a universe of continually changing forms. Making use of the analogy of a beehive, he advances a model of organic combination and development whereby simple "feeling" beings join together to form more complex ones. He doesn't go so far as to suggest that human beings are either the last or the best of these organisms—on the contrary, he takes humanity as the fascinating product of a unique sequence of cosmic events: another sequence may yet produce an entirely different and perhaps *more* sensitive animal.

> *Each form has its own sort of happiness and unhappiness. From the elephant down to the flea...from the flea down to the sensitive and living molecule which is the origin of all, there is not a speck in the whole of nature that does not feel pain or pleasure.*

Once again, Diderot takes particular interest in the human form, and especially in the nervous system that makes it so sensitive. The greater part of the second dialogue is taken up with a discussion of this issue, the result being a theory of human character based on two factors: the strength of the senses and of the nerve center that processes the impulses it receives from them.

> *If the nerve-center or trunk is too vigorous in relation to the branches we find poets, artists, people of imagination, cowards, fanatics, madmen. If it is too weak we get what we call louts or wild beasts. If the whole system is flaccid, soft, devoid of energy, then idiots. On the other hand, if it is energetic, well balanced and in good order the outcome is the great thinkers, philosophers, sages.*

And what is it that lies at the center of this living, feeling, thinking, mass of material sensations? What is it that gives it identity, character, focus, and judgment? In another stroke of brilliance Diderot once again hits upon the correct answer: memory.

Early on in the first dialogue D'Alembert and Diderot agree that personal identity is rooted in memory. If I forget everything about myself, I'll no longer know who I am. In fact, I will no longer be anybody. But how does memory actually work?

> D'Alembert: *...it seems to me that we can think of only one thing at a time, and in order to construct, I don't say*

vast chains of reasoning of the kind that range over thou-
sands of ideas, but just one simple proposition, it would seem
that at least two things would have to be present: the object
which one would say remains under the scrutiny of the intel-
lect while the intellect is concerning itself with affirming or
denying certain qualities of the object.

In response, Diderot proposes an analogy between the thought-fibers of memory and the strings of a musical instrument. While one string, already plucked, continues to vibrate, a second and even a third can be plucked in turn, setting up a relationship of greater or lesser harmony.

But vibrating strings have yet another property, that of
making others vibrate, and it is in this way that one idea
calls up a second, and the two together a third, and all three
a fourth, and so on; you can't set a limit to the ideas called up
and linked together by a philosopher meditating or commun-
ing with himself in silence and darkness.

The use of analogy in philosophical argument can be a dangerous and misleading thing, insofar as no necessary connection actually exists between the things being compared. To compare a thinking, remembering individual with the vibrating strings of a musical instrument borders on the bizarre, and D'Alembert himself points that fact out to his friend. No musical instrument makes up new tunes, after all, and very few play themselves. Diderot counters by suggesting that the philosopher is simulta-neously the player and the instrument. We feel, and at the same time we remember. In the space between the two we reason, we judge, we create. We tirelessly repackage memories into the bundles (concepts, categories) that make up our vocabulary. But the analogy begins to grow obtuse.

Nevertheless, the point Diderot is trying to make strikes me as entirely sound. In fact, it's materially indistinguishable from the remark made by the psychiatrist Israel Rosenfield recently in *The Strange, the Familiar, and the Forgotten*:

Whenever we suddenly achieve an understanding—as for example, in reading a murder mystery, when a vital clue that we have overlooked takes on a new and compelling importance—we are aware of something that escaped our attention before; we see an object or a person in new terms. What we suddenly "see" or "understand" is a new thing, neither the person or the object as it was a few minutes earlier, nor the change in either, but a fusion of the two. Consciousness, understanding, has been transformed—the realization of changes in an old friend, the recognition of the importance of a clue, the perception of hitherto unseen forms in a drawing, or even the sudden sense of familiarity as we walk along a city street. In all these cases, our consciousness...is made up neither of the new image alone nor of the old one, but of the relation between the two and our "conscious" sense of both. All thoughts, all conscious images, are a mixing of the old and the new, creations that are neither one nor the other.

Although both thinkers are making the same point, Diderot's musical analogy more clearly suggests, I think, the presence of relational fields within which we sift our memories and sensations to develop an understanding of things that's perhaps indistinguishable from its shape.

We can also learn a lot as a result of contact with events we haven't been personally involved in, of course—through books or films, for example. In describing such experiences we find ourselves occasionally referring to the resonance, the uncanny recognition, that has fascinated and beguiled thinkers since Plato's day. But for better or worse, the strings of the sensitive instrument that is ourselves will already be largely strung and tuned by the time we visit an art museum or a cinema, or crack our first history book.

I'll never forget the first time I saw Ingmar Bergman's film *Wild Strawberries*. It was at the Minneapolis Institute of Arts. My dad's parents were from Sweden—it had always been part of my "heritage"—but it didn't mean much to me beyond the sausage and potatoes in white sauce we ate on Christmas Eve.

When I saw that film, the scales fell from my eyes and I said to myself, with a mixture of astonishment and dread, "That's my family up there on the screen. That's *my* life."

Diderot doesn't appear to have been much interested in history, though it's sometimes alleged that he wrote the better part of Abbe Raynal's long *History of the Two Indies*—one of the most popular works of its time, now long since forgotten. More concerned with justice than truth, more interested in shattering a sclerotic social system than analyzing the logic and necessity of its development, Diderot's work along this line is entirely in keeping with the mode of his times.

The two brief works I've just been describing, on the other hand, are both remarkable and fun to read; they deserve to be better known.

CANZONIERE GRECANICO SALENTINO

I might describe the music of Canzoniere Grecanico Salentino, who performed recently at the Cedar Cultural Center, as mesmerizing, though it seems odd to use a word derived from the practices of an eighteenth-century Austrian physician when referring to a South Italian band singing songs from a tradition dating back to ancient times, often in a Greek-tinted dialect. Then again, that adjective—mesmerizing—has largely lost its historical associations with the early days of therapeutic magnetism, and Canzoniere Grecanico Salentino (CGS) makes no bones about the power of its music to ease the worries of daily living and elevate listeners to a loftier realm.

I'd give them a testimonial any time.

The rhythm of the music that night was driven by large tambourines, and much of it held to the same medium up-tempo beat, though there were a few ballads in the mix, and the beat also rose to levels of genuine fury from time to time. The structure seldom varied from a tonic-dominant-tonic toggle, and the tunes, such as they were, resembled plangent cries and cackling, staccato shouts held within a narrow range of intervals. Some of the songs had a dark, rich-textured, almost drone-like harmony that reminded me of some a capella songs Alan Lomax collected in 1954 in Calabria, just around the instep from the band's home region of Salento (*Rounder Records:11661-1803-2*).

Nothing in the show even faintly resembled pop.

The CGS "sound" would soon become monotonous, however, were it not for the energy and explosive insistence with which it's delivered, and the virtuosity, both vocal and instrumental, of the musicians. Bagpipes, recorders, guitar and bouzouki, accordion, fiddle, several sizes of tambourines, and on one occasion, even a bag of stones tossed in the air again and again to establish a rhythm, with dust rising into the spotlights (from the mountain paths of Salento, perhaps?)

It was easy to see, and to feel, that the musicians were grooving on the intensity of the fields of sound within which they moved. And it would not be too far-fetched to imagine that as the pulse of the music reached a pitch of intensity, we were being carried back beyond the boot of Italy, across the Adriatic to the origins of the Western musical tradition.

On a slightly more intellectual note, it occurs to me that when done well, there is something fascinating about a musical style that doesn't develop much, but draws its interest from tiny variations in short, edgy phrases happily repeated over and over again. (I think Stravinsky would agree.)

And then, from time to time, a dancer with dark, flowing hair, wearing a red dress would appear and prance—yes, that's the right word—about on the stage waving a black shawl. Her

demeanor seemed less frantic, less hyper-charged, than the music she was dancing to, but it was pleasing nevertheless. This, we were told, was the tarantella, a dance with roots extending back for centuries.

There is some confusion about the word tarantella, however. Scholars tell us it derives from the city of Taranto, yet there is also a long-standing tradition that the dance developed as a cure for the bite of a local wolf spider or tarantula—also named after the city. The belief dates back to the sixteenth century that the spider's bite was poisonous, causing a hysterical condition that would lead to death unless the victim performed a frenzied dance to exorcize the poison.

Vocalist Maria Mazzotta, a diminutive figure out of a fairy tale, reminded me of Giulietta Massina. She had a wonderful, high-pitched, open-throated, penetrating voice, like the buzz of a power saw in the garage next door—if such a sound can also be anguished and sweet and joyous and haunting. Giancarlo Paglialunga delivered a booming shout from the right hand side of the stage with less tenderness, while at the same time pounding away on his tamburrieddhu.

Emanuele Licci offered up a lighter, more flexible staccato vocal style, and when he wasn't singing, he often took off spontaneously across the stage, dancing nimbly while strumming his bouzouki. Giulio Bianco's Pan-like recorder trills were sometimes lost in the mix, but his bagpipe solos, delivered from center stage, were a treat.

Those hoping for a "O Sole Mio"-style café accordion from Massimiliano Morabito left the hall disappointed, I'm sure. He kept to a heavy rhythmic pulse in which individual notes were seldom discernible.

The band's leader, Mauro Durante, did the talking, explaining the origins of the group (it was founded in 1975 by his father) and also offering up some extraordinary fiddling. His ten-minute solo on the tambourine exhibited a remarkable range of rhythms, colors, and pitches.

A few of the numbers bore a family resemblance to the manic circus tunes in a Fellini film, but there's an important difference. Fellini's films—even *La Dolce Vita*, the best of them—are animated by a frenzied desire to return to the peasant simplicity that the characters involved never knew. Thus the music is riddled with irony and neurosis and camp. The performers in Canzoniere Grecanico Salentino have probably never tended sheep, but they've succeeded in reconnecting with the expressive impulses from which the music arose originally. The exuberance is authentic.

Not so long ago, Canzoniere Grecanico Salentino was performing in front of a hundred thousand people at the itinerant La Notte della Taranta festival in Salento. Tuesday night it put on a spirited show in front of a hundred curious and enthusiastic Minnesotans, many of whom, by the time it was over, were dancing in the dark behind the delta of folding chairs clustered in front of the stage.

Many thanks to our local treasure, the Cedar Cultural Center, and to Canzoniere Grecanico Salentino! And thanks, I guess, to the tarantula, too.

ON THE ADVISABILITY
OF ACCUMULATING BOOKS

*"When looking for a book, you may discover that you were
in fact looking for the book next to it."*
                                    – Roberto Calasso

Though often under-funded, public libraries consistently
rank among the most popular and highly-esteemed local
institutions. A library offers seemingly boundless entertainment
and information of the highest order, for free, and also a haven
of relatively quiet public space within which to pursue any and
every interest. Nowadays all public libraries have computer access,
most of them are equipped with WiFi, and many have coffee
shops attached. The Carnegie libraries of the previous century are
gradually being replaced by a new generation of stylish buildings, often with exposed birch or cherry shelving, mellow carpets,
fireplaces, and comfortable chairs with expansive views out across
suburban woods or marshes. Librarians are almost invariably
friendly and knowledgeable these days, and eager to go the extra
mile to put you in touch with those little-known databases that
take the grind out of any research project. Meanwhile, by means
of inter-library loan (easily accessed on your computer at home)
it has become possible to get your hands on almost any book,
including many that are no longer in print, for no charge, if you
have the patience to wait a little.

Perhaps the single glaring drawback of the public library system lies in the fact that you have to *return* the books. For those
who read a book diligently from cover to cover this may not be
such a problem, but for readers like me, who tend to flit from
book to book as the mood strikes them, even a long series of online renewals might not be enough. In any case, it's only natural
that the thrill we experience in the midst of a public library's

shelves is one that we'd like to feel more often. Our books are our friends. We'd like to bring them home, and have them near at hand, both the ones we've read and the ones we look forward to reading. This is why people buy books.

It seems to me that, following the pattern set down by Johns Scotus Erigena in his "Divisions of Nature," (though applying it in a different way), we can divide people into four categories. Some people buy books and also read them. Some people buy books but *don't* read them. There are some who read books but don't buy them; and some people neither buy books nor read them.

For many years I placed myself in the first category. I was an avid buyer of books, and it seemed to me that I read quite a few of them too. I would snatch up a cheesy book-club edition of *The Way of All Flesh* at the Salvation Army simply because it looked like a "classic" that I might want to read some day.

I like to think that in recent years I have moved into the category of those who read books but no longer buy them. Yet the evidence stands against me on that score. Little piles of books seem to grow like mold in stray corners of the house, and it may be that I have fallen into the dismal category of those who continue to buy books while never actually making much of an effort to read them.

I was raised in a house with books, though they were largely the detritus of my parents' college coursework. I never actually *saw* my dad or mom open the volumes of Freud, Plato, Whitehead, and Russell that sat on the shelves—maybe they'd already memorized them. In any case, my dad had long since settled into a routine of reading mystery stories, a habit which he fed by weekly visits to the public library. I would often accompany him on his Wednesday night trips, returning home with the latest anthology of Charles Adams or Peanuts cartoons, or *Dirty Track Summer*, or *Shorty at Shortstop*.

A few years later, when my mother returned to the university in pursuit of a phantom degree, I would occasionally accompany her in lieu of a day at school. While she went to classes I would eat microwave sandwiches from the purple Chuckwagon truck parked next to Morrill Hall and peruse cheap Modern Library editions of *The Trial* or *Troubled Sleep* that I'd just purchased at the Co-Op Junior in Stadium Village.

In those days the problem was to find enough books to fill the three shelves of the pine bookcase my dad had built for my use. (Edgar Rice Burroughs paperbacks don't take up much space.) My concern has long since shifted in the opposite direction, toward matters of finding shelves, rearranging books, and of determining which volumes I might actually rid myself of without lasting regret. Do I really need to be at all times within easy reach of hardbound editions of seven of Anatole France's novels? Probably not. Or the complete works of Laurence Sterne? I don't think so.

Yet the desirability of having a few books around the house has never been at issue. Books are attractive, and more to the point, they're an extension of memory. It gives me pleasure, at this moment, to glance across the desk at the shelf beyond the printer. In the shadows over in the corner I see a paperback copy of Jacob Burckhardt's *Civilization of the Renaissance in Italy* next to George Moore's two-volume novel *Abelard & Heloise*, followed by Richard Rodriguez's book of essays, *Days of Obligation*. Then comes Henri Bergson's *The Creative Mind;* a novel by the Dutch writer Cees Nootboom, *The Following Story;* and a slim hardcover edition of *Man in the Holocene* by Max Frisch. It strikes me that this is an interesting group of books, and it pleases me to note that I've read at least part of every one of them.

ARRANGEMENT

Whether they can actually be called a "group" is doubtful, however. They don't have anything much in common. Yet to my mind, part of the pleasure of looking at books comes from the odd juxtapositions and surprising associations, and nothing can kill that sensation more quickly than to discover some sort of moronic order to the arrangement. Alphabetization? How primitive! Grouping books by subject, so that all the books about architecture, for example, are in the same place? Corbusier would be appalled.

Without patterns of organization, of course, it becomes more difficult to find things, and over the years a few zones of reading matter have developed in spite of themselves. Most of the outdated travel books, seldom-used cookbooks, and nature guides have made their way to the basement, along with the genre fiction. I'm not sure that I need to keep twelve hardcover Simenon mysteries near at hand, though most of the dust jackets date from the same era, which gives the ensemble a certain interest as a design specimen. Meanwhile, the novels of Leo Perutz sit side-by-side on the shelf upstairs—I tend to get them confused with one another— and my collection of Willa Cather novels stand in a row high up in the upper corner of a wall-to-wall shelf, well out of reach. I've already read most of them, and the dull greens and browns of the cloth bindings are nothing special to look at.

To look at? Yes, aesthetics does play a part in the arrangement of books. Would anyone be shocked to discover that our newer, better couch sits in the living room, while the one our cat tore apart sits in the rumpus room? I think not. I would go further and advocate that books be arranged with due attention to height, gloss, and the color of the bindings. One pink book can shatter the appearance of an otherwise very pleasing array. And there are certain type-fonts that come close to being intrinsically offensive.

I recently came across a hardback edition (second printing) of Susan Sontag's *Against Interpretation* at a used bookstore in Hibbing. This must surely be one of the ugliest books ever designed. The cover consists of a dribbly yin-yang symbol in pale purple and bright pink. But the price was right ($1.00) and the essays are wide-ranging and also (so I told myself) interesting historically. I just now read her review of Stanley Kaufmann's anthology *Religion from Tolstoy to Camus*, which evokes a time when liberalism was in the ascendant and religion was much more on the defensive in the political sphere. In those days it was trendy to wax nostalgic about religious feeling in a world bereft of God. Sontag is criticizing this posture, which she describes as "empty piety," though she thinks it has become common in "the backwash of broken radical political enthusiasms." And the essay was written in 1961. (So much for the radical 60s!)

Matters of aesthetics aside, the juxtaposition of books from different countries and eras makes it more likely we'll begin a search for one book and end up reading something entirely different. You would think that this would be as satisfying as browsing a bookstore and coming home with a new and exciting purchase—but it isn't. It's the new book—the one we *don't* have—that will make our day, and perhaps change our life.

Alas, if reading can become a substitute for living, then buying can sometimes become a substitute for reading.

Buying

There is no stopping the expansion of books, perhaps. What retards the process—thank goodness—is that as we get older, it becomes easier to remind ourselves, when on the verge of purchasing a book, that a very similar book is already sitting on the shelf back home. Nowadays the books I buy come almost exclusively from remainder catalogs and the de-acquisition shops of public libraries.

There are few better ways to spend the tag-end of an afternoon than to thumb through a newly-arrived Labyrinth Books catalog. Labyrinth specializes in books by academic publishers that have been knocked down in price. Just reading the titles and short descriptions can be illuminating:

Zxu Xu's Reading of the Analects: Canon, Commentary, and the Classical Tradition: "During the Song dynasty Zhu Xi was foremost among scholars rereading the Confucian classics, and his interpretation of the work was considered to express the teaching of Confucius himself. Gardner shows how, for centuries, Zhu's reading helped reshape the Confucian intellectual tradition." 184 pp

This volume has been marked down from $81.00 to $14.98.

Morality: Its Nature and Justification: "Gert argues that morality is an informal system that, while limiting the range of morally acceptable options, does not provide final answers to every moral question." 456 pp

This one has been marked down from $35.00 to $11.98. (A few definitive answers might have boosted sales.)

Though such entries can be fun to scan, informative and hilarious by turns, I'm more likely to actually *buy* something from the Daedalus catalog, which trades in remaindered mainstream titles. In fact, I recently received an order from them that exemplifies the book buyer's dilemma. The three books arrived one Friday afternoon in a fine cardboard box: *The Tomb in Seville* by Norman Lewis, *Casanova in Bolzano*, by Sándor Márai, and *K* by Roberto Calasso.

Having some time on my hands, I started off with the book about Casanova. Why had I purchased it? Because I'll never read Casanova's memoirs, yet many consider him to be an interesting eighteenth-century figure. The novel brings our attention to bear on a seemingly manageable period in his life—the famous escape from the Venetian prison and the subsequent weeks spent in Bolzano. The author is described in the catalog as "one of the great modern novelists, in the same league as Gabriel García Márquez...." who succeeds in holding forth on "just about everything important in human activity: love, honor, how to live, how to die, the importance of style and dignity..."

But after eighty pages I put the book down. I didn't like Casanova and I didn't like Márai's style, which seemed to circle endlessly around events that should have been taking place at breakneck speed. In fact, the plot seemed to be largely an excuse for the author's "holding forth" rather than a means of limning Casanova's character.

As for the Calasso book, *K*, I bought it simply because Calasso wrote one of my favorite books, *The Marriage of Cadmus and*

Harmony, and I thought I ought to have this one too, though I'm not a big fan of Kafka. In all probability *K* will sit on the shelf for ages, unread and eventually unnoticed. On the other hand, the signal virtue of owning books is that from time to time we pluck some such forgotten volume off the shelf unexpectedly and are transported to new worlds of fascination and delight. But Kafka? Yes, but Calasso! And the book cost less than a glass of cheap red wine.

The third book, *The Tomb in Seville* by Norman Lewis, was a guaranteed winner. Lewis is one of my favorite writers, and the description in the catalog matched my own impressions of Lewis's work exactly:

"Acclaimed British travel writer and novelist Norman Lewis here recalls the pilgrimage he and his brother-in-law made through 1934 Spain to the family crypt in Seville. As the country began to tear itself apart, the two found themselves traveling on foot, sleeping in caves, dodging bullets while seeking a café, and taking a detour through Portugal. The *London Review of Books* hailed this final work by Lewis for its 'genial, gently ironic tone and a marvelous eye for the odd and grotesque'."

By the end of the weekend I had read the book. Fine landscapes, interesting people, more than a few adventures, daring river crossings and bullets flying everywhere. Of course I loved it. I even copied out a few passages. Here, for example, is a fine section:

> *The walk turned out to be of great interest and provided an opportunity to analyze that sense of the fantastic which the Spanish landscape seldom failed to produce.*
>
> *I came to the conclusion that this visual effect originates partly in the dryness of the air which leaves the remotest corners of the plain unsoftened by distance, and in its turn produces an almost eerie feeling of proximity with the very limits of vision. With this went a kind of suppression of irrelevant detail, a directness and evenness of coloring, and something of a stylization of light and shade in the manner of a travel poster. The hollows and hillocks, and the rare*

Accumulating Books 101

line of poplars, appeared to arrange themselves in rhythmic patterns. The fields reeled away in all directions, forming immaculate designs in pale gold and silver. Summer had long since withered away in a single week, and the sun glittered with chilly brilliance in the dark blue sky.

Yet now the question arises: If you knew you would like the book, and read it immediately when you got it, wouldn't it have been just as easy to check it out of the library? Perhaps. But this only highlights the fact that above and beyond the experience of reading a book, there is the pleasure of having it close at hand. A book's physical presence is both a comfort and a reminder that however vague and uncertain our memories of a narrative or an exposition of theory may become, they can easily be revived by simply re-opening the book. And the very sight of a book may remind us of stories and ideas that had faded from memory entirely. On the other hand, we'll probably never again catch sight of a book we returned to the library last week. And if we *do* want to see or read it again, the library quite possibly will no longer have it.

This brings us to perhaps the best source of interesting books, the bookshops of public libraries. It's a pity to see these choice volumes so wantonly discarded, yet books do take up a lot of space, even in a public library, and more new titles arrive almost daily. Ooccasionally the library's loss is our gain.

A short list of books that have come my way recently via this channel for a dollar or less would include *The City and the Country* by Raymond Williams; *Peaks: Seeking High Ground Across the Continents*, by Richard Bangs (signed); *Even in Quiet Places*, by William Stafford; *The Unknown Swedes*, by Vilhelm Moberg; *The Reasons I Won't Be Coming*, by Elliot Perlman; *The Defeat of the Mind*, by Alain Finkielkraut; *Consilience*, by Edward O. Wilson; *A Portrait of Lost Tibet*, by Rosemary Jones Tung; *Other People's Trades*, by Primo Levi; *To the Frontier*, by Geoffrey Moorhouse; *Notes from Madoo: Making a Garden in the Hamptons*, by Robert Dash; *Playing Cards and Their Story*, by

George Beal; *The Good Citizen: a History of American Civic Life*, by Michael Schudson; *Billancourt Tales*, by Nina Berberova; *Archeology and Language: The Puzzle of Indo-European Origins*, by Colin Renfrew; *A New World*, by Amit Chaudhuri; *Classics Revisited*, by Kenneth Rexroth; *Downtown: My Manhattan*, by Pete Hamill; *The Cello Suites*, by Eric Siblin; *Juan de Mairena*, by Antonio Machado; *Habitat*, by Brendan Galvin; *The Orchard*, by Theresa Weir; *The Grindstone of Rapport: A Clayton Eshleman Reader; Another Day of Life*, by Ryszard Kapuscinski; *Biology as Ideology*, by R. C. Lewontin; *The Origins of Virtue*, by Matt Ridley; and *Readings*, by Michael Dirda.

The list goes on and on. And so do the shelves of books.

WEEDING

As the books pile up, decisions must eventually be made about what to keep and what to toss. It's a time-consuming process and easily put off. The minute we take a book into our hands, it suddenly becomes interesting again, and the situation begins to take on the frustratingly paradoxical character of a fairy tale. Not only do I no longer want to rid myself of the book in my hands, I actually want to sit down and begin reading it immediately, thus short-circuiting the weeding process entirely.

To combat this effect I've developed a two-tier approach, removing books first to the basement, where they're still more or less available. Once they've moldering among the cobwebs for a decade or so, it becomes easier to convince myself that they really *don't* hold much interest for me.

It is from these subterranean stacks that I select the volumes to sell off, though I'm sometimes too lazy to scrape the bar codes off the plastic dust jackets of these double-rejects, and many of them remain unbought by the used-book dealers I show them to.

But on one memorable occasion, I got lucky. Having gathered up three boxes of books from the basement, I set off on my usual round of visits. My first stop was Biermeier's B & H Books on

4th Street (closed for good now), on the west side of the freeway in the further reaches of Dinkytown. It was a small, old-fashioned shop with wooden floors and displays of books piled high in the windows. In my college years I lived a block away and was going there before B & H sold it to Biermeier. It was easy to park right out front—an important consideration when you're lugging books around—and the owner's pricing was knowledgeable and fair. He was a quiet, circumspect fellow—we never talked—though he did seem to remember my last name. On this occasion he offered me $25 for a small stack he'd set aside on the desk.

"Has the freeway bridge collapse affected business?" I asked him as he was writing out the check.

He looked up at me and replied mordantly, "Let's just say it hasn't helped."

"The books keep piling up," I said, gesturing vaguely around the room.

"Don't I know it," he replied.

As I bent down to gather up a box of the rejects I said, "It seems like these boxes are as full as when I brought them in!"

"I snuck a few items from my own stock in there, just to get rid of them," he replied with a smirk.

With this brief exchange we had arrived at an entirely new level of jocularity.

My next stop was the Bookhouse in downtown Dinkytown, where parking meters are the critical issue. I pulled into a vacant slot on the far side of the street, crossed over to the store, and went inside. A short woman with wildly gray hair stood in front of the counter. She was engaged in an animated conversation with several other members of the staff, but when she turned and saw me she looked me in the eye and said, "Well, hello John. We don't see you around here much anymore."

"Hi, Kristen," I replied, "How have you been? I was in a few times when you weren't here."

It may have been true. But it didn't matter. By the time I'd finished that remark she'd gone back to the issue she was discussing with her staff. It appeared she was on her way out. In a momentary break in the conversation I said, to no one in particular, "Can someone look at a few boxes of books?"

"How many have you got?" Kirsten asked, turning in my direction once again, genuinely hoping to be helpful but clearly in a rush.

"Just two," I said.

"Oh, bring them in. Bring them in." So I consolidated the three boxes into two as best I could, leaving a few of the real dogs in the trunk, and hobbled back across the street with my load.

While Kirsten was looking through the books I went down to the basement to peruse the philosophy section—mostly old tired books with absurdly portentous titles involving Being, Contingency, Truth, Method, and so on. I could hear books being slapped one on top of another hastily in the lobby upstairs, and at one point I heard Kristin say to an associate, "He's a very old customer. A friend of the store."

I was rather honored by the remark, though I hurriedly drifted on around the corner to the anthropology section, fearful of what I might hear next. ("Always brings in junk.")

Finally I made my way back upstairs. "We can give you $25 in cash or $31 in trade," she said.

"Sounds fine to me. I guess I'd better take the cash."

"I'm glad we had time to take care of that," she said. And then it was back to explaining to an assistant at considerable length how to UPS a package to Toronto, and out the door she went with another assistant trailing behind her.

It occurred to me at that point that Kirsten had said nothing about the rejects. My third and final stop would normally have been the Salvation Army. But with no rejects to deliver, and $46 burning a hole in my pocket, I could think of nothing better to do than stop at Surdyk's Liquor Store to pick up a few bottles of Grange des Rouquette GSM, a powerful but affordable Rhone blend made by the Boudinaud family, who have been making wines in the Rhone Valley for five generations—or so the label reports. I don't care if they started last week, the wine is good. (In case you're wondering, the "GSM" stands for the grape varieties used to make the wine—Grenache, Syrah, and Mourvèdre.) I also purchased a Rustica baguette in the cheese shop next door.

During my hunt through the basement earlier in the morning for discardable books I had come upon a book called *History and the Humanities* by Hajo Holborn. I don't know who Hajo Holborn is, but the book looked interesting, and visions of a pleasant evening were beginning to take shape in my head involving the Boudinaud family's wine, a new collection of Mozart violin sonatas I'd recently checked out of the library, the baguette, some Hope butter, (a dairy that churns butter the old-fashioned, small-batch way) and an intriguing essay from the Holborn book called, "Wilhelm Dilthey and the Critique of Historical Reason." Now that's what I call living!

READING

Mustn't forget about the reading. Though some book-buyers fall into the category of collectors—those who buy but don't read—I don't. I might occasionally become curious about the value of my Doré Bible, my complete set of the works of Francis Parkman, or my signed copies of books by Cather, Milosz, and the Mozart scholar Alfred Einstein, but the figures you see online are not great—enough to buy groceries for a week or two—while the pleasure of having these volumes close at hand is incalculable.

No, I buy a book for only two reasons: to open up the possibility of actually reading it someday, or to have that presence nearby. A book is like a temple, after all. It contains life. Every book is limited by its chosen subject, format, and range, but within its chosen realm it's likely to be more well-balanced and complete than the lives we're living out here in the real world, beyond words, on the *outside*. That's where the pleasure of reading comes from. As we follow the words we go *inside*, bending our thoughts into new an unexpected forms of order, absorbing new visions and experiences, suffering new depths of emotion. For some, it's an essential form of nourishment.

Some twenty years ago, in *The Disappearance of the Outside*, Andrei Codrescu was already exploring the possibility that the rise of computer-gaming and various forms of virtual reality might dissolve the distinction between inside and outside, with unfortunate consequences for the human psyche. The explosion in popularity of iPods, which allows us to assemble a soundtrack for our own ongoing autobiographical drama, might be contributing to the same effect. But I'm not sure these observations and criticism differ much from the ones leveled a hundred years ago at young adults who buried their noses in books, rather than stepping out into the world to play rugby or at least collect a few butterflies. Are books an escape from reality, or are they reality intensified? I suppose it depends on what you read.

In the essay on reading that appeared in 1905 in the magazine *Renaissance latine*, Marcel Proust seemed to take greater interest recollecting *where* he enjoyed reading as a child—which room, which chair, which hour of the day—than *what* he was reading. He goes on, however, to describe reading as a pleasantly one-sided friendship in which we need not trouble ourselves wondering what the author thinks of *us*, and can laugh or become bored tactlessly, as we see fit.

Yet in Proust's view the larger value of reading lies in its power to transfer a sort of "breeding" from the author to the reader. Beyond the empty cloquence of a de Musset and the vain striving for distinction of a Fromentin, (Proust's chosen examples) writers of all sorts convey to us the "good manners" of the mind.

> *In spite of everything, literary men are still like the people of quality of the intelligence, and not to know a certain book, a certain particularity of literary science, will always remain, even in a man of genius, a mark of intellectual commonness. Distinction and nobility consist, in the order of thought also, in a kind of freemasonry of customs, and in an inheritance of traditions.*

Few of us "know" all the right books, I'm sure. In fact, the very idea that such a canon exists begins to wither as we discover, in the course of our reading, how many truly remarkable writers remain largely unknown and far removed from the media-based firmament of writers whom everyone *ought* to read.

To his credit, Proust also warns against the habit of excessive reading as a means of passive entertainment, observing that reading "is at the threshold of spiritual life; it can introduce us to it; it does not constitute it."

A poll conducted recently by the Associated Press revealed that in the previous year one in four Americans did not read a single book. Such trends are worrisome. The same poll also reported, however, that among those who *did* claim to have read at least one book, the average number read was seven. I find that impressive. Putting these numbers together, we arrive at the average number of books read per adult—five. The report, drawing on other sources, also revealed that 3.1 billion books were *bought* in the United States last year. That's ten books for every man, woman, and child in the country. Without getting too demographic about it, we can say that the average adult bought fifteen books and read five of them last year. That's a lot of new books for a nation to absorb, year after year.

I suspect that people read more books than they report. A year is a long time, after all, and it isn't all that easy to remember back. I have been surprised more than once to come upon a relatively recent journal entry referring to a book that I would swear I had read several years ago.

The bad news hidden in the study's fine print, in my opinion, is that the Bible and other religious works accounted for 67 percent of the books read. I doubt if many of these readers actually read the Bible cover-to-cover last year. More likely they read a passage or two at the dinner table before sitting down to a meal. There's nothing wrong with that. But reading the Bible to the exclusion of other books could arguably be taken as a sign of cultural regression. The study went on to report that those who read religious works are more likely to be "older and married women, lower earners, minorities, lesser educated people, Southerners, rural residents, Republicans, and conservatives." Thus all stereotypes are confirmed—and isn't that what sociology is all about?

In any case, we should remain suspicious of attempts to link fluctuations in reported book-reading with rising and falling literacy, intelligence, or moral fiber among Americans. It remains to be proven that reading a Harlequin Romance or a passage from Deuteronomy once a month makes you a better person than reading the *New York Times* every day.

For most readers the real issue will always be—too many books, too little time. It amazes me to thumb through the copy of the *New York Review of Books* that arrives in the mail twice a month. Leaving aside for the moment the excellent and comprehensive reviews themselves, I am flabbergasted by the advertisements for university and independent press publications announcing the arrival of so many fascinating studies that it makes you want to cry. No one could possibly keep up with all the fine literature, subtle lines of historical investigation, and serious political analyses being produced these days, on top of all the outdated titles that continue to pile up around the house.

Take William Dilthey, for example. I realize his name is not a household word, though Ortega y Gasset, for one, considered him the most important philosopher of the second half of the nineteenth century. He falls into the category of those thinkers who recognized the importance of the individual in historical analysis, and therefore found little use for "social" theory, yet could not rid themselves of the dream of making history a "science."

That, at any rate, is my vague recollection. I'd all but forgotten about Dilthey until I opened that stray copy of Hajo Holborn essays I mentioned a few minutes ago. Yet now that I've been reminded of his presence, I'm eager to get going on that essay. And I have a dim memory of having purchased a trade paperback of Dilthey's work from a stall in the lobby outside the Border's Bookstore in Calhoun Square—the one that closed down many years ago. It had a teal blue spine. Now where has that gone to?

The French essayist Joseph Joubert (1754-1824) once wrote:

I would like thoughts to follow one another in a book like stars in the sky, with order, with harmony, but effortlessly and at intervals, without touching, without mingling; and nevertheless not without finding their place, harmonizing, arranging themselves. Yes, I would like them to move without interfering with one another, in such a way that each could survive independently. No overstrict cohesion; but no incoherence either; the lightest is monstrous.

Stars in the sky. Thoughts in a book. Books on a shelf? Such delicacy can lead to diffidence and inertia, however, and it's interesting to note that Joubert himself never wrote a book, leaving it to his executors, including Chateaubriand, to choose aphorisms from among his letters and journals after his death and settle on an arrangement for publication. But it's easy to see what he was driving at. There are many books that might just as well have been essays, many essays that could easily have been whittled down to a paragraph or two. I sometimes wonder how much of what I know (or think I know) about books comes from the blurbs on the back of books.

On the other hand, the world that is built up in the pages of a novel draws its strength and vividness from layering, shifts in perspective, and the cumulative effect of conversations and events. The flow of ideas in an essay by Montaigne, say, can sometimes sustain an environment of thought that's more pleasing and more powerful than any of the ideas or observations contained in it.

Not long ago I ran across a passage in which the charms of "good writing" were spelled out in some detail, with the prose of W. H. Hudson being taken as a case in point:

110   BY THE WAY

> *Mr. Hudson...seems always to be meditating or remem-*
> *bering; writing for him is a means of saying what he would*
> *never say aloud. He makes his dearest friend of the reader,*
> *and confides in him with speech that has the beauty of a*
> *wild animal's eyes... He seldom says much in a single sen-*
> *tence or paragraph, but he has a cumulative power that can-*
> *not be proved by quotation, a wandering music that blows*
> *where it lists, because he never forces his inspiration or tells*
> *you what he has not got to say...*

That Hudson is a very good writer I would not dispute. (Ford Madox Ford once remarked that Hudson wrote the way the grass grows—and meant it as a compliment!) Whether his writing is *powerful* I'm not so sure. His most famous book, *Green Mansions*, is a novel, but most of his works a collections of essays. A quick survey just now of various bookshelves here and there around the house has produced copies of *Birds and Man* (1901), *Hampshire Days* (1903), *Green Mansions* (1904), *Tales of the Pampas* (1916), *The Book of a Naturalist* (1919), *A Traveler in Little Things* (1921), and *A Hind in Richmond Park* (1922). It took a little digging to locate my copies of *A Crystal Age* (1887), and *Far Away and Long Ago: A History of My Early Life* (1918).

Hudson was something of an oddity even in his own day, and one of his contemporaries commented that writers of his ilk "...are likely to remain few, for they are little encouraged We are not yet a public of readers civilized enough to demand the highest virtues of prose; we prefer 'clamorous sublimities' and phrases that ask to be noticed; we must be urged through a book by the writer's whip." Hudson is certainly not a well-known writer today, but looking at the copyright page of *Far Away and Long Ago* I notice that in its time (which happened to be immediately following Hudson's death in 1922, as is so often the case) the book went through at least twenty-three printings.

Works like these are the kind that make the accumulation of books worthwhile. They do not demand to be read cover-to-cover. Quite the contrary. But when the mood suddenly strikes you to settle into a slow-moving Anglo-Argentine essay about birds, landscapes, or people, it may be just the ticket. It's unlikely that you'll find a copy on a spur-of-the-moment visit to your local Barnes & Noble store or local library. (The large and well-endowed Hennepin County library system carries five copies of *Green Mansions,* and that's it; the older Minneapolis system, with which it recently merged, has twenty-three of Hudson's works. Not bad!) A similar argument could be advanced for books of poetry, and even those classics that you've always meant to get under your belt but seldom seem to have time for.

A slim book appeared in English translation recently, *How to Talk About Books You Haven't Read,* by the French psychoanalyst and professor of literature Pierre Bayard. Bayard has also written books about Proust, Balzac, Laclos, and Stendhal, among others, so we may presume that he's read at least a *few* books. Yet here he emphasizes the importance of the bigger picture, of the relation of books to one another, and that literary heritage Proust was talking about, which we might never get a proper bead on if we paused to actually read books cover to cover. At one point Bayard suggests that scholars own up to their incomplete educations, and begin to employ a new set of abbreviations to go along with op. cit. and ibid.: UB: book unknown to me; SB: book I have skimmed; HB: book I have heard about; and FB: book I have forgotten.

It may be only fitting for me to admit that I have never seen, much less opened the cover of this book by Bayard—I merely skimmed a review of it. In any case, it seems to me that one further abbreviation might be useful: OB: book that I own, and have right here beside me (but haven't necessarily read).

I'm sure that whatever else may be on his mind, Bayard does not advocate that we dispense with reading altogether. It's necessary to establish at least a few pillars of rock-solid reading experience before attempting to raise an edifice of literary half-truths and speculations. And most readers hope to be swept up into a new and expansive world of experience at least once in a while.

I wish that I were engaged, right now, in an absorbing literary classic that would accompany me through the dark winter months. The type of book that simply carries you along, the way I remember being carried along in earlier times by *Lord of the Rings*, *All the King's Men*, *Parade's End*, *Vanity Fair*, *Woodcutters*, *Don Quixote*, *The Makioka Sisters*, *The Charterhouse of Parma*, or *Your Face Tomorrow*.

I'm afraid I've become a dabbler. I recently made a stab at *Last Evenings on Earth* by Roberto Bolaño but it didn't take. I thoroughly enjoyed *The Interpreter of Maladies* by Jhumpa Lahiri—vivid, economical, penetrating, and more than occasionally wise—but these are short stories, and she's just too *young*. I thoroughly enjoyed Louise Erdrich's *The Round House*, but I'm not sure I would have kept going were it not that a bout of the stomach flu kept me in bed for two days. I'm grateful that it did.

It would appear that I have only limited time for any one human voice or predicament. There are so *many* voices, insights, and perspectives available to us these days, and they stretch back for centuries.

I recently got the opportunity to examine that essay on Dilthey by Hojo Holborn. Near the end of his critique, Holborn underscores Dilthey's belief in "the relativity of every metaphysical or religious doctrine," and cites Dilthey's description of history as "a vast field of ruins of religious traditions, metaphysical positions, demonstrated systems of all sorts."

Such brief quotations can hardly serve as a summary of anyone's thought. Yet it strikes me that while the word "ruins" may apply to the history of architecture, it would never be appropriate when applied to the vanished religious traditions, philosophical systems, and individual works of art that make up the historical record. These things are certainly not in ruins. They're all around us still. In fact, they're right here on the shelf. And the relativity of which Dilthey speaks could never be one of aimlessly shifting sands or a wilderness of mirrors. Rather, it must refer to the relativity of a developing perspective that continues to claw its way, by means of reading—and living—toward a transplendent but ever-elusive ideal.

Gabriel Marcel : E. M. Cioran

The friendship sustained for many years by E. M. Cioran and Gabriel Marcel must rank among the most improbable and appealing of the twentieth century. According to Cioran's report, the two were neighbors and went to the theater together regularly. The conversations they had while wandering the streets of Paris after a performance likely fall into the same category as Aristotle's dialogues—precious artifacts that have been lost to history forever.

Though neither thinker would be considered mainstream today, Cioran is probably the better known. His aphoristic writings, collected in works such as *The Trouble with Being Born* and *A Short History of Decay*, are relatively easy too find, though as the titles suggest, they're steeped in pessimism and bile. But they're also leavened by an acrid humor and a lyric sweetness, as if Cioran were really a disappointed sentimentalist rather than an angry scourge.

Though Marcel earned his living as a theater critic and wrote quite a few plays himself, it's as a philosopher that he's best remembered today. His writings along these lines differ radically from Cioran's in both tone and shape. Marcel was adept at crafting lengthy, meditative essays that were often assembled into collections with lofty titles such as *Creative Fidelity* and *The Existential Background of Human Dignity*. His goal, when baldly stated, takes on a whiff of grandiosity: to tease out the reality and (perhaps divine) significance of finding ourselves in the presence of other people in the world.

Nowadays Marcel seldom appears in surveys of philosophy, and when he does, it's usually in a footnote or subordinate clause, as the thinker who coined the term *existentialism*. With the passage of time, and the rise in stature of his younger contemporary and sometime student Jean-Paul Sartre, Marcel himself grew dissatisfied with that association, preferring to describe his work as "neo-Socratic," and this term may give us a clue to the foundation of his long-standing friendship with Cioran. Marcel craved dialog, had an explosive temperament, and loved thoughtful opposition. Cioran may well have been a perfect foil. The two men were both temperamentally religious and both tended to push ideas to extremes—albeit in opposite directions.

In his eloquent though occasionally long-winded essays, Marcel offers us his entire train of thought as he ponders some seemingly quotidian event or situation—a child bringing a flower to show her mother, for example. He develops his lines of reasoning cautiously, prodding and poking, circumnavigating and re-examined the situation from every angle in Socratic fashion. The end result is usually a modest set of assertions expressed in everyday language. Like Socrates, Marcel is comfortable acknowledging when the heart of an issue under consideration may have escaped him, though he leaves open the possibility that the investigation might nevertheless offer flashes of insight to those who follow along, regardless of its inconclusive character.

Cioran more typically gives us the end-point of his dire ruminations in a few caustic sentences:

I anticipated witnessing in my lifetime the disappearance of the species. But in this the gods have been against me.

Read somewhere the statement "God speaks only to himself." On this specific point, the Almighty has more than one rival.

Such relentless teeth-grinding would soon grow tiresome, but Cioran also has his appreciative moments.

Music is an illusion that makes up for all the others.

For Mallarme, who claimed he was doomed to permanent insomnia, sleep was not a "real need" but a "favor." Only a great poet could allow himself the luxury of such an insanity.

The son of an Orthodox priest, Cioran was born and raised in a small village in the Romanian mountains. He attended the university in Bucharest, where, along with playwright Eugene Ionesco, essayist Mircea Eliade, and other young intellectuals, he fell under the spell of the fascist ideology of the Iron Guard—an enthusiasm he later regretted and eventually disavowed.

On the strength of his first book, *Tears and Saints,* a set of idiosyncratic reflections on the Christian mystics, Cioran received a scholarship to study in Paris from the French Institute of Bucharest. He remained in France for the rest of his life, avoiding starvation until the age of forty by eating in student cafeterias. In 1949, he published *A Short History of Decay,* his first work to be written in French. The book, in the context of the fashionable existentialism of the postwar era, was a success, and with the proceeds Cioran moved into a small garret apartment in Paris where he lived for the rest of his life.

Reflecting on his own background, Cioran once wrote, "I come from a corner of Europe where outbursts of abuse, loose talk, avowals—immediate, unsolicited, shameless disclosures —are *de rigueur,* where you know everything about everyone, where life in common comes down to a public confessional, and specifically where secrecy is inconceivable and volubility borders on delirium."

The son of a high-ranking government official, Marcel was raised in a typically haut-bourgeois Parisian environment, though the death of his mother (a non-practicing Jew) when Marcel was four cast a shadow over his early years. He excelled academically as a teen, in part due to the incessant demands of his step-mother, and eventually specialized in philosophy. But he found the mechanized character of his education chilling, and the relative emptiness of the material itself was brought home to him in the course of World War I, during which he was employed by the Red Cross to locate missing soldiers and inform their relatives of the often unhappy results of his researches.

Marcel published his first play in 1914 and established himself as a thinker of note during the 1920s with a series of essays and books culminating in "On the Ontological Mystery," and the *Metaphysical Journal* (1933). He converted to Roman Catholicism in 1929, but orthodoxy had little place in his researches, which remained grounded in common experience to the end.

Although the subjects Marcel addresses vary widely, they all impinge in one way or another on questions of the meaning and value of personal life. If a single phenomenon lies at the heart of his reflections, it's *l'exigence ontologique*, which might be translated as "the need to exist," or "the need to be." On the face of things this expression seems absurd: after all, we already exist, we already *have* being. Yet Marcel detects within himself, and also notes in the thoughts and actions of friends and colleagues, a degree of doubt on this score, which manifests itself in a compelling urge to exist more fully.

Several of Marcel's eminent contemporaries devoted their careers to highlighting the alienation and absurdity of human existence, but Marcel found such veins of thought, when stripped of their rhetoric, neologisms, and bizarre totalitarian undercurrents, to be self-dramatizing and shallow. Yet he didn't deny that the condition of alienation presented a genuine problem to be examined and overcome. "Being and life do not coincide," he once wrote, "my life, and by reflection all life, may appear to me as forever inadequate to something which I carry within me, which in a sense I am, but which reality rejects and excludes." Such a disjunction is not only unpleasant; it can also be life threatening.

> *Despair is possible in any form, at any moment, and to any degree, and this betrayal may seem to be counseled, if not forced upon us, by the very structure of the world we live in. The deathly aspect of this world may, from a given standpoint, be regarded as a ceaseless incitement to denial and to suicide. It could even be said in this sense that the fact that suicide is always possible is the essential starting point of any genuine metaphysical thought.*

The allure of negation has become the stock-in-trade of modern philosophy. Cioran himself once remarked:

> *The trouble with suicide is, it always comes too late.*

Marcel singles out Nietzsche, somewhat dubiously perhaps, as one thinker for whom such a turning toward despair was "the springboard to the loftiest affirmation."

Marcel's own investigations led him in a different direction: toward the realization that although "I" am inseparable from "my body," I begin to participate in a higher order of being when I make myself available to, interact with, and come to love others. Cioran would no doubt acknowledge the importance of such a quest, while denying that any progress toward its fulfillment is possible. Thus:

> *Of all that makes us suffer, nothing—so much as disappointment—gives us the sensation of at last touching Truth.*

In Marcel's view, the pursuit of what we might call transcendent value is far from futile, though he would be the first to point out that the word "transcendent" should never be taken to mean "divorced from life." First to last, he remained committed to exposing the distinctly personal and *incarnate* character of the realm he was exploring. That being the case, it's interesting to note that the love for others Marcel describes seldom takes the form of a man loving a woman. Far more often he couches this "incarnation" of spirit in terms of friendship, family life, or the goodness we come upon in unexpected places.

> ...I cannot stress too emphatically that the word "fulfill-ment" can take on a positive meaning only from the point of view of creation. Moreover, it is clear, as we have already suggested, that creation is not necessarily the creation of something outside the person who creates. To create is not, essentially, to produce...I think that we must all, in the course of our lives, have known beings who were essentially creators; by the radiance of charity and love shining from their being, they add a positive contribution to the invisible work which gives the human adventure the only meaning which can justify it. Only the blind may say with the sugges-tion of a sneer that these individuals have produced nothing.

"Oh, isn't he sweet?" "Oh, isn't she a saint?" We hear such sen-timental remarks from time to time and even make them our-selves when acts of thoughtfulness and selfless generosity take us by surprise. Look closer (Marcel is saying) and you will see here a more ample manifestation of "being" than there is to be found in any phenomenological reflection or alienated aside.

From such observations Marcel arrives at the conclusion that truth itself is participatory rather than empirically verifiable. Here Cioran might well agree, in his own way.

> It is never ideas we should speak of, but only sensations and visions—for ideas do not proceed from our entrails; ideas are never truly ours.

Early in his career Marcel, reflecting on the buoyant and invigorating potential of human interactions, sensed the emer-gence of a presence to whom he cautiously granted the epithet divine. Thus, to the arsenal of everyday terms he had developed to limn the character of being—availability, participation, love,

MARCEL : CIORAN   119

fidelity, embodiment—Marcel found himself reaching again and again for yet another: faith. This concept served him—I may be putting words in his mouth, here—not as a substitute for reason, but as a means of describing an orientation of the personality toward the good.

To some readers this will all sound somewhat imprecise, not to say *mushy*. What is goodness, after all? And how much can we expect to accrue by means of an availability that seems to be largely passive? But Marcel's own essays are far from mushy. On the contrary, his reflections flesh out several aspects of the movement of being toward goodness. His problem lies not in conceptual mushiness so much as in rhetorical prolixity. As he moves from everyday experiences into more numinous regions, Marcel peppers his train of thought with phrases like "Great is the temptation to..." "But it will be objected that..." "I am inclined to think that there is..." "We cannot go on to a deeper analysis of this suggestion without..." and so on, to the point that we wish he would *just get on with it*. At some point we might yearn for a dash of Cioran's brevity:

> *The essential often appears at the end of a long conversation. The great truths are spoken on the doorstep.*

The unorthodoxy of Marcel's religious views may be suggested by the following remark:

> *I can say no more than that between God and me there is the relation of one freedom with another.*

Yet this supposed freedom notwithstanding, Marcel occasionally oversteps the range of conclusions that follow logically from his analysis, tiptoeing into the realm of dogmatic assertion that he's keen to avoid. The remark previously quoted, from the *Metaphysical Journal*, leads on to a long-winded analysis of the relation between love, faith, and God, during which he lets fly with several curious assertions:

> *When faith ceases to be love it congeals into objective belief in a power that is conceived more or less physically.* [So far, so good.]

And love which is not faith (which does not posit the transcen-
dence of the God that is loved) is only a sort of abstract game.

At this point we're starting to leave the track. Don't we all love
plenty of things that aren't God? It might be said, on the contrary, that love rooted in an act of *positing* anything is *ipso facto* an
abstraction. Unless we're merely loving an idea inside our heads.

In any case, Marcel is at his most interesting when he leaves
God in the wings and takes up the analysis of feelings. One
notion that I find appealing, though it's never become part of
mainstream philosophical vocabulary, is *gaudium essendi*—the joy
of existing.

This experience has not gained a place alongside Sartre's *ennui*
or Heidegger's *Dasein* in the vocabulary of existential catch-
words, but it's more than worthy, I think. I experience it often.
For example, if I happen to be out raking the leaves on a fall day,
I stop every four or five minutes to assess my progress, ponder the
universe, lean on the rake, and pat myself on the back for being
alive. I have had this problem ever since I was a child. (Just ask
my dad.) Some would call it laziness. On the other hand, such
moments of aimless reverie are good for the soul, I think. It's
important to touch bottom every once and a while—to reground
ourselves in that cosmic, purring *je ne sais quoi* which is the source
of both life's meaning and its delight. I liken the experience of
relishing a little *gaudium essendi* to taking a catnap with the gods.

The essay in which Marcel makes use of this phrase carries the
ponderous title "Authentic Humanism and Its Existential Pre-
suppositions." The phrase appears in a parenthetical aside Marcel
is apparently directing at one or two of his colleagues.

*The central deficiency in existentialist philosophies of
anxiety, I think, is the completely arbitrary overlooking of
a fundamental experience I like to call the* gaudium essendi, *the joy of existing. A certain threat does, in fact, menace
this* gaudium essendi; *a serious shadow is projected upon
it. And there is the tragic aspect of our situation. But if this*

primordial fact of the gaudium essendi *is overlooked, then we will have only a mutilated and deformed idea of our situation.*

There are plenty of lively emotions that serve to illuminate our condition. The joy of existing is one of them. Marcel goes even further, calling it a primordial fact.

It seems to me that there is no way that any of us can "reason" our way into a state of joyfulness, however. Joy comes upon us, gurgling up from who knows where. We may be raking the yard or enjoying a meal with friends, or perhaps doing nothing at all... when we're struck by a sensation that takes us beyond the situation at hand to a subtle awareness of the all-encompassing *coolness* of existing in the midst of life's ongoing stream. It's a great feeling—a metaphysical feeling. A mind game, perhaps, but one that's loaded with significance. Wouldn't it be worthwhile learning how to play this game well?

I don't have an answer to those questions. I don't have a method. But it might help if we made an effort to differentiate *gaudium essendi* from other similar emotions.

It needs to be differentiated, for example, from the ego-centered satisfaction of have won something. Winning things provides us with a blast of self-worth, and that's important, but it also separates us from others...and from life.

By the same token, the sensual pleasures we sometimes enjoy certainly add interest to life. But such experiences are invariably transitory, and they're also bound to a particular time and place. *Gaudium essendi*, on the other hand, has nothing to do with either pride or pleasure. It's a secret thought, an inner glance, a bemused recognition of...what? Life's basic goodness? It's a quiet emotion, unlike the brash assertiveness of a Whitmanesque embrace. All the same, it may make us want to sing, or at least to whistle. In a word, *gaudium essendi* is less a matter of feeling good about ourselves than of feeling good about everything.

You may object that the act of feeling our oats existentially—of relishing the richness of being alive—*means* little. The energy seems to be everywhere, but when we bring our fingers delicately to our lips to cradle that infinitesimal kernel of vibrant and precious perfection with which our heart and soul is pulsing, perhaps it's only a gurgle of selfish emotion after all, like the call of a robin under the window in the pre-dawn light.

I suspect that one reason the concept of *gaudium essendi* has not figured prominently in existential disputes is that an individual in its grip would be more likely to write a poem or simply succumb to reverential awe than take up a line of analysis on its behalf. Those who lie in its grip don't need to define it's significance very carefully. They feel no need to philosophize.

One thing is certain: *gaudium essendi* is very imperfectly distributed. Some individuals seem to bath in it while others have never caught even a fleeting whiff. Perhaps it was not quite fair for Marcel to suggest that his colleagues have casually overlooked the phenomenon. No, the joy of existing doesn't lie before us all like a fleet of sailboats in which the wiser among us sail off to explore the Isles of Bliss, while the rest remain inexplicably on shore, gnawing mindlessly at their guts. There are plenty of good-hearted, good-natured people among us for whom it is a daily struggle to enjoy life even slightly. Cioran might well be one of them.

By choice, Marcel was never a systematic thinker, and it's not easy to summarize his positions. Such glosses are prone to vacuity and abstraction, and no doubt I've succumbed to the same faults here. The beauty of Marcel's work lies in his patient analysis of interpersonal relations, which expose their profound import with a delicacy that approaches lassitude. Yet from that domain springs all the things we value, and all the things that endure.

By way of contrast, in one essay Cioran praises playwright Samuel Beckett, like him a misanthropic emigre in Paris, in the following terms:

> *To fathom this separate man, we should focus on the phrase "to hold oneself apart," the tacit motto of his every moment, on its implication of solitude and subterranean stubbornness,*

on the essence of a withdrawn being who pursues an endless and implacable labor…as relentlessly as "a mouse gnawing on a coffin."

Cioran himself was a similarly "withdrawn being." Marcel was quite the opposite. It's a curious fact that although Marcel lived through a turbulent era in European history, and spent much of his time reviewing plays, evaluating works of fiction for a Parisian publishing house, and translating foreign authors into French, relatively few of his opinions on specific aesthetic and political issues are available to us. It's as if, being beset by issues of a deeply personal nature, the middle ground of value in its specific manifestations—art, politics, history, *belle letters*—was of only secondary concern to him. But we know this is not the case. Marcel took an avid interest in conversation, travel, music, art criticism, and other activities.

The Spanish philosopher Julian Marias tells the story of attending a conference in Peru at which Marcel was also present. During a break in the sessions, Marcel sat down in one of the lounges and started to play the piano. Unbeknownst to him, a peacock wandered in through an open window and stood quietly at his side, listening intently.

I'd like to hear more stories like that about Marcel.

As for Cioran, just read him and weep…and then laugh…and then weep.

POETRY – UNCERTAIN

Charles Simic was in town recently to give a lecture on the subject of translating poetry. I enjoy reading Simic's articles and essays in *The New York Review of Books*, and also the poetry he's written over the years. I went to the talk to see the man, to find out what he's like, how he stands, how he speaks.

The small auditorium at the Loft, in the urban wastes between the university and skyscrapers downtown, was half-empty. Simic stood at the front, off to one side, in full view, looking somewhat askance, almost embarrassed, while the crowd was assembling. He was wearing jeans, a dark blue shirt with open collar, and a scruffy wool sport coat. His rounded wire-rimmed glasses appeared to be slightly tinted—pink—and although his face is a little fleshy, at first glance you might mistake him for John Lennon's older brother. One of the festival directors went over to speak with him, then someone else stepped to the microphone to give an introduction.

"Winner of the Pulitzer Prize, finalist for the National Book Award, author of more than sixty books and anthologies. etc. etc. Won't you please welcome Mr. Charles Simic." (Applause.)

Simic walks up to the microphone, hands stuck awkwardly in his pockets. He pulls some papers out from under the podium and sets them in front of him on the lectern. He adjusts the microphone, then waves his arms vaguely in the air at his sides.

"Well, translating..." he muses, as if he hadn't really given the subject much thought. Or as if the topic were so towering and formidable that it would be folly to even attempt an assault. But little by little the thoughts, the anecdotes, the observations and judgments begin to flow.

Simic himself was born and raised in Yugoslavia, though he spent one year of high school in Paris before coming with his mother to the United States more than fifty years ago. His first attempt at translation, he tell us, was from the Russian of Maya-kovsky's difficult surrealist poem "The Cloud in Trousers." "This is not a book I could translate even today!" he exclaims, laughing.

And so the halting, rambling, self-depreciating monologue begins. Simic speaks with an accent, turning all "th"s into "d"s, as if he had a bad cold, so that the word "the" becomes "de" for example. Before long he's brought Robert Bly into the picture, whom he refers to as "your local boy Bob." Very early in his career Simic had taken some work to Bly, who was then in New York editing *The Fifties*, the magazine that gave many young American writers and readers their first exposure to foreign poets.

"He poured me a big glass of Chevas Regal," Simic reports. "I don't remember a single word that either of us said," he laughs, "but I do remember that big glass of Scotch." He goes on to note that Bly disliked the French surrealist poets, preferring the earthiness of the Spanish and Latin American poets. Simic likes the French.

To anyone familiar with Simic's poetry, the tone of his lecture would not, perhaps, have come as a surprise. His poems are usually brief. They're often more like fables than lyrics, but they lack a clear-cut didactic thrust, and in the end we're left with the imagery itself, which is almost invariably bizarre, and often appallingly so. I might suggest that where French surrealist poems are dreamily and erotically bizarre, and Spanish modernist poems are bizarre in mysterious, earthy, and child-like ways, Simic's imagery is an oblique reflection of wars, urban poverty, and ethnic atrocities. This makes it all the more surprising that his poems often have great humor and lift.

The Partial Explanation

Seems like a long time
Since the waiter took my order.
Grimy little luncheonette,
The snow falling outside.

Seems like it has grown darker
Since I last heard the kitchen door
Behind my back
Since I last noticed
Anyone pass on the street.

A glass of ice water
Keeps me company
At this table I chose myself
Upon entering.

And a longing,
Incredible longing
To eavesdrop
On the conversation
Of cooks.

In the course of his talk Simic told us tales of Slavic specialists he worked with at the New York Public Library who would be gone for days tracking down a volume in the stacks for him. He described working on anthologies with titles like *2000 Years of Armenian Poetry*, compiled at great expense by one government agency or another, though destined to be bought by no one, which left him wondering whether the translations were uniformly bad, or whether the nation itself was peculiarly lacking in poetic genius. Little by little, in the course of these anecdotes, he brought the challenges and rewards of translating into focus.

The gist of Simic's talk can easily be guessed, because translating is by nature both a dubious and a worthwhile undertaking. Citing Pound, he suggests that the sound of a poem can seldom be recreated in a second language; the concrete imagery often comes across well, but conveying the "logos" or sense of the poem is usually an iffy proposition. He doesn't approve of those self-proclaimed "imitations" that draw upon some original while being blatantly unfaithful to it in one way or another, and he mentioned the terrible temptation many translators feel to improve on the original by changing the word "arm" to the word "leg," for example. Near the end of his talk Simic reiterated that well-known saw, "Poetry is what gets lost in translation," but he added boyishly, "And so it is the ideal situation. It simply can't be done...Yet people do it every day!"

The next morning Hilary and I returned to the Open Book to hear the Zen poet Jane Hirshfield speak—her topic: "Poetry and Uncertainty." The New York Yankees were in town for a divisional play-off game, however, and to avoid the congestion near the stadium we parked near the Plymouth Avenue Bridge and rode our bikes through the warehouse district and then through downtown, stopping along the way to peruse the merchandise in a Finnish home furnishings shop and to peer in at the ice rink that's being refurbished in the old train station.

The auditorium was even less crowded than the previous morning—forty people at most. (I suppose the other 50,000 were at the Metrodome watching the game.) I immediately spotted Hirshfield, a thin woman with long, wiry brown hair and slightly beady eyes, quivering, darting, alive with curiosity and intelligence. She was sitting in the front row, chatting amiably with three women sitting in the row behind her. Following the traditional introductions she stepped up to the podium, and began her talk by announcing, a little nervously, "Those of you who know what my talks are like will know that I write neat little speeches that I read very carefully, so I apologize for the formality and look forward to questions after the talk, which can be about anything you want, not just the topic at hand." And then she began to read.

I couldn't tell you what Hirshfield said in so many words, but the thrust of the talk was clear—certainty is a bad thing, poetry rises out of uncertainty, questioning, ambiguity. Strange as it may seem, considering the topic, I had the feeling that every

128 BY THE WAY

well-crafted remark she made was true. I enjoyed listening to the phrases, the sentences, well-turned and riddled with quotations from poets I particularly like—Pessoa, Milosz, Stafford—as well as one or two Japanese poets I was unfamiliar with. She spoke of Heisenberg, and referred to Bohr's intriguing remark that the opposite of precision is clarity. And yet, although I felt I'd heard it all before, I couldn't actually track her argument, her direction, and I said to myself more than once before the talk was over, "I'll read it when it comes out in a book."

My own theory of certainty can be expressed in a few words: We have all been certain of things that have turned out not to be true. Therefore, certainty is not an attribute of truth. Once you come to realize that truth can never be certain, it requires no great leap of thought to accept that poetry need not be certain. It also needs to be pointed out, however, that although truth is never certain, we sometimes are. Certainty is a feeling we sometimes have with regard to our ideas about things. It's a feeling we ought to be suspicious of. This, I think, is the point Hirshfield was driving at.

At the same time, it needs to be stressed, I think, that poetry harbors truth, clothed in a personal utterance which invariably presents a view, a vision concocted of images, feelings, and reflections. (Quite the opposite of Wittgenstein's often trivial analytic propositions, for example.) The value of a poem derives from its arrangement, texture, fidelity to experience, and imaginative élan, all of which are intuitively arrived at—and no less intuitively responded to by the reader. Neither the certainty nor the uncertainty with which a poem is conveyed contributes much to its beauty or its depth. In fact, beauty often depends on the effectiveness with which the poet conveys the glorious uncertainty, flux, and bewilderment of life's irrepressible energies.

Hirshfield's eloquence was dazzling, but she gave herself away near the end of her long talk when she remarked: "It's really very simple..." and I thought to myself, "yes, it is." I noticed that several listeners were cradling well-worn copies of her book of essays, *Seven Gates*, and it almost made me want to go home and pull my own copy down from the shelf. As for the poetry itself, it strikes me that Hirshfield's poems are often explorations and exercises through which she attempts to shake off that intensely analytic part of herself:

White Curtain in Sunlight and Wind

More and more
wanting to learn
how to leave things be.
To live as the Dutch painters
looked at a fish:
all of it eaten but leaving no sign.
Or if so much cannot be given,
then to enter as Chuang-tzu's butcher
entered an ox—slipping completely through;
each cut, sinew and fat, sharpening
the knife. Nothing taken, or left behind.
Heart returned to the granite mountains of its home.
After, it could almost walk away.

LOVE SONGS AT THE WOMANS' CLUB

Two events, exactly a week apart: We stopped into the auditorium of the Minneapolis Woman's Club with some friends on a Sunday afternoon to watch a music video being filmed of Chan Poling and the New Standards. I'm not much of a rock-n-roll fan, but I'm old enough to remember the Suburbs, and I even have some nice Super-8 (or is it Straight-8?) footage of that band performing in Loring Park—no sound, of course, but if you put "Hobnobbing with the Executives" from *In Combo* on the turntable as you watch it, it's fairly exciting.

We sat near the back of the small dark auditorium looking up at the stage, which was draped with a stylized winter scene painted on a sheet of canvas by the video's director, Wyatt McDill. A plug-in campfire was burning to the left, the strips of orange cellophane fluttering upward under the impetus of an electric fan. A few Christmas trees stood to the right. Further to the right, out of the camera's view, stood a grand piano.

Maybe fifteen people were standing around on stage, either chatting idly with one another or giving advice or directions. Some of them were gaffers, I suppose; others were grips

Several thin young women were sitting in the audience, notable for the fact that they were all wearing stocking caps. (It was 95 degrees outside.) Chan and his musical cohorts were also sitting there in the dark, watching the goings-on in silence.

It's amazing how much time can go by while you're waiting for something to happen, not bored, but vaguely titillated by the creativity pulsing through the darkness.

At one point Wyatt stopped by to say hi, and his wife Megan, who was very calmly producing the shoot, graciously did the same. (Full disclosure: we aren't famous; we were sitting with Wyatt's parents, Dana and Mary, who have also produced a vast flotilla of wooden bathtub boats—no two are alike.)

Finally the dancers were assembled on-stage. They were all wearing roller-blades. Wyatt, in Twins cap, sitting comfortably a few rows back in front of two monitors that we could also see, said "Action" or some such word. The music started to play. Vibraphones or marimba. A singer.

The two cameras, mounted on a little track, began to move slowly back and forth under the impetus of the gaffers (or the grips) who were pushing both the cameras and the cameramen along. Everyone on stage (all of them under thirty, I suspect) started to skate around in a circle as little snowflakes descended in a steady stream from the rafters.

The song was something about, "The only way your heart will mend..." Needless to say, thoughts of Chan's late wife Eleanor Mondale came to mind.

They played it two or three times. I never got tired of it, though it reminded me of the soundtrack to *American Beauty*. One of the cameramen said, "Can we do it one more time?"

Wyatt said, "No, we've got to keep moving ahead."

We were waiting for the musicians themselves to take the stage but they never did. At one point some members of the crew assembled the undercarriage for the vibraphone. That was a good sign. I also saw the bass player bring his big instrument up onto the stage. Then, with a hand-held camera, the crew started to film one of the dancers—a dead ringer for Reese Witherspoon— doing pirouettes for about half an hour.

Then we drove down to the Ice House with Dana and Mary to sample the $5 whiskey menu.

A week later, Hilary and I returned to the Woman's Club to hear operatic baritone Gabriel Preisser in recital with pianist Mary Jo Gothmann. I'd never heard of Preisser, but the price was right ($5) and the program, which featured Brahms, Ravel, Villa-Lobos, and Ives, looked enticing.

To our surprise, the event was staged not in the basement

auditorium but in the parlor. Tall Palladian windows to the right, an elegant bar to the left. Relatively comfortable, free-standing, high-backed chairs, well-spaced. There might have been fifty people there.

Following a well-meant but inaudible introduction by the club's president, Preisser entered from the long staircase in the rear, singing a tune about "lonely towns" from a musical I'd never heard of. It was obvious from the get-go that he was a ham—he looked a little like Senator John Edwards—but he had a deep, rich voice and a winning, almost ingratiating manner.

Preisser referred to each group of songs as a "set," which confused me at first. The Brahms set consisted of three love songs, on the order of "…and my beloved is fair like the sun/ which shines upon the lilac bush…" Only the final number had an element of gravitas. Things haven't gone well for the lad, and he reports that "the lonely tear flows trembling, burning, down my cheek."

For some reason, I'd gotten it into my head that Preisser would be performing Brahms's "Four Serious Songs," almost the last thing he wrote, very stern, all about death. But why, on a Sunday afternoon in a sunny, well-appointed parlor, should it be so? I'd never heard the ones he did sing, though I immediately felt I'd heard them a thousand times. German lieder. Nice…

The second set was the opposite. Although I've heard Ravel's trio of songs titled *Don Quichotte a Dulcinée* a thousand times, they're still as fresh as ever. And Preisser did them justice, though with echoes of Gerard Souzay's version echoing in my head, I did notice a few casual moments. The dramatic flair Preisser put into his performance more than made up for them, and I also began to appreciate how shifty and difficult the entrances were, seldom anywhere near a recognizable "beat." Few song sets in the repertoire, I suspect, are as lovely and fun (and deceptively difficult) as this one, while still holding up to repeated listening.

Ravel himself was a native of the Pays Basque—still a long ways from Cervantes's La Mancha, but it's worth mentioning. He completed the songs in 1933 as part of a competition to supply the soundtrack for a film the German director George W. Pabst was making about Don Quixote. Manuel de Falla, Darius Milhaud, and Jacques Ibert were among the other contestants. Ravel lost out; he didn't compete his work on time. He was already suffering from the ataxia and aphasia that would soon make it difficult for him to compose anything.

The song cycle closes with a drinking song, a robust *jota* in triple time that Preisser delivered with admirable brio, leering and staggering. "I drink to joy! Joy is the one aim for which I go straight...when I've drunk."

Ravel himself never finished another piece.

The third set consisted of tribal songs from Brazil arranged by Villa-Lobos. Mary Jo Gothmann, a fearless and very musical accompanist, informed us in the course of her introduction that alongside he other talents, Preisser is fluent in Brazilian Portuguese—a nice touch, though in the program notes we're told that the songs are in the Bantu dialect. They were lovely pieces, no matter what language. The kind of thing Villa-Lobos does best.

The Ives songs carried that anti-classical, vernacular tone for which he's justly famous, and Preisser hammed up the cowboy tune involving Charlie Rutlage to good effect.

> *Another good cowpuncher has gone to meet his fate,*
> *I hope he'll find a resting place, within the golden gate.*
> *Another place is vacant on the ranch of the XIT,*
> *'twill be hard to find another, that's liked as well as he.*

The words on the page cannot even hint at how vigorous and dramatic the tune is. It's what live performance is all about.

I left the event convinced that an expansive parlor is the perfect place to hold a recital, especially when it's open to the public at a price cheaper than a hotdog at the ballpark. But my conviction was also confrmed that it's a mistake to mix show tunes with classical compositions. Preisser ended his recital with a very long encore from *Carousel*. Different tone, different attitude, different level of musical sophistication. As if to say, 'You've endured the longhair stuff, now I'd like to sing something you might actually enjoy."

❧

BEEHIVE CLUSTER

While vacationing on the North Shore over New Years, I added a few elements to my knowledge of the night sky, including the Beehive Cluster in Cancer—rudimentary to many, no doubt, but entirely new to me. Perhaps even more interesting, along the lines we're pursuing here, was a passage I came upon in a little book called *The Meaning of It All*, by the physicist Richard Feynman:

> *It is a great adventure to contemplate the universe, beyond man, to contemplate what it would be like without man, as it was in a great part of its long history and as it is in a great majority of places. When this objective view is finally attained, and the mystery and majesty of matter are fully appreciated, to then turn the objective eye back on man viewed as matter, to view life as part of this universal mystery of greatest depth, is to sense an experience which is very rare, and very exciting. It usually ends in laughter and a delight in the futility of trying to understand what this atom in the universe is, this thing—atoms with curiosity—that looks at itself and wonders why it wonders.*

This is a simple and beautiful description, I think, of an experience many of us have had at one time or another. Feynman goes on to suggest that the sense of awe he's describing is so deep and impressive that conventional religious explanations—for example, that our presence here on earth has been arranged by God for his own glory, or so that he can watch the struggle between good and evil—are simply inadequate.

I would agree. Perhaps we could go further, and argue that such explanations are not merely inadequate, but misleading, because they posit an overlord whom we have difficulty meeting face to face, or even limning the contours of. This shadowy figure tends to drag us down into a muddle in which exuberance and wonder compete with a sense of personal inadequacy and conscience. The laughter and delight diminish.

Yet such notions of deity do serve a purpose, I think, exposing a reality that Feynman's intuition doesn't go *quite* far enough to include. For when we posit the inanimate universe from an "objective" point of view and then reverse our attention back to ourselves, we don't see "man." We see ourselves. More specifically, *I* see *me*. Unique, sentient, curious, mysterious, and fraught with contingency.

This is the source of the *frisson* Feynman is describing. Matters of gender bias aside, it's important to remove the abstraction "man" from the equation, and it also might be just as well to remove the references to matter and atoms. Everything is made out of atoms, I guess. So what? The question is, *How* is it made? What is its structure? That, after all, is what makes it interesting, excellent, unique. Calling a sentient being "atoms" is like calling a soufflé "flour and eggs."

It might be worth pointing out, furthermore, that when we turn from the remarkable universe "out there" and refocus our attention on the no less remarkable whatever-it-is "in here," we find ourselves face to face not only with personal awareness, but also with a bevy of unruly drives and interests, cavorting in a rickety pen we sometimes refer to as the "ego."

The negative connotations of that word, "ego," are nearly the opposite of those that give a troubling luster to the word "God." If we tend to see God as unduly portentous and dour, we too often see the ego as irredeemably crass and shallow. Both appraisals are superficial, but they're also complimentary, working together to form the common, yet wrongheaded, notion, that to enjoy oneself is evil, while to give selflessly with obsequious deference to the Almighty is right and proper.

Perhaps there is a more fruitful way to set these elements against one another. Without diminishing the wonder and delight that Feynman describes, a more complete inventory of the emotions associated with "existential awareness" might also include a vague sense of obligation to exert ourselves on behalf of the greater world in the midst of which we find ourselves. The two feelings don't conflict. Rather, they support and fuel one another.

In other words, conscience is a natural result of self-awareness, and it becomes stronger yet when we begin to attend to the beings who surround us on all sides, each of whom have different, but similarly unique, "windows" on the universe.

The universe is fueled by dolor and exuberance, self-aggrandizement and sympathetic concern—and by a fellow-feeling that's usually governed less by an urge to love our neighbor indiscriminately than by personal affections and preferences.

Such concepts are difficult to articulate and I suppose I've made a hash of it here. But it seems to me (returning to the subject at hand) that the rituals and revelations of the world's religions expose a variety of public responses, enshrined by tradition and exalted by art (though also defiled occasionally by superstition and politics) to this very interesting mess of impulses.

Less widely recognized nowadays, but of equal importance, I think, is the long tradition of rational inquiry into these matters. Plato's early dialogue *Euthyphro* may be taken as a case in point. Though the dialogue ends inconclusively, along the way Socrates asks the question whether the gods love something because it's good, or whether something is good because the gods love it?

Translated into religious terms, we might ask whether we're being good when we do what God tells us to, or whether the injunctions offered by religious authorities are designed to help us clarify and aid the natural bent of the spirit toward the good. Reduced to essentials, it's a distinction between obedience and conscience.

But no sooner does the word "bent" appear than I'm reminded of Kant's remark, "Out of the crooked timber of humanity no straight thing was ever made." That's a grim statement, and also an exaggeration, but it points to an aspect of the issue that I've been neglecting. Some people don't seem to *have* much of a conscience. And even the best among us are often wracked by guilt when reflecting on things they might have done better, or perhaps should have done but never did at all.

When we ogle the night sky on the shortest day of the year, this is probably not the direction our thoughts will take, however. Something far simpler is likely to surface as we feel the cold air in our nostrils and shuffle our feet back and forth in the white snow—wonder and delight, accompanied, perhaps, by a vague sense of gratitude directed toward we know not who or what, that we're actually here in the dark with a trillion miles of empty space in front of us.

✦

World Press Institute

For many years the World Press Institute invited a select group of young foreign journalists, under the auspices of Macalaster College and other local organizations, to visit the United States. They stayed with host families in the Twin Cities area and traveled together by bus to various parts of the United States, including Washington D.C., New York, Detroit, Atlanta, Miami, Los Angeles, and Chicago. They spent three days at farms in rural Minnesota and three days in the news environment of regional centers like St. Cloud, Duluth, and Rochester.

My friends Lee and Judy were among the host families for many years, and they sometimes invited me to the closing festivities, at which the participants were given the opportunity to share something of their experience with the public. Each journalist was given five minutes to speak. Two things came out in these reports with some regularity: the United States contains far more ethnic and cultural diversity within its borders than anyone from abroad would guess from watching American television. And it also has produced far greater income disparity than one would expect to find in a nation ostensibly dedicated not only to individual initiative but also to equality of opportunity.

As far as journalism is concerned, it was generally agreed by participants that while the coverage of international news on the highest levels is quite good in the U.S., there's is a good deal of parochialism to be found in smaller markets; and that television news of all stripes is marred by efforts to be safe, balanced, and entertaining, rather than genuinely informative or penetrating.

Here are some of the distinctive comments made by participants during one of these events held during the Bush era:

Bertrand Tchoumi, Cameroon: What is all this about tips, tipping everyone all the time? In Camaroon we don't have tips, we have bribes. People tell me, 'You must tip the woman who makes your bed, she's not well paid.' But isn't this America? These people should be out on the street, demonstrating for higher wages!

Lars von Törne, Germany: One great thing about the United States is all the political memorabilia. I went down to Ruminator Books, and I bought this pack of playing cards (holds up deck) with Saddam Hussein and his henchmen...and then I bought this deck (holds up other hand) with George Bush and his cabinet on them (laughter from the audience). I find it amazing how much latitude there is here for the expression of criticism toward government—although it seems that the current administration has not been held to account as rigorously as it might be. I am also amazed at how well the United States succeeds in incorporating people from all over the world into its body politic—this is something we in Germany must learn to do better.

Patience Rusere, from Zimbabwe, referred more than once to the fact that people in the United States seem to take for granted the great personal freedoms they possess. These comments took on added significance later that evening, when we learned that Patience's apartment back home had recently been ransacked by the government—she had refused its request to write inflammatory letters against the U. S. before her departure. For the time being she'll be remaining here in the United States with friends.

Olivér Kiss of Romania was the comic of the group. When asked by moderator Cathy Wurzer whether Romania would be among the nations aiding the United States in their efforts to rebuild Iraq he replied: In Romania people make $100 a month. How are they going to help the U.S. build Iraq? He brought his speech to a close with a joke he'd borrowed from someone else: What is the capital city of the U.S? Obesity.

During her allotted five minutes Teresa Bausili of Argentina described how impressed she was with the strength of regional, religious, and even sports loyalties among Americans. The group had been in Chicago during a Cubs series with

140 *By the Way*

the Marlins, and Teresa found the enthusiasm there even more extreme than that of the most rabid South American soccer fans. (Somehow, I doubt it.)

Jinmei Lu of China was asked to comment on the widespread concern here in the United States about excessive control of media outlets by a few major corporations. She paused politely, a little bewildered by the question, then replied, "Well, you must know that in China the government controls *all* the media. I don't think you have a serious problem here yet." When asked what surprised her most about her visit, she replied, laughing, "What surprises me most is that, wonderful though the United States is, I still want to go back to China!"

Shujaat Bukhari of Kashmir expressed his disbelief that in a Sunday edition of a major eastern newspaper he could find no mention of the fact that the Indian minister of defense had just resigned. "If the American defense minister had resigned, it would be in all of our papers!" he exclaimed. (This comment left me wondering if he had been reading one of those Sunday editions that appear on news stands *Saturday* morning.) Near the end of the program the moderator asked Shujaat what advice he would give our president if he ever got the chance. Here, I thought, is a chance to speak out. The participants had been circumspect all evening with regard to recent shortcomings in American policy, both foreign and domestic. Shujaat might well have said "Repeal the hideous and harmful tax break you've just given to the rich," or "Quit trying to impose your quasi-religious political beliefs on the rest of the world," or "Get your act together in the Middle East and end your petty quarrel with the U.N." But what Shujaat said was "Solve the problem in Kashmir."

I realize this was a spontaneous, off-the-cuff remark, but it seemed to reflect the same sort of parochialism that several members of the panel had noted in America's approach to world affairs.

In the lobby after the gathering I asked Shujaat what he thought of Pakistani president Musharraf. The gist of his reply was that Musharraf was a pretty good guy among the dictators of

WORLD PRESS INSTITUTE 141

the region. In fact, he'd actually saved Pakistan in the years before the war in Afghanistan. Lars von Törne was standing nearby, and I asked him if he had any hopes that the European community would ever be able to put together a coherent and effective foreign policy. "It's true, we have had much difficulty doing this in the past, and we are very grateful to the United States for acting in the Balkans at a time when we were able to do nothing," he said. "But I do have some hope that in the future we will be able to solve these problems." I asked him how he felt about Gerhard Schröder's recent campaign for re-election, which was the first anti-American campaign in post-war German history.

"I was not happy about that," he relied. "In some ways Schröder is like Bush. His policies are superficially popular but very short-sighted."

As THE CROWD IN THE LOBBY was thinning that night, and we retired along with most of the participants to the home of one of the event sponsors, where we settled into more intimate conversations that—for me, at any rate—combined the fascination of learning about other cultures with the pleasant illusion that our own daily lives are actually worth describing.

I thoroughly enjoyed hearing from Finnish correspondent Kaius Niemi about the origins of the Finnish people, and the year he spent in military service in Lapland. Kaius speaks four languages fluently and was named Finland's Journalist of the Year in 2002 for his reporting in Afghanistan, but if he found my questions jejune he never let on. During the presentations earlier in the evening he had remarked, "I have had America in my head for as long as I can remember." He also commented that what surprised him the most during his visit was "how many Big Macs I could consume," so I suppose he was enjoying one more encounter with a *bona fide* American. When I apologized for my lack of linguistic expertise he replied: "No, no. Why should you learn other languages? Do you think the French know other languages? We in Finland must learn, because *nobody* knows Finnish. Why should they?" I made mention of Bo Carpelan, the only Finnish writer I could think of, and was informed that he wrote in Swedish. (How was I to know?!)

When I asked Kaius about the Northern Lights in Lapland, his eyes lit up as he began to describe the evening when he was showing some of the "boys" how to activate... (What is the word in English?) *flares*. As he spoke he held his hands in front of him, about to pull the imaginary pin, then looked up toward the ceiling. "I looked up, and there were colors everywhere. It was dazzling, extraordinary. There was no need to light a flare that night."

"Did you ever experience that Arctic hysteria they talk about, during the months of darkness?" I asked him.

"I'm crazy anyway," he replied, laughing. But then he added, "Yes, it can get rather unhealthy. I need the light. Everyone does."

Nevin Sungur of Turkey has reported from Iraq, Afghanistan, Indonesia, Eritrea, and Sarajevo, but she was similarly inquisitive and relaxed as we sipped our wine and munched on pieces of candy corn. I asked her about the likelihood of a Kurdish state being formed from the northern part of Iraq, and she agreed that it was likely. Sixty years? I asked. Sooner than that, she replied. She took umbrage at my suggestion that Turkey represented a model of democratic sophistication in her part of the world. "The military protects the constitution, the military has the ultimate power." She also acknowledged that the election of Recep Tayyip Erdogan, whose Islamic orientation is well-known, as prime minister, was a troubling development. On the other hand, she seemed delighted when I told her about an expression we use here in the United States to describe a group of innovative newcomers who shake up a staid and conservative situation: we call them "Young Turks."

But for me the highlight of the evening was my conversation with Teresa Bausili of Argentina. She described some of the dramatic regions and landscapes of her country, and we discussed the effects of the IMF policies on the troubled Argentine economy. We evaluated the works of Borges, Paz, Machado, and other stars of Spanish-language literature, and she expressed her enthusiasm for the Italian Marxist Antonio Gramsci. I was at a loss, however, when she asked me to recommend some contemporary American writers to her. Everyone I came up with happened to be from somewhere else. But when I mentioned the Spanish novelist Javier Marias she said, "You mean *Julian* Marias?"

"No, Javier."

"It must be Julian's son."

"How do you know *Julian* Marias," I asked in some surprise. I had never before met anyone who had heard of that rather obscure Spanish philosopher and historian, author of *Philosophy as Dramatic Theory, Reason and Life, Understanding Spain* and other classics.

"He was a good friend of my father."

"You're talking about Julian Marias, the protégé of Ortega y Gasset?"

"Yes, my grandfather was a good friend of Ortega's. My father and grandfather are Spanish. They came to Argentina with Ortega and Julian Marias during the Civil War."

I was flabbergasted by this revelation. Ortega y Gasset, though not widely read today, is a thinker comparable in stature to Heidegger, Croce, or Wittgenstein. He died in 1955. Marias carries on the tradition of "vital reason" that Ortega pioneered. I would never have imagined that I would be sitting at a dining-room table discussing politics and literature with someone for whom these names evoked personal memories. It seemed to me that Teresa was perhaps no less surprised to be discussing these matters with an American stranger. She may, in fact, have been pleased to be sharing associations that had meant a great deal to her father and grandfather. "I was so young then," she said, tearing up a little. "I wish I remembered more."

She did tell me about the discussions that went on in her house, and of her grandfather's library, so vast and venerable and obscure that the only thing to be done when the old man died was to sell it. She promised to get more detailed information about those times from her father before he forgot everything.

"One story I do remember my father telling me. He was a young man, sitting at the table with his father, Julian Marias, and one other man, and his father said to the group, before pursuing a line of argument 'Well, we're all intelligent adults here.' My father was very moved. It was the first time my grandfather had given him praise of any kind."

In the course of these (to me) fascinating exchanges I noticed that a somewhat heated discussion was taking place in the kitchen between Nevin, Kaius, and Olivér. I found out later that the subject had been Iraq, and Olivér had been defending the American involvement. "Even if the invasion is 99% about politics and oil, and 1% about freedom, I still support the American action," he was saying. "You do not know what it's like for an entire generation to starve."

As the party broke up people began exchanging cards. "Drop me a line if you're ever in Helsinki." The journalists returned to their hotels, with other adventures on the road ahead, and we Americans returned to the dining-room table, where, over a bottle of port from Galena, Illinois, we discussed such mundane topics as the assault charges that had recently been brought against the son of the St. Paul police chief following an altercation in a bar.

❦

KUNDERA AND HANDKE

Milan Kundera has charmed readers with his tale-telling for decades. His recent efforts—*Slowness*, *Identity*, and *Ignorance*—have been shorter than the early masterworks but hardly less engaging. Since the collapse of the Soviet Union, such "Eastern European" offerings have lost some of their cache, and Kundera himself was denounced as an informer a few years ago. But he keeps finding new things to occupy his attention. In the seven-part essay *The Curtain* (2005), he re-examines, from a more mature perspective, some of the material he first dealt with a quarter-century ago in *The Art of the Novel* (1986).

One section of *The Curtain* originally appeared as a free-standing essay in the *New Yorker*, and at the time I found it so brilliant that I cut it out and stuck it in my copy of *The Art of the Novel*. In that essay Kundera defends the practice of reading literature in translation, even going so far as to assert that it is *only* through translation that literature from small countries will ever escape the tyranny of nationalistic enthusiasm to make its mark on the wider world. The broader theme of *The Curtain* is the history of the novel itself, and Kundera makes a stab, very early on, at underscoring why that art form is so important.

"…human life as such is a defeat. All we can do in the face of that ineluctable defeat called life is to try to understand it. That— that is the *raison d'être* of the art of the novel."

Kundera's approach to the subject is freewheeling; he refers again and again to a fairly small selection of authors, jumping back and forth in time to suit his purpose: Cervantes and Rabelais, Sterne and Fielding, Balzac and Flaubert, Tolstoy and Dostoyevsky, Musil and Broch, Kafka and Gombrowitz. At one point he contrasts his approach to the more strictly chronological one we often find in conventional histories.

" 'History as such,' the history of mankind, is the history of things that no longer exist and do not join directly in our lives. The history of art, because it is the history of values, thus of things we need, is always present, always with us; we listen to Monteverdi and Stravinsky at the same concert."

This analysis is not entirely sound. History of every sort concerns itself with things that remain both valuable and conjoined to us. But in the history of art those connections become blatant.

Kundera analyses the density of Dostoyevsky's plot-constructions, Flaubert's attempt to de-theatricize fiction, and Tolstoy's success at exposing the largely random musings that pass through a character's mind, even during moments of extreme crisis. He explores the significance of the fact that until recently, the French language had no word for "kitsch," and jostles Hegel's theory of lyricism just to see what falls out.

Music and poetry, Hegel says, have an advantage over painting: lyricism. And in lyricism, music can go still further than poetry, for it's capable of grasping the most secret movements of the inner world, which are inaccessible to words. Thus music is actually more lyrical than poetry itself. From this we can deduce that the notion of lyricism is not limited to a branch of literature. Rather, it designates a way of being. And a lyric poet is only the exemplary incarnation of man dazzled by his own soul and by the desire to make it heard.

Yet just a few pages further on, Kundera underscores the anti-lyric conversion a novelist must undergo to establish distance between himself and his characters. He credits Cervantes for tearing through the curtain of self-identification. "..his destructive act echoes and extends to every novel worthy of the name: it is the identifying sign of the art of the novel." At one point he observes: "Humor is not a spark that leaps up for a brief moment … to set us laughing. Its unobtrusive light glows over the whole vast landscape of life."

Kundera's own novels carry that jaunty music, and this spirited critique of the modern novel does, too. Few writers, I think, can match the estimable brevity and heedless courage with which he explores such issues as depth, soul, tragedy, history, lyricism, and meaning itself.

When Elfriede Jelinek won the Noble Prize for Literature in 2004 she is reported to have said: "They made a mistake. Peter Handke should have won it." She's probably right.

The critics, with their perchance for schools and categorization, have put Handke into the German Neo-romanticism pigeonhole, and *Across* definitely fits the bill. It's the personal narrative of a man who's left his family and his job as a teacher to work out some things in an apartment above a supermarket in a village on the outskirts of Salzburg. A good deal of the book consists of minute and exacting descriptions of the buses arriving and departing at the village station, the noises arising from the street, the character of the light that glances through the apartment at various times of the day, the quotidian activities the narrator witnesses on his incessant walks, and the shifting appearance of the nearby mountains. For example:

> *I sat in my usual corner, with a view of the two small groups, and also, through the cleft of the curtains, out into the open. There in the northern sky gleamed the gray prison wall of the castle, toward which the canal flows in gentle meanders, in the foreground traversed by one of its many bridges. Two cars were standing side by side on the hump of the bridge, the drivers talking to each other through open windows as if they had just met. Between them slithered a moped, whose rider's body while on the bridge seemed airier for a moment. The bridge was empty. An old man and an old woman sat on a bench on the embankment, which oddly enough, like all the benches along the canal, faced away from the water....*

One long section deals with a card game. But the central event is this: the narrator, while walking in the mountains, comes upon an old man painting a swastika on a tree trunk. He

148   *By the Way*

kills the man in a fit of rage with a stone and tosses the body off the edge of a nearby cliff.

Near the end of the book, the narrator receives a kind letter from his former mentor requesting that he return to his post at the school.

> *The reader of the letter sat down and wept; not over the praise, but over the salutation, "Dear Andreas." for it seemed to me that for years no one had called me by my first name.*

❧

ART BOOKS AND BOOK ARTS

We caught the "Graphic Design: Now in Production" Show at the Walker on the afternoon of its last day. Plenty of color posters, digital gimmicks, magazine layouts, and branding displays. As we entered I caught sight of a big display of books in a gallery to the left and skirted past the introductory bulletin board with nary a glance.

Why? Because I like books—precious, hand-made books and those with eccentric, avant-garde designs. The books under the Plexiglas display cases at the Walker reconfirmed my long-held belief that many such productions are fascinating to look at but difficult to read. When a book becomes a mere vehicle for design, or beyond that, a piece of sculpture, I begin to lose interest.

You may argue that there's no need for us to chose between "books" and "book arts." As the saying goes, "It takes all kinds (of books) to make a world."

True enough. And I have books scattered all around the house that seem precious to me, at least in part because they're so exquisitely crafted. I recently pulled off the shelf a fine copy of *The Book of Tea* by Okahura Kakuzo, for example, with heavily textured paper, encased in one of those sturdy boxes. Opening it at random, I read:

> ...*But when we consider how small after all the cup of human enjoyment is, how soon overflowed with tears, how easily drained to the dregs in our quenchless thirst for infinity, we shall not blame ourselves for making so much of the tea-cup. Mankind has done worse...*

By the same token, the squared format, quaint illustrations, and scattered type-setting of the anthology *The Cubist Poets in Paris* which sits here on the shelf is entirely appropriate to the subject. And what about this tiny cased edition, two inches square, of *Findings* by Ursula K. Le Guin? It was published by Don Olsen at Ox Head Press in 1992 in the Minnesota Miniatures Series. You could hold not only the book, but the press on which it was printed, in the palm of your hand.

All good stuff. But at the point where "design" or "innovation" begins to obscure the literary import, I become queasy. Such creations often exhibit the same delectable textures that make a fine-press book so, well, *fine*. But I'm not sure whether I ought to read them or put them on exhibit above the piano. Most such examples of "book arts" are out of my price range in any case, so I guess the question is moot.

It strikes me that this issue of cross-purposes extends even to blank books. I've bought a few exquisite, hand-made blank books in my time, but have difficulty writing anything in them. Nothing that's going on in my head seems worthy. Eventually I take the plunge.

I'm looking now at a book I bought in a little shop called Il Tourchio in the Altarno neighborhood of Florence. Opening it at random, I read:

Dec 4, 1992

Poulenc and wine. Just having finished Judge Dee and the Chinese Lake Murders. *And I don't like this pen.*

Music by the moods. What would you be reading if you were listening to Ravel's Scheherazade? *There's an essay by Cocteau that I wish I had but do not have. Don't know the name of.*

I rest my case.

On yet another glorious evening I drove downtown to hear a talk at the Minnesota Center for Book Arts. The featured publisher was Univocal, a small outfit that's been in operation, so I gathered, for hardly more than a year. The firm makes its own books locally, printing the guts digitally on linen stock and doing the covers by hand.

The publisher, Jason Wagner, opened the program with a brief description of the hands-on, boutique philosophy of the press, followed by a 4-minute video of the presses at work. At that point Wagner turned the presentation over to director Drew S. Burk, who delivered a fairly lengthy spiel about the demise of the printed word, how children no longer like to read books, and why philosophy, art, and life don't really need to be sequestered from one another.

Burk is from St. Louis, and he also riffed on the Mississippi flowing past us a few hundred yards to the north, the ancient Nile, and the use of linen to mummify corpses in ancient Egypt. It's all part of the message Univocal is trying to get across. Everything is organic. Everything connects.

Burk went on to describe the five books Univocal has published recently in some detail—all of them translations from the French. He devoted special attention to a forthcoming work called *Biogea* by a former bargeman, now a professor at Stanford, named Michel Serres, and read a few passages dealing with the Garonne River.

Although Michel Serres's work has been characterized as a

unique amalgam of poetry, philosophy, science, and biography, the paragraphs Burk shared were poetry through and through. Not a concept or hypothesis in sight. They reminded me by turns of Jean Giono and Andre Breton (in *Arcanum 17*, for example), with elements of the great French biologist Rene Bubos perhaps waiting in the wings.

During the Q & A Wagner revealed the Univocal books are distributed by the University of Minnesota Press, a publisher already well-known for French translations. That's a major coup for them. Other questions from the audience, most of whom were "book-arts" people rather than book people, ran the gamut from "Why don't you do ebooks?" to "Why don't you number your books like art objects and double the price?"

I was tempted to buy a copy of *Biogea* but in the end did not. Just the other day I placed an order at Daedalus, a remainder house in Maryland, for a few books, including *The Carbon Age: How Life's Core Element Has Become Mankind's Greatest Threat*, *The Thoreau You Don't Know*, and Joyce Appleby's history of capitalism. And to tell you the truth, my shelves are already brimming with contemporary works translated from the French, few of which I've read. (For my money, Vincent Descombes is the best of the lot.) It seems to me that for the most part, the infatuation on this side of the Atlantic for French thinking has been a big mistake.

Alongside his concern for the environment and the future of the printed word, Drew also raised the question: Whither the humanities in this increasingly technical and capitalistic ethos? Yet it wouldn't be too much of an exaggeration to say that the humanities were weakened from within and rendered irrelevant at least a generation ago by the sloppy, fashion-minded jargon of the post-modern academy.

Such caveats aside, I rose from my folding chair at the end of the presentation full of admiration for the Univocal enterprise—both its principles and its methods. And the Michel Serres book did sound interesting. (Maybe I'll buy it on-line.)

As I wandered the beautiful gallery of the Center on my way out, ogling the wonderful paper-based projects on display, admiring the evening light streaming in through the window, and pondering the massive river churning away just down the street, though out of sight, it occurred to me that Univocal ought to consider scuppering its white covers and the austere, digital-looking design qualities in favor of more colorful, and perhaps even florid creations worthy of the cosmic rivers of life, death, poetry, and insight flowing across the pages inside.

JAMES CARTER AT THE DAKOTA

James Carter was a phenomenon at seventeen, a virtuoso on several reeds at twenty-one, and now that he's 43…it sometimes seems that he still hasn't quite got it altogether.

The show he put on at the Dakota Sunday night was dazzling, frustrating, and almost boring by turns, yet the final impact approached greatness. Or so it seems to me. That greatness was musical only in part. The rest came from the good feeling in the room, between the musicians and also from with several members of the audience who mean a great deal to Carter. He referred to them repeatedly in the course of the show, with great affection, as "Pops" and "Moms." By the time the second set was over, they were both up on stage performing.

I ought to confess here I'm not a James Carter expert. I heard him at the old Dakota in St. Paul many years ago in a quartet setting. It was a wild show, utter cacophony, Coleman Hawkins riffs,

New Orleans roars, coming out of both horns in a riotous tangle of sounds. It was one of the best shows I've ever heard.

I believe the man on the baritone sax that night was Donald Washington, the man in the audience whom Carter referred to the other night as "my musical father"—or simply "Pops."

But the few Carter recordings I've heard seldom rise to that level. Carter seems reluctant to keep to any one tone or style for more than a minute or two, other than the honking free jazz mode, before he starts making strange noises, worrying and drawing out the notes, or heading off in a self-mocking, comical direction. It seems he can do anything on almost any horn, but he's suspicious of ballads and he obviously prefers bluesy riffs to challenging Bebop chord changes. As often as not, he doesn't seem to be playing from inside the music, but merely joking and raging through it.

The same attitude can be felt in his on-stage patter, an odd mix of insouciance, charm, sincerity, and affectation.

The presence of ever-smiling drummer Leonard King, Jr. Sunday night was a blessing, and the rich tonal backdrop provided by Gerard Gibbs on the B-3 organ also helped to sustain that "Hey! Jazz can be fun!" mood, though Gibbs's own solos took a long time to gather steam.

Carter delivered flashes of brilliance throughout the first set, along with plenty of feverish high-energy riffs. He played a fine, pure intro to Ellington's "Come Sunday" on the flute, and King delivered an extended scat solo on one of the up-tempo numbers.

If we'd left at intermission, I'd have considered it an engaging evening but musically schizophrenic and not entirely satisfying. But Dakota impresario Lowell Pickett assured the audience that there were seats available for anyone who wanted to stick around.

We went out into the lobby to secure our seats for the second set, then wandered Nicollet Mall for a block or two in the evening twilight. We discovered they'd been serving crawfish buckets out on the patio—that would have been entirely in keeping with the fun-loving and rather "Southern" first set.

Back at our table, I got to talking with the young man who'd

been sitting next to us. I'd seen him chatting with one of the men sitting at the table behind us with Moms and Pops.

So, do you know those people?" I asked him.

"He's my teacher, Kevin Washington. His parents were sort of mentors to James."

"Then you must be a musician."

"Yeah, I play the drums."

When his mother returned from the bathroom the truth came out. This shy young man was Miguel Hurtado. He plays with several groups around town. He was booked for a late-night set at the Dakota with trumpeter Jake Baldwin the next week.

By this time Carter himself had come over to chat with Moms. (I don't know where Pops had gone.) I went over to say hello, but didn't want to interrupt their conversation. James was telling Moms about his flute, pointing at things as she held it in her hand. From what I could tell, he'd bought it in a pawn shop in Winnipeg. There was some note he could hit on that thing that he'd never hit before.

Finally, I said, interrupting, "I don't mean to interrupt…but I hope you don't mind my talking your picture."

"Not at all, go right ahead," he said graciously, turning his head.

They both smiled and I got my shot. (It was very low light.)

"Thanks very much," I said, "I loved the first set…"

But before I could make my exit, Carter said, "How about you taking *our* picture?" He pulled out a little camera.

JAMES CARTER AT THE DAKOTA   155

"OK, sure," I replied, taking the camera. "Get closer together, scrunch up a bit, this will be good." And I took the shot.

James began his intro to the second set talking about the bucket of crayfish he'd just eaten. I couldn't hear much of what he said, but clearly he'd been enjoying himself. Finally he said, "But enough of this colored humor...We're going to open the second set with a number off my Caribbean album."

From the first note, the band was in a higher groove, and the energy only increased when Carter invited Pops up onto the stage. A twenty-minute explosion ensued, not unlike the set I'd heard in St. Paul—though this time we were sitting farther from the stage.

King sang a mellow rendition of the ballad "I Wonder Where Our Love Has Gone," with Carter adding a few rich choruses. And even Gibbs started to put out a little more, moving beyond the funky chord-rattling and repetitive hi-jinks into a more inventive vein.

The ballad came at just the right time, and when Carter invited Moms up on the stage to sing some scat and play the flute, it seemed the evening was finally complete: music, love, honoring the elders, crayfish, religion, energy. Lots of hugging and smiling on stage, lots of grinning in the audience. I knew my ears would be ringing when we stepped out into the night.

Carter's showmanship often gets in the way of his musicianship, but in the course of this four-hour display of artistry, both elements gave way to vibrant expressions of hospitality and good-feeling.

The Thoreau You Don't Know

To some, Thoreau is an icon of environmental insight and political conscience, a keen social critic, and a paragon of self-sufficiency. To others, he's a fraud, a misanthrope, and a dour, holier-than-thou stick-in-the-mud who took his washing to be done by servants at his mother's house, week after week, that is, when he wasn't actually living there.

To me, Thoreau has been a hero of sorts since I was in high school, though at a certain point it occurred to me that I had never actually read *Walden*, but only thumbed through a few pages here and there. I believe I was more profoundly influenced by *In Wildness is the Preservation of the Earth*, a Sierra Club book of photos by Eliot Porter with quotes by Thoreau attached. Even today, when I come upon a beautiful, densely textured forest scene, not classically picturesque but bristling with subtle patterns and shafts of light, I say to myself, "Now there's an Eliot Porter scene."

The only book by Thoreau I've read cover to cover is *Cape Cod*. But it was obvious to me from the first that Thoreau was better with words than the common run of mid-nineteenth century prose stylists. His sentences are clear, evocative, and riddled with irony and humor in the best "modern" style. What can sometimes grow tiresome are his gripes against his fellow man. And his paradoxical turns of phrase at times seem merely facile or clever rather than genuinely insightful.

In his recent biography, *The Thoreau You Don't Know*, Robert Sullivan has done a good job of reminding me of the Thoreau I once admired. He paints a portrait of a joking, musical character who not only criticized those of his neighbors who were living "lives of quiet desperation," but also expressed admiration for the ones who knew their land well and managed it wisely.

Far from being a misanthrope, Thoreau gave lectures, managed the family pencil-factory, surveyed most of the area around Concord at one time or another, hosted a popular watermelon festival every summer, and in general, led a very town-centered life, even when he was conducting his experiment at Walden Pond—a twenty-minute walk from Concord.

Against Thoreau's famous remark that "in wildness is the preservation of the earth," Sullivan counterpoises another that he finds more Thoreauvian. "The wilderness is simple, almost to barrenness. The partially cultivated country it is, which chiefly has inspired, and will continue to inspire, the strains of poets, such as compose the mass of any literature."

But as Sullivan stresses in the introduction, his book is less a biography of Thoreau than a "look at the times and the conditions under which he wrote, and a look at him as a free lance writer..." This turns out to be a fruitful perspective. The Panic of 1837, the vast influx of Irish immigrants, the resultant increase in domestic servants, and the rising popularity of Martha-Stewart-like home decoration and management books, are all phenomena that Thoreau was well aware of and often refers to obliquely in his work. At a distance of almost two centuries, it's sometimes difficult for the modern reader to discern when Thoreau is being serious and when he's gently lampooning a fashion or attitude of his own day. (Scholars have been saying the same thing about Socrates for centuries.) Sullivan gives us the background to do so, and in the process he fleshes out a more nuanced and interesting portrait of the man than we're accustomed to, complete with love interests, social commitments, and ecological analysis a century ahead of its time.

Along the way Sullivan also offers shrewd portraits of Thoreau's parents, his brother John, and lifelong friends including Emerson, Hawthorne, Horace Greeley, Bronson Alcott, Orestes Brownson, and Ellery Channing. He describes Thoreau's growth as a free lance writer as perhaps only a fellow free-lancer could. Nor does he neglect to explore at length Thoreau's approach to observing "nature," which seems to be as much about farmers, ice-cutters, and woodchoppers as it is about frogs, hazelnuts, and northern lights.

As we approach the end of the book, we feel we've been thoroughly exposed to Thoreau's cranky side, too, though his superlative awareness of everything going on in his neighborhood shines through repeatedly. In the last chapter Sullivan decides to walk the short distance from downtown Concord to Walden Pond, where the plaque reads, in part: "...I did not wish to live what was not life, Living is so dear."

Sullivan has succeeded in bringing the man's liveliest moments to the surface. It's a Thoreau I once knew, but had somehow forgotten.

✺

New Orleans Way

It was in the news every day during the spring of 2011: millions of gallons of water barreling down the Mississippi. In early May we saw the swollen river from the bluffs in Natchez and Memphis, awesome and dangerous. But when you're driving around amid the bayous of southern Louisiana, you don't get the news much. And whatever the media may report, you notice there's still a lot of dry ground south and west of New Orleans before you get to the Gulf of Mexico.

One day during our visit, we wandered the backroads that parallel the bayous on the way south from Houma to Cocodrie. Though utterly flat, much of the landscape is covered with tall grasses—it looks like a very unkept corner of the Netherlands.

The houses and shacks that line the bayous are all perched fifteen feet in the air, with cars and boats stored in the open air underneath.

At one point I spotted a least bittern fly into a roadside marsh and then run delicately along the tops of the reeds in pursuit of a fish. I'd never seen one before. Forster's terns were flying overhead, and helicopters also passed repeatedly much higher up, carrying men and parts out to the oil rigs in the gulf.

A young lawn-service worker at a shaved-ice stand along the canal told us they were going to open a spillway and flood the town of Morgan City, which we'd passed through the day before. We told him we were headed for New Orleans and he said: "They're also going to open up the Bonnet Carré. You'll be going right over it."

"Can we get through?" I asked.

"Of course," he said, "There's bridges."

From the waterfront in New Orleans, the river looked like a mile-wide rapids, and river traffic had been curtailed for fear the wake might breech the levees. But music was still playing on the Riverboat Natchez. They were serving beans and rice and beer and hurricane drinks at a dozen restaurants in the French Quarter. It was 90 degrees, and it was fun.

II. ACADIANA

The part of Louisiana known as Acadiana was often in the news as the river rose, because that's the region that would be bearing the brunt of the Mississippi flooding if and when they opened the Morganza Spillway. The term wasn't coined until the 1960s, but the French-speaking Acadians to which it refers began to arrive in the region in the eighteenth century, having been expelled from Nova Scotia by the British for "security" reasons, even though they'd maintained a posture of vehement neutrality in the colonial wars of the era.

Today few people in southern Louisiana speak French, I suspect, though I could be wrong. (Perhaps their grandmothers did.) Yet the culture of the region is distinctive, with shrimp boats, Roman Catholicism, jambalaya, bayous, alligators, and the Cajun two-step adding to the fun. On the map the entire area looks to be a maze of rivers, swamps, bayous, and canals, but anyone who pays a visit will see that most of Acadiana consists of flat, dry fields planted with sugar cane, wheat, and rice. As you travel south down the minor roads that parallel the major bayous, the fields turn to grasslands and water.

During the three days we were in the area, we caught a bit of the local flavor. I think our most pleasant morning was spent in St. Martinville, where we toured a plantation and ate some fabulous *beignets* at Le Petit Paris Café. A group of women were having breakfast when we arrived. One of them told us that they attend Mass every day at 6:30, arriving 30 minutes early to do a few rosaries. On Saturdays they have breakfast together after Mass at the café across the street from the church. That's where we ran into them.

"St. Martinville is a dying town," one woman told us. "You can see for yourself." And she gestured toward the empty storefront of Hebert's Jewelry store next to the café. "When they built the freeway from Lafayette to Baton Rouge, the businesses began to drift north to Breaux Bridge." All the same, she was born and raised there, and today she lives next door to her brother, who has taken to shooting the armadillos that tear up the yard with their snooting and shoveling.

Breaux Bridge is famous for its Café des Amis, an unassuming place that serves some very fine food and holds a Zydego brunch every Saturday morning. We ate lunch there and caught some of the Zydego action the next morning. Mulates, a more traditional Cajun roadhouse out on the highway, has a dark interior and low ceilings, murals of the bayous on the walls, a bustling atmosphere, frequent live music, and a much bigger dance floor. (If you rent the German film, *Shultz Gets the Blues*, about a melancholy retiree and amateur accordian player who travels from Germany to the American South, you'll get a few glimpes inside the place.)

A few miles south into the backcountry (presuming you know the way) is Lake Martin, the shores of which are ringed with half-submerged cypress trees.

At Lake Martin it's easy to spot alligators near shore, and at one point the shrubs support a rookery where we watched little blue herons (that's a species, by the way, not a term of endearment) feed their babies as roseate spoonbills flew back and forth from their nests in the pines further out in the swamp.

Back in Breaux Bridges, we parked downtown and wandered the streets north toward the Crayfish Festival. It turned out to be a far more elaborate event than I'd anticipated. We took some free dancing lessons in 90 degree heat under one of the many white tents that had been set up alongside the freeway, and later ordered three pounds of crayfish at another pavilion. That may sound like quite a feast, but once you've torn the heads off and peeled away the legs, there isn't much left to eat. (The real connoisseurs suck the fluids out of the heads.)

We would have danced some more—there were bands playing on several stages—but I couldn't figure out where to put our lemonade glass that guaranteed an unending succession of $1 refills.

III. New Orleans: Jazz

I have heard more than one person say recently, "New Orleans is my favorite city." A cyclist we met on the Natchez Trace said, "New Orleans. You either love it or you hate it," and then she added, "I want to be there right now!" My sister Nancy is an adventurous traveler, but her one-sentence appraisal of the city is, "It's smelly and dirty: I hate it."

To each his (or her) own, I guess.

After having spent a mere two days on foot in the French Quarter, I'm in no position to call New Orleans my favorite city. (New York? London? Rome? Duluth?) But I can say that New Orleans is fascinating and full of history and energy and music and color. If the Minnesota State Fair were held on the Left

162   BY THE WAY

Bank in Paris, the atmosphere would perhaps resemble that of the French Quarter in New Orleans.

To which remark the learned might reply, "There is very little French architecture in the French Quarter. The neighborhood is largely a reflection of Spanish building and decorative techniques." All well and good. Let's just say that the open-air bohemian café-sitting, the street musicians, the various little shops and museums, the urban intimacy created by the side-streets and courtyards and grade-school kids in uniform marching toward the waiting bus, give the place an attractive European ambiance, while the affordable and unfussy Cajun cuisine and the ubiquity of tourists in flip-flops and tank tops divest the area of the slightest whiff of pretense.

Here's a theory: The French Quarter is the anti-Las Vegas. Everything is small and closed in, some of it is venerable and most of it (dare I say it?) is sort of "real." Yet it shares with Las Vegas the sense that fake is fine, and those who come here know precisely why they came, and they know how to have a good time while they're here.

Ten minutes after we'd hit the streets, slightly overwhelmed by the age and glitter and grit of the Quarter, we turned a corner and happened upon the Smoking Time Jazz Club, a brass band that was playing some old-time tunes like "Sweetheart on Parade" and "Livin' in a Great Big Way." A lithe young couple was doing the Charleston (or something) on the street in front of the band. They were part of the band, in fact. The musicians were equally loose and the soloists took to their sixteen bars of fame with brash and joyous aggressiveness.

Sweltering heat, trumpets blaring, limbs flaring—it was a great introduction to the city. We even bought one of the band's CDs, a self-produced item *sans* label wrapped in a sheet of yellow construction paper. (I'm listening to it now. It's good.)

That night (after returning to the room for a nap, a shower, and a glance at the laptop in search of entertainment ideas) we wandered back down to Bourbon Street, which was just coming alive. Monday is probably the quietest night of the week, but there

was still plenty of music blaring out of doorways, block after block.

Folks were wandering here and there with green hurricane drinks in hand, though they weren't staggering yet. It was exhilarating to thread that gauntlet, though nothing I heard sounded all that tempting. The Dixieland bands were less youthful and brash than what we'd heard at noon, and though the Cajun band we listened to for a while from one doorway was good, we'd been hearing that kind of thing for days and the dance-floor inside was already packed. The ubiquitous blues noodling of white guitarists that drifted into aural range, block after block, were uniformly dreadful. (That's just my opinion.)

Eight or twelve blocks east toward downtown, we finally wandered into the marble-lined, fern-festooned halls of the quiet, largely empty, and unmitigatedly staid lobby of the Royal Sonesta Hotel.

The choice was neither arbitrary nor escapist. We'd come to the Irvin Mayfield Jazz Playhouse to hear The Original Tuxedo Jazz Band, which has a continuous record of performing in New Orleans dating back to 1910. A few of the original members have "passed" by now, of course, but drummer Bob French has led the group since 1977, which isn't bad. The band was good-natured and eager to please. The guitarist (who, to judge from his

solos, might once have been a protégé of Johnny Smith or How-
ard Roberts) looked like he'd just stepped off the set of *I Dream
of Genie*. A black torch-singer in a white spaghetti-strap gown
stepped up onto the stage to do a few songs, and at one point the
trumpeter cut loose with a brief but startlingly inventive solo. All
in all, the set was "good enough," considering there was no cover
and only a one-drink minimum.

It was made more interesting by the fact that an uninhibited
middle-aged woman joined us at our table. She'd spent the previous week at the New Orleans Jazz and Heritage Festival with a
Gold Pass. She was thrilled to have heard Sonny Rollins at the
final concert, and was a little surprised to learn that we Northern-
ers had heard Rollins—Yes, "live"—several times during the '70s
in Minneapolis, when he was still in his prime.

She called the San Juan Islands home, but evidently she didn't
need money and wandered where she willeth. She seemed to
have roots in New Orleans, too: as it happens, she was dating the
bassist—a tall, elderly, black man with a well-trimmed mustache
and courtly manners. He joined us after the set. The two of them
re-lived the exciting moments they'd heard or participated in at
the festival while we finished our $6 pints and prepared an exit.

"How long will you be staying in New Orleans," the man
asked us genteelly as we rose to depart.

"We've only got one more day here," I replied. "We're due back
in Minneapolis on Sunday."

"But that's four days from now!" he blurted out, somewhat
surprised.

"We'll be doing a lot of zigzagging through the Ozarks," I
replied apologetically.

The next day was walking tours and museums and beignets
and blackened catfish po'boys. I was exhausted by the time
we got back to the room, and was surprised, a half hour later, to
see Hilary putting curlers in her hair. It never occurred to me
we'd be going out again that night.

New Orleans Way   165

Bourbon Street was a bit more animated, and there were quite a few more women of all ages and shapes in fringed bikinis leaning from doorways toward the passing businessmen. We got to the Jazz Playhouse at the Royal Sonesta before the opening set started and listened in as the drummer Jason Marsalis chatted with the reedman Rex Gregory about the chord changes on some obscure Art Blakey LP from the mid-1950s like a couple of precocious frat house boys who were keen on bop.

From where I sat in my Victorian chair fifteen feet from the stage, the talented but self-effacing bassist, Peter Harris, looked like a Wilson that was too clean-cut to join his older brothers in the Beach Boys. Marsalis himself looked like a young Will Smith. And Rex looked like a thin white guy trying to be hip by wearing a cap. I mention the strangely collegial appearance of these folks as a prelude to declaiming that the set they played was one of the best I've heard in years. They *are* hip.

As I remember it now, the play-list included a Charlie Parker tune ("Barbados"), a Monk tune ("Nutty"), a Hoagy Carmichael tune ("Stardust"), and "All of Me." But Jason Marsalis, like his older brother Wynton, is not only a fine musician but also a musical scholar. Therefore, he felt compelled to grope ever deeper into the past to come up with "St. James Infirmary," "You Are My Sunshine," and finally, even "Bourbon Street Parade." But there was nothing academic about these performances. Marsalis provided the percussive energy and Gregory sustained the lyric spark, sounding a lot like Pres and Hawkins sounded back in the 40s when they still had energy and spark. I kept saying to myself, (like Redford or Newman), "Who *are* those guys?" The absence of a piano was a blessing. Genius in our midst. Egoless expression. These people don't know how good they are. (Probably they do.)

166   *By the Way*

THE GARDEN GATE

The violets are healthy and happy and spreading everywhere, and nothing that I or the neighborhood rabbits can do will keep them back for long. All the same, on a sunny morning I sometimes enjoy spending a few minutes in the back yard with a hand trowel and a bucket, digging up those little clusters of heart-shaped leaves. It may have rained the night before, in which case the air will be cool and fresh, and the sweet smells of earth and vegetation will be everywhere.

We have lived in this house for close to thirty years, and during that time the garden in the back yard has become shadier. A visit to the nursery is largely an exercise in nostalgia. We wander among the lovely flowering plants, and as we scrutinize a particular cultivar our unspoken thought is, "We tried that one. It died." "That one died." "That one didn't do so well." Now it's astilbes and hostas. Kirengishima, goatsbeard, Siberian bugloss. Clematis recta. Ligularia. I've been moving ferns over from the terraced garden under the window for quite a few years now.

On the other hand, weeds don't grow very well in the garden shade either, and I find the absence of color largely compensated by the variation in leaf pattern we've succeeded in establishing. We scatter impatiens here and there for a little color. A few daylilies bloom in June and July. Some black-eyed susans show up later in the summer. As the painter and sometime gardener Robert Dash once put it, "I am predelicted toward shape, mass, and form, and have learned that the predominant color of all gardens is green...."

The great triumph of this gardening season has been the wrought iron arbor I bought recently to gather the wild grape vines that thrive in the shade under the spruce trees on the south east side of the yard. That portal is so handsome! Every time I walk through it I feel the freedom and ease of not having to brush aside all the vines and elderberry branches that used to crowd the path. It's true, I don't go that way very often, unless I'm pushing the lawn mower from the front yard to the back yard, in which case the magic of the moment is somewhat undercut by the noise of the machinery and the sensation of dead, dry pine needles flying at great speed against my unprotected shins. All the same, I love that arch.

It may be wisdom or sheer laziness—I don't know—but these days I take particular interest in noting the plants that just happen to show up in the garden. This is true, in particular, of that part of the back yard I refer to as "the woods." We were originally attracted to the house, in part, because of this band of uncontrolled vegetation, which stretches along the back of the lot and varies in width from fifteen to twenty feet. For many years it gave us the impression we were living a long way from town. But when the neighbor kids were young they trashed it mercilessly, breaking off trees and trampling the woodland wildflowers that had been planted by the previous owner. I don't blame them. I did the same myself when I was their age. And the local deer also played a part in thinning the screen. As the ash and box elder trees got taller, the leaf cover got thicker, the understory got feebler, and the screen became thinner. Forest succession.

Meanwhile, as the trees got taller, the power company got more diligent in trimming back the branches that were threatening the wires running along the back of the lot. Two years ago they really went to town on our woods, trampling underbrush and severing tree-trunks at ground level. For the first time in twenty years, sunlight reached the forest floor.

Though saddened somewhat by the loss of privacy, I also saw this turn of events as a golden opportunity to plant a few species that would (or so I thought) become tall thick bushes in a few short years, thus re-establishing the screen of vegetation without unduly threatening the power lines. To that end I purchased and planted two nannyberry bushes, a gray dogwood, and a red-twigged dogwood. I watered them faithfully throughout the hot summer months. I watched weedy plants spring up on every side and eventually begin to steal the sunlight. I pondered the dense clay-like soil that I had removed while digging the holes for these sophisticated species. And throughout the winter months I looked forward to the day when they would sprout again, well-established, thrifty, secure, and ready to expand by leaps and bounds.

I don't remember quite when it was I noticed the deer had eaten down the tasty branches of these dormant bushes considerably. By May I had to admit that one of the four had died and the other three were now smaller than when I bought them. I crafted some chicken-wire tubes to keep the deer at bay. *And this summer*, I said to myself, *they'll really begin to show their worth.*

I took a stroll through the woods earlier this evening, to see how my *babies* were doing. Well, they're still alive, though they don't exactly stand out in the midst of all the verdure. I still have hope for them, but it's also interesting to note who else has moved into the neighborhood. I see honeysuckles, Virginia creeper, and some kind of mint that looks a lot like ragweed. There are low-lying jack-in-the-pulpit everywhere, box-elders, buckthorns, and one small tree that looks for all the world like an apricot. There are serviceberries here and there, and Canadian elderberry. And I spotted one hearty plant that looks like rhubarb, though it isn't red and it's already five feet tall!

It's fun to stroll through the woods after a long hard day at the office, then settle myself at the table on the deck, looking out at all the vegetation as it catches the late afternoon sun, forming lush, complex layers of green and yellow and gold. If the woods were thicker, that luscious light would not be filtering through.

THE GARDEN GATE 169

The word paradise comes from the Persian word for an enclosed park, or garden. And the garden (unlike the farm) has appeared throughout history as a locus of both romance and meditation. Gardens have springs, fountains, shade, peace, pleasant scents, and colorful accents. Relaxing at our ease, it's difficult to resist the thought that this is what life ought to be like *all* the time.

I recently came across a scholarly analysis of the peculiar wild-yet-wonderful effect that gardens often establish.

> *Places of this kind represent a compromise, a fusion of elements of city and wilderness, symbolical of a harmony between reason and the forces of the subconscious. A fitting climate, then, for naturalism as revaluation of instinctive life in a rational framework... an appropriate introduction for a gentle opening of the mind—without a direct, sudden, and drastic exposure—to those subterranean phenomena of life, those forces of matter and of the unconscious, which, in their full bloom, could but frighten and repel....*

Yet it strikes me that the relationship between reason and wildness we find in a garden is less of a compromise than an abiding reality that accompanies us, taunts us, delights us, and challenges us, whether we're in the city, on the golf course, wandering an upland pasture, or out in the bosom of wilderness itself. We bring an element of civility to the wilderness simply by being in it. By the same token, there is no drawing room, garden, or church in the world, however refined, that doesn't have an element of *wildness* to it, simply because we are there.

The comedian Jerry Seinfeld once observed sagely that the pleasure we take in driving around in cars can be attributed to the fact that we're inside and outside, moving and stationary, all at the same time. It might similarly be pointed out that when we're in a garden, we're in the midst of wildness that has been somewhat tamed, tailored, and beautified by human effort. We're clearly outside, yet protected by an enclosure of sorts, thus bringing another set of evident contradictions to life.

Wild/tame-inside/outside. Philosophers have been struggling for centuries to establish a hierarchy amid these interfaces. It can't be done. Everything raw and open and beautiful in life erupts from the midst of this cauldron of confusion. In fact, it may be that we feel "grounded" in life only to the degree that we can feel the tussle taking place within us, and have some idea of the direction we want to take it.

The garden must certainly rank among the most pleasing end-results of that drama. We retire to the deck, following our satisfying spell of work with the plants, and stare mindlessly off into the underbrush. We admire the curving branch of the buckeye tree for perhaps the fifteenth time, though we know we'll have to cut it down soon. We find ourselves at home in this inside/outside wild/tame environment that closely resembles, and in fact includes, ourselves.

But make no mistake. The plants we cultivate and enjoy may become our friends, but they stand somewhat removed from us. Like us, they have elevated themselves above the random molecular activity of the interstellar regions. Yet their habits, forms, and colors continue to startle and impress us, because we see in their visage creative achievements that we could never conceive of on our own and will never match. The irregular pattern of a single nasturtium leaf, with its spoke-like ribs, may, on occasion, fill us with a child-like joy. As for the tender tissue of the soft orange flower hiding underneath, it can sometimes be almost shocking in its appeal.

❦

SCANDINAVIANS IN NISSWA

The Nisswa-Stammen is a low-key festival held each summer in an outdoor "pioneer village" in the lake country a few miles north of Brainerd, Minnesota, a few thousand miles up the Mississippi from New Orleans. Fans of Nordic culture drop in, often in costume, to listen to musicians play. There are amateurs and professionals, Scandinavians and home-grown talent. Dance and performance workshops are held throughout the day on Friday, there's a concert that night, and the next day the musicians play a rotating schedule of 30-minute sets at three outdoor stages, with additional dance instruction being offered (to live accompaniment) to beginners like us, in a log cabin "dance barn" so small it might better have been named the "dance shed." On Saturday night a smorgasbord is offered in a nearby church, followed by a genuine dance that can run into the wee hours of the morning.

Or so I'm told. We've been to two such festivals now—the Saturday portion at any rate—and have taken a few dance lessons ourselves. But we're not sufficiently adept to make it worthwhile lingering at the evening dance. Besides, after a long drive and a day of listening (and eating) in the open air, we're pretty much worn out by the time that last meatball disappears from the smorgasbord plate.

Last year the Scandinavian headliners put on outstanding shows—Geitungen (from Norway), Faerd (from Denmark and Sweden), and the Polka Chicks (from Finland). This year the groups were smaller and slightly more traditional in their approach.

The Näsbom brothers, for example, learned to play from their musician father, and listened to Eric Sahlström, Viksta Lasse, and other eminent fiddlers perform in their childhood home in

Norway at an early age. Torbjörn took up the nyckelharpa as well, and though Pär moved to Switzerland two decades ago, the brothers have continued to perform and tour together, playing the Uppland tunes they first learned as children.

At one point I spotted Torbjörn tuning his nickelharpa over by a split-rail fence and went over to chat.

"It's hard to keep this in tune in the Minnesota weather," he said, in his clipped, slightly nasal tone of voice. "It's a lot hotter and more humid here than it is in Norway. But I think the instrument has finally gotten used to it."

"How long have you been in Minnesota?" I asked.

"Almost a week. We got here Monday."

"Really? What have you been doing?"

"We went fishing on Mille Lacs Lake." He smiled.

"Any luck?"

"Yes, we caught quite a few walleyes. Some were so big that we had to throw them back." And then he explained to me carefully, as if *I* were the newcomer from Norway, how the law requires that the really small and the really big ones could not be kept.

"I hope you managed to keep a few," I said.

"Oh, yes. We ate quite a lot of them. We even had enough to invite the Danish girls over for a fish fry."

The Danish "girls" to whom Torbjörn was referring were the members of Fiolministeriet. So casual is this annual event that by the time we heard this trio perform I'd already had the pleasure of dancing with Kirstine Sand, the group's violinist. She'd been teaching Danish dances in the "dance barn" and she stepped in line along with everyone else for the ensuing "mixer." It was crowded in that confined spaced, and as I did my level best with Kirstine, the conversation went as follows:

Me: There's no place to turn.

Her: Take smaller steps.

And then we were moving on to the next partner.

Kristine is joined in Fiolministeriet by a violist and a cellist, and all three of the women sing. The cello gives their arrangements added richness, and though many of the tunes come from their home islands of Funen and Bornholm, they often seek out irregular rhythms and sudden dynamic contrasts, which also adds to the interest. At times the very richness of the string sound brought a classical feel to the performance, unlike the Nasbom's, whose austere and even creaky sound evoked log huts, long winters, and goats on the roof.

Norwegian Hardanger fiddler Britt Pernille Frøholm teamed up with freebase accordionist Linda Gytri for a couple of lively sets, though I was no less mesmerized by the fiddling of Loretta Kelley, sometimes referred to as America's foremost Hardanger fiddler. She did a few haunting tunes at one point with vocalist Arna Rennen, who lives on the North Shore. Arna, in turn, did some story-telling numbers in the Summer Kitchen Stage with Georganne Hunter.

We know Georganne because I worked on a book with her husband, the herring fisherman Stephen Dahl. But such connections didn't help when we tried to get past the Viking gate-keeper into the Summer Kitchen, a log cabin a quarter of the size of the Dance Barn. (We listened at the window for a while, and

Georganne later filled us in on the gist of the stories they were telling.)

Out on the Allspel Stage, veteran Finnish soloist Arto Järvelä (who founded the groundbreaking string band JPP almost thirty years ago) also put on quite a show, drawing some slow, delicate stuff from the fiddle and letting loose on one or two raucous vocals, too. He later took the stage with the American group Kaivama—one of the few groups at the festival with both a guitar and keyboard.

As you may have guessed, I couldn't tell a *polsk* from a *jenkka* or a *hambo* from a *nigvals*, not if my life depended on it. (I could easily distinguish between a *siguireas* and a *soleá*, but that's a different story.) Still, I love the music—both the cheerful "regular" tunes and the strange, irregular ones. Something precise and lively and as simple as a children's game, yet steeped in piney forest mists and the brooding spirit of Swedenborg and Hamsun.

How can you explain it? Yet music and dance and food and landscape and heritage *must* come together from time to time. At the Nisswa-Stammen they do.

By the time the afternoon performances were winding to a close, the temperature had risen to 90 degrees, and though we were sitting in the shade, the heat had begun to take its toll. So we drove out to the public access on Lower Cullen Lake to dangle our feet in the water before redeeming our 5:15 ticket to the smorgasbord at the VFW.

Salmon, herring, deviled eggs, pork, au gratin potatoes, beets with apples, meatballs, cucumbers, baked beans. At the smorgasbord we sat across from a Francophone couple from Thunder Bay who'd come down for the festival—a ten-hour drive. We got to talking about the Acadians in Louisiana and they told us about a Celtic festival they attend in Thunder Bay. Later we all headed north to the town hall at Pequot Lakes for the big dance. You can't miss the place: it's just off the highway, under the water tower painted to resemble a fishing bobber.

SCANDINAVIANS IN NISSWA   175

This blending of music and dance is the essence of the experience, of course. If you add the ambiance of a cool summer evening—with or without nighthawks—the memory sinks deep. And if you can't do the dances, you can still enjoy watching. They do some "mixers" that everyone screws up, due to how crowded the dance floor is (and also due to the fact that some people just can't count to eight). It's fun, regardless of the confusion, to find yourself dancing with an eminent fiddler or a twelve-year-old girl with braids and braces for a few minutes, before the routine carries you on to your next partner.

By nine we were back at our motel in Baxter, nursing a bag of potato chips and listening to the passing traffic on Highway 371. A train would occasionally rumble past, heading to Fargo and places beyond, just as they've been doing since 1871. Snatches of nickelharpa and fiddle were also ringing in my ears.

Oh! That's Hilary, googling things on her iPad.

A FEW RECOMMENDED RECORDINGS

Britt Pernelle Frøholm: *Eins*
Frøholm's fiddling benefits from the rich freebase accordian accompaniment of Irene Tillung, and the top-flight recording gives these numbers an electric liveliness.

Geittungen: *Langt Ute*
Three kids—strings, fiddle, accordian—offering simple tunes that sink as deeply as a pine forest.

Færd: *Landmark*
Songs from Denmark, Sweden, and the Faroe Islands, irregular rhythms and touches of jazz.

Torbjörn & Pär Näsbom: *Upptakt*
This set of fiddle-nyckelharpa duets is hardcore ethnographic stuff, and no one would describe it as cheery, but...

❦

SEVENTEEN MILES ON THE RUM RIVER

We had no idea what to expect, beyond what could be gleaned from the window of a fast-moving car on Highway 169. But we wanted to get to know the Rum River better. Internet sources were few and all but worthless. The DNR's map of the river was better, giving accurate mileage and a few comments about hazards, campsites, and points of public access. The Falcon guide *Paddling Minnesota* was little help. Thomas Waters' classic *The Streams and Rivers of Minnesota* was useful to a degree, though it came out in 1977, and things have changed.

For example, Waters writes that the stretch between Onamia and Princeton "is not wild—it is crossed by many roads…The riverside is not heavily wooded, and much of the area is in pasture or open fields."

Well, the seventeen-mile stretch we canoed in early June is *entirely* wooded. And discounting three or four bridges and the mile or so just before you arrive in Milaca, it's entirely wild. During the first two hours we were on the water we saw nary a person, a pasture, or any other sign of human activity, aside from three or four isolated cabins. In fact, during that interval we couldn't even find a convenient place to come ashore and ponder the beauty of the scene.

When Louis Hennepin negotiated the river in 1682 it could hardly have been more wild.

As for the water level, it was high, and that was a good thing. The official DNR reading available online was two months out of date—not worth much, considering all the rain that had fallen in the central part of the state the previous month. Then again, the Rum River gets most of its flow from Mille Lacs Lake, which is a very steady source. We learned more from the attendant at the wayside rest on Highway 169 fifteen miles north of Milaca,

THE RUM RIVER 177

where a path down the hill through the woods led to the river.

"The river's high, so you shouldn't bang around too much," he told us. "Some people in kayaks went down yesterday."

When I suggested a three-hour transit time to Milaca he hesitated, then nodded his head in a sort of doubtful affirmation.

Waters writes of this stretch of river, "Upstream from Milaca, the Rum is clear so that canoeing or wading is a real visual pleasure." That much is true. It might have been nice of him to add, "Most of this stretch is rapids."

Now, there are rapids and there are rapids. Not much of the river we ran was "whitewater" per se. But here's the way I look at it. On many mid-sized rivers, you mostly have the freedom to drift, springing to attention occasionally when the sound of riffling water approaches. On the upper Rum River, you're moving pretty fast, and there are very few stretches when you *aren't* looking ahead, charting your immediate path, looking for Vs and protruding rocks, or actually negotiating a Class One rapids. The hazards are ever-present, and the swift current is relentlessly carrying you toward or through them. There is little time to pause or ponder anything.

None of these rapids are terribly dangerous or difficult. But what you begin to notice is not the rapids, but the rare two-minute interludes when the river ahead looks calm and you can relax, look at the map, or extract the camera from its plastic bag and take a picture. Such moments are few and far between.

Waters tells us that the Rum River drops 145 feet during its 140-mile journey from Mille Lacs to the Mississippi, and half of that descent is along the 30-mile stretch from Onemia and Milaca.

Along this stretch I suspect the Rum is seldom more than five feet deep, and there's little danger of serious injury. What you want to avoid is hitting an isolated rock square-on in the midst of a rapid, spinning sideways in the swift current, and dumping.

Even this could well end up being fun—we were both wearing swimming suits, after all—except for the camera and binoculars we'd brought along. I was also concerned about the straps and foam cushions required to fasten the canoe to the shuttle-car once we reach the end of the journey. I would really have hated to see that stuff go floating off …

During our journey we were accompanied by an osprey that rose from the overhanging branches and flapped away downstream time and again. We also saw several bald eagles at very close range, a few chattering kingfishers, and about a thousand cedar waxwings darting out and back across the river.

We'd been paddling for two hours through the gorgeous, silent hardwood forest before we found a decent place to stop. It was a rocky spit about two feet across and ten feet wide. Hallelujah!

Hilary went swimming. I ate some cherries and drank a can of lemonade. Then we watched two iridescent green damsel-flies chase one another back and forth across our "beach." It was a lovely sight—one of those little moments when you say to yourself: "I've never seen anything like *that* before." (Might these have been the Ebony Jewelwing?)

Another thing you notice is that some rapids have lots of water in them, and though everything's moving fast, you feel that if you choose the best channel you're going to whisk right through. Then again, other rapids give off a chattering sound that tells you they're shallow and full of rattling rocks and no matter which path you take, you're going to bottom out once or twice before you get to the bottom. As you race through these riffles you sing the praises of the Grumman Aircraft Corporation. (They made the indestructible aluminum canoe you're sitting in.)

For quite a while we kept an eye out for the Old Whitney Log Dam Site, which was marked on the DNR map, but once we started to hear the traffic on 169 again we knew we'd long since passed it. By that time our map had gotten soaked and stained and I wasn't paying much attention anyway.

Meanwhile, the river had developed the habit of separating into two or three strands; there were more backwaters and side channels—maybe a cuckoo bird lurking?—some of them

THE RUM RIVER 179

carrying a good share of the river's flow and thus rendering the "main" channel that much shallower.

During the first half of our trip, we bottomed out five times—during the second half, maybe fifteen times.

On only one occasion did we hit a rock in the middle of a rapid and spin sideways. Too deep for me to disembark and steady the craft, our only hope at that point was to push off the rock and complete the spin. As a result, we found ourselves going backward down the rapids. This called for a further pirouette, which we executed deftly, brushing a few more rocks broadside in the process but completing our 360-degree circuit without going over. Bravo!

The temperature had risen above 90 degrees and I was getting tired when we spotted a communications tower above the trees ahead of us. Next the manicured fairways of a golf course came into view. Then teens in swimsuits appeared riding turquoise inner-tubes—indolent slackers a third our age who sometimes inadvertently clogged the best lanes down the ever-threatening rapids.

Then I saw the lights to the Milaca baseball field and I knew we were only a few minutes from the car. Seventeen miles. Four hours. (In case anyone's wondering how long it really takes, the way I was until today.) A beautiful and occasionally thrilling pre-4th of July event.

Heading down the Rum River, we had no idea what to expect. All we knew was that once we set off, there was no way to turn back.

I find it difficult to imagine the Dakota, the Ojibwe, or anyone else, taking this stretch of the river *upstream*. But of course they did. In his memoir recounting events that took place three centuries and more ago, Louis Hennepin recalls: "these Indians sometimes make 30 or 40 leagues (120 miles) by water when they are hurried by war or wish to overtake enemies."

❦

180   *By the Way*

Steiner and Croce
at Leech Lake

The modern age is no less rife with ignorance, superstition, and silliness than any other, I suppose. (The "post-modern" age is merely an academic fashion, an afterglow at best, and ought not to be considered an epoch in itself.) And among the silliest of its theories is the one suggesting that our expressive capabilities are somehow limited, and perhaps even dictated, by language. The idea is that because the language we use has a finite number of nouns, verbs, and adjectives, some parts of our experience will remain unexpressed, and perhaps inexpressible, due to a lack of vocabulary. It has even been suggested that our experiences themselves are flavored, and perhaps even shaped, by the terms we have at our disposal when committing them to memory. The French have eighty words for "love, "but no word for "child." Certainly this must affect how they see and describe the world?

I was reminded of this odd and misguided, but widely-held notion not long ago while sitting in the lobby of a motel in Walker, Minnesota, on the shores of Leech Lake. It was 5:30 in the morning, and I had begun to thumb through a book of essays by polymath George Steiner that I'd brought along to peruse at just such an hour. I had delved briefly into an essay called "Heidegger's Silence," hoping it would shed light on his experiences alone in his rustic cabin. The actual subject, Heidegger's troubling silence concerning the Holocaust, didn't much suit my mood, so I moved on to an essay called "The Retreat from the Word."

Here Steiner suggests that the Western tradition has been guided since ancient times by the idea that, as he puts it, "all truth and realness—with the exception of a small, queer, margin at the very top—can be housed inside the walls of language." Following a brief discussion of musical expression and Tantric transcendence, Steiner spends the greater part of the essay examining how the rise of mathematics as a symbolic language since the seventeenth century has eroded our faith in the primacy of words and changed our understanding of the cosmos. That argument was not very interesting—not to me at any rate—because Steiner was setting it in opposition to an initial premise that was wrong-headed to begin with. Language does not "contain" thought.

In our effort to explore the issue, I think it would be a good idea, first of all, to divest it of the clumsy metaphor Steiner has draped it in: Truth housed inside the walls of language. Is that what thinking is? To cast about for a suitable "house" within which to settle our thoughts? I don't think so. But if it were, then there are many, many such houses available. The English language, which is the world's richest in vocabulary, has upward of 650,000 words; the average speaker knows perhaps 20,000 and uses 2,000 in an average week. Few of us can be said to be testing its limits.

But in any case, when we attempt to express ourselves, we don't simply look around for a suitable single-family dwelling on a good-sized lot. No, we build a new structure, making use of whatever scraps of vocabulary we have at our disposal. And when we poke our nose into a new book by Steiner, Nietzsche, Melville, Joyce, or anybody else, we're looking for entertainment and enlightenment...but we're also looking for building materials. Such materials are virtually limitless, as I noted a moment ago, and the instant we begin to combine words into phrases, sentences, stanzas—which is what writing is, after all—we enter new and uncharted territory, putting the stamp of our personal experience on the production.

Steiner opens his essay with a reference to the famous passage from John, "In the beginning was the Word...." He goes on to suggest that this Word, this Logos, is the Hellenistic concept to which Western civilization owes its essentially verbal character.

Monoglot though I may be, I fear that Steiner (who speaks

182   *By the Way*

nine or ten languages fluently and probably read the *Iliad* in the original Greek at the age of eight) has somehow missed the boat here. For what is the actual meaning of the term "logos?" We translate it as "word," but it's clearly a very special word, if it's in the presence of God, and is, in fact, God, as the evangelist suggests. Everything came about through this "word," according to the text, and the life which is the light of mankind came about within it. This word is not just any word.

No doubt Steiner was making use of this reference as a rhetorical trope, a means to open his essay about language, but the richness and indefinability of the word "logos" as it functions here might better be taken as an example of the opposite case—of how powerful and inexplicable language, and even a single word, in a foreign language no less, can be.

Consulting an on-line dictionary at random, I am confirmed in my understanding that "logos" carried a wealth of meanings in ancient times. To the pre-Socratics, it was the principle governing the cosmos, the source of this principle, and the human reasoning that struggled to illuminate it more fully on a personal level. The Stoics held a similar view, though they more explicitly associated it with God as the source of all activity and generation, and with "mind" (nous), which, through the power of reason, develops the wherewithal to bring order to experience and even, on occasion, make an associative leap to the divine. Among the Sophists, "logos" took on a more arid meaning of the topics and necessary implications of rational arguments—in other words, formal logic

What we derive from all of this is that "logos" is not merely "the word" or language, but a form or logic that unites the cosmos and the individual in some sort of quivering harmony. I am reminded here of the quivering mosquito twins in *The Book of the Hopi* that sustain the universe, and the musical meters which, in the Satapatha Brahmana, are the cattle of the Gods.

But perhaps I've begun to nod off here, as the sun rises over Leech Lake and the TV news creeps in from the motel breakfast room. I've begun to dream of the mosquitoes we swatted and the

cattle we passed in the course of our bike trip through the Shingobee Hills south and west of Walker yesterday. (And where does
the word "Shingobee" come from?)

Let me return to my point: the Western tradition doesn't rely
overmuch on the "word." In the *Lysis* Plato takes up precisely the
question of the "logos" in relation to the "ergon," the word in relation to the deed, and this theme runs throughout the history of
the West from that day to our own. What this amounts to, for
example, is a consideration of the goodness of an act, as opposed to
the logical rigor of an ethical theory defining what goodness is; the
beauty and power of a phrase or an entire novel, as opposed to the
correctness of a grammatical theory defining the limits of what we
can express. It may be true that among linguists and theorists such
as Steiner himself, "language" can sometimes be a more interesting phenomenon than the things that have been expressed with it.
Indeed, as Benedetto Croce once observed,

> *The revolts against logicism in theory of language have*
> *been as rare and have had as little effect as those against*
> *rhetoric. Only in the romantic period...did there develop,*
> *among certain thinkers, or among certain circles, a vivid*
> *awareness of the imaginative or metaphorical nature of lan-*
> *guage and its closer tie to poetry than to logic.*

Herein lies the crux of the issue. Speech, writing, the use of
language to cloth and preserve our thoughts, is a deed, not a word.
Every utterance we make expands the language—or has that
potential. The words and syntax we have at our disposal act, not as
a limiting force, but as a powerful set of tools or an expansive field
of play, if you like, within which we express ourselves through
verbal dance, choosing this or that phrase, this branch, that flower,
to construct a new hut which reflected the logos of our personal
experience no less than that of the surrounding countryside. Anyone who knows the language is welcome to enter, to join us, and
share in the music.

TETTEGOUCHE BACKCOUNTRY

A hundred-year-old cabin on the shores of a pristine lake in the boreal forest of Northern Minnesota? It sounds like the height of luxury, and beyond the reach of most of us. Let me complete the picture by adding that the cabin has mice, but neither bathroom nor running water—there's a creaky hand-pump fifty yards away. It's heated by wood. The rustic furniture is only marginally comfortable. And did I mention that you have to walk almost two miles through the woods to get to the place?

My hat goes off to those backpackers who cram five days worth of equipment and supplies into a pack and set off up the Superior Hiking Trail. We had trouble getting a weekend worth of supplies into our packs. No tent, no foam pads, no cooking equipment required—just sleeping bags, clothes, and food. And then there were the books, of course. A thick terrycloth towel? Yes, we brought one. A cribbage board? Why not?

The cabin does have a modern two-burner electric stove and a little fridge (with ice). The building itself was originally part of a logging camp that was later sold to a group of Duluth businessmen, back when cars had cranks and fighter pilots flew bi-planes. Some of the buildings fell down eventually and the state of Minnesota bought the rest of them. There are four cabins left, along with a variety of sheds and a single large lodge that anyone who trudges in can hold a picnic in.

Each of the private cabins comes with a canoe, and there are fishing rods lined up in one of the sheds. No lures or bait, however. That took me by surprise. Though I haven't fished in thirty years, there are two Rapalas sitting right here—one gold, one silver—in the front drawer of my desk. Why didn't I bring them? They're made of balsa wood: I think I could have borne the weight.

I ended up fishing from shore with a bobber, using raw chicken or slices of andouille sausage for bait. No luck.

Cabin B, which we reserved about a year ago after spending a night in cabin D, is by all accounts the best of the four. It's located beyond the others at the end of the trail, making it the most private by far, and it's also the only one that sits right on the lake.

Micmac Lake is only five feet deep in many places, but it's surrounded by lofty hills and sheer cliffs that in Minnesota might almost be mistaken for little mountains. There are swamps at either end—always fun to explore. On our second night we paddled a circuit around the lake's shoreline in half an hour, spotting a deer in the distance at one point and later surprising a huge beaver who was sunning himself on the shore a few feet from our passing canoe. He waddled down the grassy embankment and eased himself onto the water, paddled a few feet from shore, then took a dive, slapping his tail—twice! On the east side of the lake fifteen turkey vultures were soaring and diving together in the evening light. They looked almost majestic.

The first night it dropped below fifty and we got a fire blazing in the cast-iron stove. The next morning broke bright and sunny, and we were on the hiking trails by 8:30. Ovenbirds and black-throated green warblers were singing away by the hundreds. Though we never spotted either of those species on the hike, we did get a very good look at a magnolia warbler, a red-eyed vireo, and a least flycatcher.

The trail we took circles around Mic Mac Lake through the hilly terrain, joins the Superior Hiking Trail for a while, diverges north to swing around Nipisiquit Lake, crosses Mosquito Creek, and ends up back at the hunting camp. It took us three hours, and was unspeakably pleasant from beginning to end. The leaves weren't fully out yet and we could see ample chunks of sky. The trailsides were an unending succession of starflowers, clintonia blossoms, sarsaparilla, emerging ferns, bedstraw, and forget-me-nots. The temperature? A delectable 65 degrees would be my guess.

We took a spur at one point out to Raven Rock, an exposed

ridge that offers a spectacular view out across the hills south to Lake Superior. The air was so clear that with binoculars we could see the channels separating the Apostle Islands on the far side of the lake, maybe 60 miles away.

During our hike back to the car Sunday morning, we stashed our packs in the woods at one point and took one final side-trip up to Mount Baldy. Another sunny morning, another great view across the hills to the sea.

BLY AT BLUE MOUND

On August 25, 2012, Robert Bly gave a reading at Blue Mounds Interpretative Center in the southwest corner of the state as part of a year-long series honoring the 100th anniversary of novelist Frederick Manfred's birth. I reserved a walk-in campsite at the park, stuffed the backpack with the bare necessities, and was on the road by eight, hoping to reconnect not only with Bly but also with that relatively untouristed part of the state.

South of Belle Plaine I saw a man chasing a horse down a gravel road—always a funny sight. Two police cars and a pick-up were parked along the highway. I suppose the man was transporting the horse in the pick-up, and when the cops pulled him over, the horse jumped out. But I have no idea what's *really* going on in rural Minnesota. It's a whole different universe.

The skies were gray but the route along Highway 169 up the broad floodplain of the Minnesota River Valley toward Mankato was lovely. The rosemary-apple scone I picked up at the River Rock Coffee shop in St. Peter was also topnotch. I'd dropped a recording of Claudio Monteverdi's Seventh Book of Madrigals into the CD player; angelic voices, both male and female, were intertwining with tireless bright emotion in pleasingly incomprehensible Italian, and I said to myself, "I could listen to this all the way to Luverne!"

By the time I got to Windom, I'd taken a wrong turn down 169, driven through a patch of heavy rain, and was thoroughly sick of Monteverdi. The expansive sea of corn through which I'd been driving, dotted with islands of thick woods as far as the eye could see, was impressive. All the same, I was happy to depart Highway 60 onto a county road where the landscape was hillier and the shoulders were narrower or non-existent.

I was on my way to Kilen Woods State Park, tucked into a fold of the Des Moines River. I'd never been to this park before and found that there isn't much to do there, especially with the hiking trails being so wet. The park does offer some views down into the valleys, and the largely treeless "prairie" campground loop has a few nice sites looking out across the countryside.

At noon, having passed a fair number of wind-turbines in Jackson County, I was sitting in the parking lot at a Burger King in Worthington under a gray sky, looking out the windshield at a Walgreens, a Hy-Vee gas station, and an O-Reilly's Auto Parts. (The main street downtown is now dominated by Hispanic grocery stroes and beauty salons.) I was listening to jazz pianist Brad Mehldau trying to breathe life into "Still Crazy After All These Years" and I was also struggling to keep mayonnaise from dripping out of my hamburger onto my shirt.

Half an hour later I was in Luverne, scoping out the Art Rocks art fair on the county courthouse lawn. I listened to a woefully off-kilter rendition of "Under the Boardwalk," then went inside to the Brandenberg Gallery to look at the same ten Brandenberg photos—nice photos—I've been seeing for the last fifteen years.

I was crossing the street on my way back to the car when I was stopped by a woman in a passing SUV who asked me where the Brandenberg Gallery was. "It's not in this building here," I said, pointing, "but the one next to it." Then I noticed Robert Bly was sitting in the passenger seat.

"Robert," I said, as if we were old friends, "I drove down from Minneapolis to hear the reading. I'm camping at a walk-in site at the park." (As if he needed to know that!) He nodded his head, smiled wanly, and tried to look pleased.

Blue Mound State Park lies just a few miles north of Luverne, and I doubt if there is a better time to see it than in late summer under an overcast sky. The "mound" rises a hundred feet and more from the surrounding countryside. It's made of pink Sioux Quartzite, one of the hardest rocks on earth; local farmers found it impossible to cultivate the thin layer of soil scattered on top of it. Hence patches of virgin prairie remain amid the exposures of quartzite, and quite a bit of it is now used as grazing land for the park's buffalo herd.

Three hiking trails cut along the length of the mound at different levels from one end of the park to the other. That afternoon I hiked a few miles of the middle trail, moving along the crest of the mound, then cut down through a break in the cliff face to get a view from the grassland below. The pink slabs of exposed rock veritably glowed, and the lichens, the grasses, the stunted sumac, the cactus, and other flowers and shrubs roundabout all took on a remarkable intensity in the filtered light.

Touch the Sky Prairie, established in 2001 by the Brandenberg Prairie Foundation, can be reached via gravel roads three miles east of the park. It lacks the drama of Blue Mound's pink cliff-face, but the site seems more remote and windswept, and the prairie grasses more all-encompassing. The peculiar positioning of the quartzite chunks scattered here and there call to mind Zen gardens or menhir alignments, though I have little doubt they've been sitting that way for eons. A mini-Garden of the Gods?

Communing with these solitary, elemental environments put me in a good frame of mind for the Bly reading, and even the

BLY AT BLUE MOUND   189

tired lettuce in the salad I bought for dinner at the local supermarket couldn't dispel it. Bly isn't a "nature" poet, but he does draw much of the imagery for his illogical, fabulous musings from the plant and animal kingdoms—mice, dogs, birch trees, the sea. Benedetto Croce once described a work of art as "a compendium of universal history" and as far as Bly's poems are concerned, the definition almost fits: guilt, love, infatuation, vanity, deceit, longing, all bundled up with dream-images from the farm and allusions to classical literature.

But I don't care to analyze Bly's style here. Some like it, others don't. I will say that he's a marvelous reader of his own poems, giving them a conversational yet musical emphasis that renders the "meaning" almost secondary. He's also good at pacing an evening of readings, leaving long breaks between poems and reciting others twice.

Yet there has always been a compulsion underlying Bly's work, not merely to assert his personal genius, but to get us to *change*—like a Biblical prophet, but with a far more eclectic pantheon. And though he peppered the evening with little quips and jokes, it's clear that he thinks it's important for us, as listeners, to dig deeper into our relationships with our parents, children, and neighbors, and also into our religious beliefs.

I found some of the quips endearing. After reading the short poem "Clothespins" (reprinted below) he remarked, "That says about as little as a poem can say, I suppose."

> *I'd like to have spent my life making*
> *Clothespins. Nothing would be harmed,*
> *Except some pines, probably on land*
> *I owned and would replant. I'd see*
> *My work on clotheslines near some lake,*
> *Up north on a day in October,*
> *Perhaps twelve clothespins, the wood*
> *Still fresh, and a light wind blowing.*

After reading one poem he said, "I have no idea what that means." Then he added, "You write a book of poems, and years later you look at it again and say to yourself, 'Did I write that?'"

But perhaps the most touching aside came at the conclusion to "When My Dead Father Called." Robert read it twice. He honed in on the line, "He was stuck somewhere." Then he asked the crowd, "Maybe your father has been stuck somewhere. What would you do?" There was a pause, and then he said, almost dismissively, "Write a poem, I guess." The sense of resignation with which he delivered this remark left me with the impression that this is what he did...and it wasn't an adequate response. And it still pains him.

David Whetstone provided beguiling sitar accompaniment throughout the reading—he was skilled and relaxed and congenial, adjusting Robert's microphone, stopping and starting on command. And Robert's wife Ruth helped him pick out selections to read, eventually coming on stage to sit behind him. "It's nice to have a wife who likes *some* of your poems," he remarked at one point. It was a truly loving scene, and the thirty or so guests sitting alongside me down in the pit, most of them from Luverne and the surrounding countryside, I suspect, were lapping it up. (But as I mentioned earlier, I have no idea what's really going on in rural Minnesota.)

The Laverne Area Chamber of Commerce sponsored the event, if I'm not mistaken, and they also provided the free bottled water—and ice-cream bars!

At one point Bly, uncomfortable dominating the proceedings, asked the audience to contribute, to say something in response. This is an awkward moment. We've all been thinking about the words Bly has been reading. We're going to have a hard time coming up with a response to:

> ...*You become whatever*
> *steals you, the tree steals a man,*
> *and an old birch becomes his wife*
> *and they live together in the woods.*

Bly had stolen us. But we had not yet become Bly.

I was going to say something about the thick flock of night-hawks circling outside the building, or the blue grosbeak I spotted before the event on a dead tree down in the valley below the interpretive center. But I held my tongue. Saw some birds? Where's the import? Where's the catch?

It was not yet dark when I made my way down the path through the woods to my little campsite. A lump of Sioux Quartzite about the size of a tank sat just beyond the fire ring, half-covered with wild grapevines. The Rock River gurgled through the woods in the shadows nearby. I'd purchased a load of firewood at the ranger's office and I sat on the picnic table staring into the fire, sipping the Irish whisky I'd brought along in a little metal flask, thinking about nothing.

A vast contingent of Southeast Asian families had occupied the group camp a few hundred yards away, and the pleasant shriek of children chasing one another and playing games came wafting through the woods in the dark.

❦

NATURALIST FOR A DAY

One April afternoon I received an email, out of the blue, inviting me to give a keynote address at the annual meeting of the Minnesota Naturalists' Association to be held the following October at a remote environmental learning center near Longville, Minnesota. It sounded like fun. I said, "Sure."

I set off one Friday morning in November and arrived at the Deep Portage Learning Center eight hours later—not an impressive travel time when you consider the trip is only 170 miles long. But it occurred to me that I might as well explore a few new places along the way. I had planned to visit Onigum, situated on a peninsula on the west end of Leech Lake, but made it only as far as the village of Boy River (also on my list) before deciding I'd better head back south to Deep Portage. Earlier in the day I also checked out Rum River State Forest and the contiguous section of Mille Lacs National Wildlife Refuge.

I was on the lookout throughout the day for winterberry, a species of native holly that Hilary and her mother use for holiday decorations; much of the low, wet, backcountry I was moving through seemed like perfect habitat, but I spotted not a single berry all day. I did harvest a few twigs of red dogwood and spotted quite a few swans here and there. They often had their heads down, and they looked like immaculate white pillows floating on the silvery gray water, far more brilliant than anything else in sight. Oh, the leaves of the red oak were very fine, and the dead, dry grasses were also in their autumn glory in the swamps and along the shorelines of many lakes in the region. But it's a subtle pallet, a connoisseur's pallet. The most dramatic color in the landscape these days is flaming, deer-hunter orange.

After taking a few wrong turns on Cass County 46, I finally arrived at the center in near-darkness and was graciously welcomed by Katie Pata, the woman who'd arranged to have me speak. She was my guide and sometime companion throughout the evening, and that was a good thing, because most of the eighty-odd people attending the event were under forty, and they all seemed to know one another already.

How could that be? I learned in the course of the evening that many naturalists work part-time, take several jobs in different places, or have full-time jobs with a park system that send them from one nature center to another like a circuit judge. Lots of naturalists get to know one another that way. On top of all that, many of them attend this event annually, where they "network," see old friends, and make new ones.

Any celebrity cachet I might have had was dispelled immediately upon my arrival, as I walked with Katie down the long halls to the auditorium with my laptop slung over one arm and a big white pillow under the other. (We had been advised to bring our own linens.) But naturalists are a friendly lot, and I got involved in quite a few interesting conversations before the evening was over. I learned a great deal in ten minutes from Elaine Evans, who's finishing up her Ph.D. in entomology, about the bees of Minnesota and North Dakota. Her ambition is to establish a population baseline for the hundred-odd bee species in the region—something that hasn't been looked at for ninety years.

I'm one of those lay-people who use the word "bee" to refer to anything that might sting you badly—bees, bumble-bees, wasps, hornets. I'm pretty sure Elaine figured that out right away, so she probably wasn't surprised when I asked her if she'd been stung a lot. "Not often recently," she replied. "I kind of miss it."

Josh Leonard, the education director at Belwin Outdoor Science Center in Afton, had some funny/sad stories to tell about the city kids who visit his facilities. Some of them are so curious that during an entire nature walk they only make their way a few feet from the building. "I wanted to take them over *there*," he told me, pointing to a spot in the middle distance, "but they were happy looking around *right here*." Other kids are so obstreperous that he ends up feeling more like a policeman than a naturalist, and expends much of his energy just trying to keep them from running off into the woods.

Although I'm not a naturalist myself, I (perhaps presumptuously) spent a few minutes at the start of my spiel trying to underscore the notion that one of a naturalist's chief goals ought to be to instill a sense of affection and appreciation for nature in his or her students. This may seem obvious, and perhaps it is, though it seems to me naturalists sometimes dwell overmuch on the ways nature is being destroyed or upset or obliterated, which is not quite the same thing. Affection can be engendered through scientific observation and analysis—the web of interactions we call "nature" is staggering in its complexity and beauty. But there are other methods that might sometimes work better, including poetry, crafts, food, and sheer recreation—kayaking, fishing, geocaching. (By in large, naturalists already know these things.)

Most of my talk was really a slide show devoted to highlighting places around the state that are worth visiting—a glorified road trip, if you will, condensed into 60 minutes. But I had never before given it to a crowd assembled from all over the state, and it was fun to find that someone in the room hailed from, or worked at, nearly every place I mentioned.

I showed a slide of the Mayo House in Le Sueur and a women sitting near me said, "I run that site." I showed a panorama from the top of Eagle Bluff, near Lanesboro, and someone remarked: "I work there."

When I showed a photo of the hardware store in Big Falls, several people said "Katie," and Katie Pata owned up to the fact that she'd been brought up in that remote part of the state.

My biggest gaff was when I ingenuously remarked, "What I don't like about this DNR map is..." and someone said, "Be careful what you say. The DNR is here."

Well, of course I love the DNR. And I also love the map in question. All the same, it's hard to figure out where you are on the DNR map because there are no towns marked. So I used that map to make a slightly more informative map, based largely on DNR research and cartography but adding the relief from another source and improving the colors a bit.

After the show, a number of people came up to chat. Mara Koenig, who works for the Minnesota Valley National Wildlife Refuge, informed me that a photo I'd shown of a woman leading some kids down a path at the Bass Ponds was *her*! Now there's a coincidence. A colleague of Hilary's who also works at the Nye Nature Center near Henderson introduced herself. I conversed with several pleasantly rambunctious young men from Dodge Nature Center, and Katie filled me in on her early years in Max, Minnesota, a town marked only by a reduced speed limit—no sign, no commercial buildings, population nine.

I had several interesting chats with Steve Robertsen, the forest service naturalist in Tofte, who also owns some rural property near Moorhead. I even volunteered to help him figure out the new Adobe design program he bought recently for the office.

But eventually people began to form into groups of five or six, often sitting in a ring on the floor with a three-litre box of wine in the middle. It was 11 p.m.. I was exhausted. I felt like I was back in the dorm—though I've never lived in a dorm. Clearly, it was time to call it a night.

At breakfast I sat across from a geology grad student—the perfect guy to discuss the "snowball earth" hypothesis with. His curly-haired companion, who's studying soil science, helped me with the pronunciation of "loess" soil. And Jim Bradley, whom I'd met the night before, stopped by my table to say, "So, you want to canoe the Boy River? I've done it. It's great!" And he shared some information about where to get in and out, and how long the trip would take.

HEARTLAND FALL FORUM

The Heartland Fall Forum, sponsored by the Midwest Book-sellers Association, got off to a memorable start with a dialogue-performance by local luminaries Garrison Keillor and Louise Erdrich. These two authors are not only internationally renowned; they both own bookstores in the Twin Cities.

Hans Weyandt, co-owner of Micawbers Books, delivered a pithy and heart-felt introduction in which he underscored the fact that books are here to stay and described a few of his adventures while on the road gathering data for *Read This,* his book of interviews and book-lists. Keillor and Erdrich then took the stage, and engaged one another in a less straightforward dialogue that mostly consisted of Keillor pumping Erdrich for details about the early years of her bookstore, Birchbark Books. They also discussed when it first occurred to each of them that they might actually succeed in fashioning a career based on the written word. Erdrich's most telling response to Keillor's queries, perhaps, was, 'I don't know that many writers…You're right across the river, and I don't know you."

But for the most part, Louise came forth with a long string of interesting details about the early days of Birchbark Books. For example, in the early years she made the mistake of hiring staff that didn't read—they just happened to need a job.

"Everyone was on anti-depressants," she said. But sometimes someone would go off them, which heightened the tension. There was so much bad energy in the store that they began to burn large quantities of sage to improve the vibe. People started to think that the store was a head shop selling marijuana—after all, the sign above the door said Books * Herbs * Indian Art.

A good part of her clientele also frequented the nude beach on nearby Cedar Lake, which added to the stoner mystique. The former occupant of the bookstore's small retail space, located in a tony residential neighborhood west of Lake of the Isles, was a dentist who had no patients, but large quantities of nitric oxide. The dudes Louise hired to finish the floor the night before the grand opening passed out during the night, and in the morning she found that all the change had fallen from their pockets and gotten embedded in the polyurethane. "That was the most money we made in our first year," she commented with a straight face.

Keillor was far less forthcoming with details about the origins of Common Good Books and its recent move to a second, above-ground location. In fact, there were fleeting moments when his ever-so-slightly domineering interrogation almost gave him the sound of an old-fashioned cad. But underneath it all, you could tell that Keillor was a true booklover, and he expressed his admiration for Erdrich lavishly in the first few minutes of the dialogue.

He also contributed a few comments of his own when Erdrich admitted that she had no idea how to run a bookstore in the early years. She'd never heard of "returns" or refreshing the stock, for example. "Neither had I," Keillor replied, in his soft, low, booming voice. "I thought that if you kept a book on the shelf long enough it would sooner or later find that single discerning buyer who would give it a loving home."

By the time the program was over, a third of the audience had left the room. Perhaps they'd come to hear a different kind of talk, with fewer references to nudists and potheads. Or maybe they wanted to catch the start of the Romney-Obama debate. Well, I've heard plenty of authors talk about their books. How much more revealing it can be to hear people of well-developed imagination spin tales about themselves on the spur of the moment. If you'd been merely eavesdropping on a private conversation between these two at a bank, you'd cherish the experience 'til the end of time.

But we all heard it. It was odd and interesting and unique. And in the end, it was entirely appropriate to the occasion—a dialogue about bookstores and idiosyncratic people and the writer's life and the love of books by two local giants who know quite a bit about such things.

At the Wednesday night event I'd picked up a freebee of *Read This!*, and it turned out to be a nifty little volume, though it isn't really the kind of book you'd sit down and read. It contains *lists* of favorite books compiled by bookstore owners, book buyers, and employees of independent bookstores around the country. It also has a few choice anecdotes and personal remarks from the contributors about individual choices.

Thumbing through the book, I was once again reminded how little I've read in recent years—and how many books I've started but failed to complete. To be honest, I hadn't heard of quite a few of the titles listed. I also spotted a number of titles I meant to read at some point in the past but then forgot about—for example, Lampadusa's *The Leopard*. And I also came upon a few titles that I did read and love…and then forgot about entirely. It's like running into a long lost friend—very nice.

This happened to me, in fact, as I glanced at the first list in the book, compiled by editor Hans Weyandt of Micawbers Bookstore. Number six on his list is *Running After Antelope* by Scott Carrier. Now there's a brilliant, humorous, and very low-key collection. Thanks, Hans, for reminding me!

It occurred to me that I ought to return the favor by compiling a list of my own. I have never worked in a bookstore but perhaps warehouse work might qualify me. Categorical thinker that I am, I divided up my selections by type, so the reader (presuming there is one) would find it easier to apprise unfamiliar selections.

Literary Non-fiction (my favorite category)
Literature and the Gods: Roberto Calasso
Walter Benjamin at the Dairy Queen: Larry McMurtry
Islands and Books in Indian Country: Louise Erdrich
Voices of the Old Sea: Norman Lewis
The Gameskeeper at Home: Richard Jefferies
Vertigo: W. S. Sebald

Son of the Morning Star: Evan S. Connell
Six Memos for the Next Millennium: Italo Calvino
Running After Antelope: Scott Carrier
The Book of Disquiet: Fernando Pessoa
London Journal: James Boswell
In Bluebeard's Castle: George Steiner
Desert Solitaire: Edward Abbey
Essays: Montaigne (the motherload)
Prague Pictures: John Banville
Around the Day in Eighty Worlds: Julio Cortazar
Otherwise Known as the Human Condition: Geoff Dyer

Long Novels
Parade's End: Ford Madox Ford
Your Face Tomorrow: Javier Marias
The Makioka Sisters: Junichiro Tanazaki
Don Quixote: Cervantes
Vanity Fair: Thackerey

Novels
Repetition: Peter Handke
A Heart So White: Javier Marias
Out Stealing Horses: Per Petterson
Montauk: Max Frisch
The Periodic Table: Primo Levi
Far Afield: Susanna Kaysen
Growth of the Soil: Knut Hamsun
Philosopher or Dog: Machado de Asis
Lord Grizzly: Frederick Manfred
The Book of Laughter and Forgetting: Milan Kundera
The Charterhouse of Parma: Stendhal

Short Novels
Runaway Horse: MartinWalser
Solo Faces: James Salter
Hunger: Knut Hamsun

Wittgenstein's Nephew: Thomas Bernhard
The Assault: Harry Mulisch
Farmer: Jim Harrison
A Thousand Cranes: Yasunari Kawabata
The Blue Flower: Penelope Fitzgerald

Short Stories
Sketches from a Hunter's Album: Ivan Turgenev
The Interpreter of Maladies: Jhumpa Lahiri
Dance of the Happy Shades: Alice Munro
The Moccasin Telegraph: W. S. Kinsella
Collected Stories: Frank O'Connor
Five Tales of Ferrara: Giorgio Bassani
By Night Under a Stone Bridge: Leo Perutz
Once in Europa: John Berger

The list betrays an obvious bent toward postwar European literature. Well, what can I say? I've read quite a few of Willa Cather's
novels but I'm not sure which one I ought to include. The same
goes for Conrad and Chekhov. I've become a dabbler, dipping
into Thoreau, Audubon's Journals, books of poetry scattered
around the house. Recent triumphs (meaning I got to the end, or
close) include *Darwin's Lost World* (Martin Brasier), *The Bullhead
Queen* (Sue Leaf), *Falling Man* (Don Delillo), *The Round House*
(Louise Erdrich), *A New World* (Amid Chaudhuri), *The Bark
River Chronicles* (Milton Bates).

What next? Looking over at the bookshelf, I suddenly spot a
book I forgot I had. It has a pale green binding, easily lost in the
mix. Mavis Gallant: *Across the Bridge*.

It troubles me that I read so many of the books on this list
decades ago. Maybe Geoff Dyer is right when he writes:

> *If reading heightens your responses, shapes your idea of
> the world, gives you a sense of the purpose of life, then it
> is not surprising if, over time, reading should come to play
> a proportionately smaller role in the context of the myriad*

possibilities it has opened up. The more thoroughly we have absorbed its lessons, the less frequently we need to refer to the owner's manual.

RUNNING AFTER ANTELOPE

Those of us who came of age during the 1960s (which began in 1968 and ran mostly during the 1970s) look back on that era with varying degrees of fondness, embarrassment, and regret. In those days we lived in "houses" with an ever-shifting constellations of male and female friends. We volunteered at the coop and ate brown rice at the Earth Kitchen, convinced that it was not only healthy but somehow virtuous to do so. We communed with nature, hitchhiked with heedless abandon, read Alan Watts and D. T. Suzuki, marched against the government, and studied arcane and even frivolous academic subjects and languages not because they were practical but because we found them interesting. The voting age was lowered and the drinking age was raised. Paranoia was rampant among the young (sometimes with good reason), radicalism was chic, and plastic recycling bins were a welcome novelty—a sign of better things to come.

I remember one late-summer evening in the early 1970s. My brother had just rented an apartment on 4th Street in Dinkytown, and I had gone down to spend the night with him. Antiwar protests had taken place that afternoon, and as we drove through campus we saw a large pack of growling police-dogs behind the fence at the impound lot of Kohler's Towing Service.

202　BY THE WAY

As it turned out, they were never unleashed, but that image of potential violence stayed with me.

Later that evening, as I was helping my brother clean up his new apartment, I noticed a phrase penciled faintly, but precisely, onto the pale green paint of the kitchen wall in capital letters.

– LESS IS (MORE OR LESS) MORE –

Thirty years later, that adage still returns to me from time to time. Beneath the vision of new-found simplicity that inspired the hippie movement lay the awareness that in the end, life can be complicated. There is humor in this line, I think, and self-depreciation, and perhaps the recognition that when the sons and daughters of affluent suburbanites go to college and learn how to "drop out," a degree of contradiction, evasion, and delusion may be involved. But also a degree of truth.

As it turned out, the age of Aquarius didn't blossom with quite the inevitability that some of us imagined it would. Where did disco come from, anyway? And what about Farrah Fawcett Major's hair-do!! Did we really need those Pershing missiles in West Germany? And how did it happen that average SAT scores and gasoline mileage started to drop?

Looking back on it all, it seems to me that the instincts and values that animated those times were sound. Nor did the youth of my generation fall away from them with quite the materialist gusto you see in a conservative manifesto like *The Big Chill*. On the other hand, take a look at the 50-somethings we've become. Jobs, mortgages, kids, summer camps—is it really that much different from the way our parents lived?

One of the pleasures of reading Scott Carrier's *Running After Antelope* is that it reacquaints us with the dangers, the freedoms, and the truths to be met up with on the fringes of bourgeois American life. Carrier writes with deadpan sincerity about his experiences as a journalist, his hitchhiking treks, and the various unglamorous jobs he's taken to make ends meet, making no attempt to make them sound more adventurous or important than they were. It's as if he were committed, with every line of prose, to say to us, "This is what happened to me then." or "This is how I felt," without elaborating overmuch or making an effort to extract any deeper moral or sociological significance out of the events. Though many of the themes are the same, Carrier's style bears little resemblance to Gonzo journalism. His book spans thirty-five years, from 1963 to 1997, but as a result of this terseness, it can be read in an hour or two. In this case, less is (more or less) more.

Some of the stories collected here appeared originally in *Harper's* and *Esquire*, and some were broadcast on National Public Radio's All Things Considered and Public Radio International's This American Life. But Carrier himself appears dead-center in all of them, and the pieces are arranged in chronological order. This gives the book the flavor of a *bildungsroman* rather than a miscellaneous collection.

In one early story, the narrator, captain of his high school defensive football squad, has a moment of transformation:

> *I was standing there spacing out with everyone else, and then I had this new feeling: I was conscious of being inside a shell, and looking out at the world like my uniform and even my body were just protective packaging. I was in love with the air, the smell of the grass, the warm light in the cottonwood trees and the edge of the field.*

Inspired by this intuition, Carrier calls a new "haiku" defense. The team will line up in a 6-3, then start moving around at random while he (the captain) recites a haiku. "The wind brings dry leaves, enough to build a fire."

The coach immediately blows his whistle and asks Carrier what the hell is going on. Carrier explains that it was a Haiku defense.

"It was just an idea," he tells his bewildered coach, "It didn't really work out like I thought it would. I'm ready to move on, if you are."

Several stories describe Carrier's less-than-exemplary climb up the employment ladder. At one point we find him working as a carpenter for his younger brother's construction company. The work itself isn't so bad, but he's distressed to find, again and again, that the men alongside whom he's pounding nails are inspired by one or another religious cult. As an attempt to come to grips with this phenomenon, Carrier explores the idea that these men are so uniformly extreme in their religious views because they, like Jesus, are all carpenters. But this theory leads nowhere.

> ...these men were not interested in philosophy or meta-physics. And they were not even interested, it turned out, in stories about Jesus and his teaching of compassion. Far from it. They were all into the Book of Revelations; they were all religious for reasons of revenge.

The author eventually realizes that at this point in his life, he's a lot like them—an unhappy slave with no real idea of what to do about it.

In one piece Carrier hitchhikes from Salt Lake City to New York to see a publisher about some assignment or advance. (Why not just call him on the phone?) Along the way he gets picked up by a Serbian truck driver. They have some trouble at a weigh station when the authorities spot Carrier in the passenger seat. After conferring with the officer, the trucker returns to the cab.

"....it's against the law, even in my own truck," the driver says, "for me to give you a ride. He told me to drop you at the next exit, and I told him I wouldn't even consider it. This country is becoming a police state. I know, I've seen it all before."

During the long lonely cross-country trip the two get to talking about music, eternal forms, and religious art, and the trucker reveals that his cousin is a painter. Carrier eventually agrees to go to the trucker's Pennsylvania home to examine his cousin's paintings, which are on display in an upstairs gallery. (How could he refuse? The guy has just risked his license to driven him a thousand miles.)

RUNNING AFTER ANTELOPE 205

While the two of them are viewing the works a tactful conversation takes place, on the order of—

"Your cousin may be a great genius...but it seems like he might be insane as well. He paints like he has fire in his eyes and lightning shooting out of his fingertips."

"Yes, it's true, he does." The trucker agrees.

Carrier asks how much the cousin is asking for his canvases.

"For the larger ones, between one and two hundred thousand dollars."

'It seems like a lot,' I said. 'but I suppose if you were rich, and wanted one, then it would be nothing.'

In the end Carrier admits to becoming a bit flummoxed.

I didn't really know what to say—the Old Testament done in the Dutch Baroque by a modern-day Serb and hung in a former pizza parlor in Hazelden, Pennsylvannia, by a truck driver... this seemed beyond my ability for comment.

The experiences described in this collection are diverse, ranging from childhood memories to travels in Cambodia and Chiapas. In the travel pieces Carrier wisely avoids making sweeping judgements of a political nature. As always, he contents himself with describing what he sees and how he feels, though rumblings of moral outrage are everpresent.

One unusual thread resurfaces repeatedly in the course of the book—a quest to run down an antelope. Carrier's brother had come up with the idea as part of a graduate program in physiology or biology. The theory, based on a few scattered anthropological records, is that humans used to capture their prey by chasing it until it collapsed due to exhaustion. Carrier himself—by his own admission not a very good runner—is recruited to help with the experiments. It's an interesting project, and Carrier keeps at it intermittently long after his brother has moved on to other things.

Does he ever succeed in chasing the svelte pronghorn—the fastest mammal in the Western Hemisphere—to the point of collapse? I'm not going to spoil the fun. Let it suffice to say that these antelope tales, like most of the others in the collection, have an element of latent absurdity which Carrier sweeps aside in his efffort to forge quietly ahead in pursuit of truth.

But perhaps it would be more accurate to say that absurdity is simply the flip-side of convention, and Carrier has little time for either.

✳

Twin Cities Book Festival

The Twin Cities Book Festival has always been a stimulating (and free) event, regardless of the venue—the old Munsingwear Building, the Minneapolis Technical College downtown, the state fairgrounds. Exhibitors of one-of-a-kind fine press books are lined up cheek-by-jowl with self-published poets promoting their slim volumes, internationally ambitious distribution firms like Consortium, used book dealers, literary presses from Graywolf to Nodin Press and Holy Cow!, and arts organizations from all over the map. Meanwhile, the people at Rain Taxi book a succession of speaking events that ranged in 2011—to take a recent example—from Steven Pinker (one of *Time* magazine's 'top 100 intellectuals in the world') to panels of local talent dilating on "A Sense of Place" and memoir writing.

I'm not sure how many books are actually sold during the day—perhaps not many. But I can think of no event where you feel more strongly you're in the midst of that bubbling current of intelligence that makes books possible. And a seemingly limitless cadre of Rain Taxi volunteers makes sure that people are ushered into and out of the events in an orderly way, that everyone finds the booth they're looking for, and all the rest.

Part of the fun, for me, is simply to reconnect briefly with old friends from the book world.

Over at Consortium, for example, old buddy Bill Mochler was excited about the prospects of two of the books on his table—a children's book for adults called *Go the F**k to Sleep* and *Wing-shooters*, which I gather is Wisconsin's version of *To Kill a Mockingbird*. Nice cover.

It was a pleasure to meet poet Cary Waterman, finally, after having worked with her during the summer on her new book of poems, *Book of Fire*. "I feel like I already know you," she said. The feeling was mutual, though the author photo I'd been working with didn't do justice to the sparkle of the real thing.

Later in the day I ran into a figure from the more distant past—Brett Laidlaw. We worked together on the Bookmen loading dock decades ago. He has a new cookbook out called *Trout Caviar*. I read his foraging blog occasionally, so I knew a little about what he'd been up to recently. He assured me that the book had plenty of prose along with the recipes. "I'm a writer, not a cook," was how he put it.

The two authors whose talks I sat in on were both promoting works of non-fiction or *belle-lettres*. Both talks were well-attended and thoroughly engaging, though in different ways. Steven Pinker made use of a power-point presentation to hammer home the thesis of his new book, *The Better Angels of Our Nature*, that the world has become progressively more peaceful with the passing centuries. In a seemingly endless succession of charts and graphs he offered proof that violence is in decline (while I.Q.s are on the rise) and he tossed out some intriguing theories as to why this might be so.

Against the oft-repeated (but never substantiated) contention that WWII was the most destructive event in history, he countered with evidence that it ranks merely ninth. During that bloody era perhaps 3% of the population died violently. The Mongol invasions of the thirteenth century were five times bloodier. Expanding the range of reference, the evidence of forensic anthropologists suggests that in pre-historic times, 15% of the population died violent deaths.

How are we to explain this trend? Pinker offered a few suggestions, including the rise of the state, the expansion of international trade, the decline of self-righteous and wrong-headed ideologies, and the rise in human empathy due to increasing literacy. (Hurray for books!) In brief, he's lending support to the theories of progress and fellow-feeling promulgated by Condorcet, Turgot, Shaftesbury, and other Enlightenment thinkers—but with more evidence to back them up. To judge from the reviews I've read, the book is far more complex and fascinating than the author's one-hour gloss could possibly suggest. Pinker did a good job of sticking to the basics, at the risk of underselling the merits of his thesis.

Meanwhile it occurs to me that the author, with his long silver locks, looks a lot like an Enlightenment thinker himself.

A few hours later I wandered into a smaller room to hear Lawrence Wechsler read from his new book of essays, *Uncanny Valley*. Where Pinker had been eloquent and to the point, Wechsler (for twenty years a staff writer for the *New Yorker*) was rambling, soft-spoken, nimble. At times it seemed he was simply thinking out loud as his stood at the podium pondering everything from the challenges of digitalizing the appearance of a glass of milk to the broader significance of the phrase "We hold these truths…"

At one point he quoted from a Transtromer poem titled "The Outpost":

> *Mission: to be where I am.*
> *Even in that ridiculous, deadly serious*
> *role – I am the place*
> *Where creation is working itself out.*

He described an afternoon he spent with another Nobel Laureate, the Italian playwright Dario Fo, in a manic attempt to see twelve Broadway plays in a single day. This reminiscence led him on to a discription of a Russian film shot in a single ninety-minute take, and then an elaborate series of associations that included "The Ride of the Valkyries" scene from *Apocalypse Now*, Custer's Last Stand, *The Birth of a Nation*, and the music criticism of Theodor Adorno.

After a few remarks I failed to catch, Wechsler read a piece in which he watched an ant laboriously line up three piece of grass end to end, and then vanish into the desert gloaming. From there it was on to an analysis of America's efforts to tank the legislation that established the world criminal court. A little later he was recommending that we all go home and watch the YouTube piece "Marcel the shell with shoes on," which he claimed had greater merit as a piece of animation than Avatar.

All in all, it was a wild ride.

❦

CULTURE WEEK:
FRAZIER, ALEXIE, DYER

In the aftermath of the announcement on November 14, 2012, that two writers who call Minneapolis home had won National Book Awards—that's half the total—arts-journalists were eager to riff on the vibrancy of the local literary scene. And with good reason. There always seems to be something going on hereabouts in the line of readings, tweet-ups, and other arts-related events, sponsored by various alliances, bookstores, libraries, art centers, and publishers. Of course, the correlation between literary awards and book events is a little shaky; Louise Erdrich didn't learn to write as well as she does by taking classes at The Loft. All the same, Twin Citians can be thankful for a seemingly endless stream of opportunities to listen to, and rub shoulders with, literary and cultural luminaries—both visitors and home-grown talent.

My thoughts were already drifting in this direction on a Sunday afternoon a few days before the awards were announced, as I sat in a plastic folding chair and watched Garrison Keillor wander forlornly into Common Good Books (which he owns) wheeling a small black carry-on bag behind him. Hilary and I were among perhaps fifty people who'd gathered in an open space in the center of the store to hear Ian Frazier read from his new book, *The Cursing Mommy*. During his introductory comments Keillor remarked that "very funny people often don't like to be referred to as 'very funny'... so I'll say no more about that." He went on to draw attention to Frazier's substantial book about Siberia, which "has not yet found its audience."

Frazier, in turn, began his intro by remarking that he spent a lot of time traveling to small towns, where he marveled again and again at how great Keillor's influence has been on that hue of the American demographic spectrum. "These people know they like living in small towns, but Garrision has made it possible for them to actually be proud of that fact."

Once he got into the reading, Frazier was very funny indeed, bringing to life the personality of the cursing mommy in ways the printed word can only hint at. During the question-and-answer period, he talked a lot about growing up in Ohio, and characterized his latest literary creation as "a cross between Sylvia Plath and Phyllis Diller."

◆

It snowed during the night, and the next morning we headed up to Maple Grove to see the new nature center at Elm Creek Regional Park. That's another outstanding municipal amenity we Twin Citians have long appreciated—all the green and wild open spaces. The new nature center proved to be very fine and airy, adding some sparkle to a creek-bed that can sometimes be a little skanky.

Snow on the ground affects your mood in subtle ways; it tends to make you more withdrawn, and more poetic. Maybe you end up reading more? In her *Star-Tribune* interview following the award announcement, Erdrich remarked, "People elsewhere think that it's cold and desolate around these parts, but that cold is good for literacy and reading and culture."

Inspired by the Frazier reading, we went downtown that evening to hear Sherman Alexie speak at Plymouth Congregational Church. The church sponsors a fine and very popular Literary Witnesses program, and Alexie drew such a large crowd they had to set up chairs in another part of the building to manage the overflow. The disparity between the Frazier crowd and the Alexie crowd seemed a little odd to me. Then again, aside from being a literary and a nature capital, Minneapolis is also considered the urban capital of America's Native American population.

Alexie himself, who's from Spokane, WA, admitted as much, and to underscore the point he added, "I think every Indian in America has gotten laid in Minneapolis at one time or another."

Such was Alexie's monologue—raw, funny, antagonistic and affectionate by turns, droll, insightful, intense. Once again, the human voice and personality took us beyond anything to be found on the printed page. Alexie's prose may be harsh, but his comic timing was superb, his improvisational genius remarkable. He delivered an extemporaneous monologue about house fires (he's been in three or four) and Claude Van Damme movies that deserves a place in the Library of Congress. At the root of it all there was clearly a troubled soul who's learned to modulate and temper his emotions, though he's nowhere near finished working through them.

It occurred to me later than Alexie has a lot in common with Richard Pryor. (And if you haven't seen *Richard Pryor Live*, you should. Might as well see Alexie's film *Smoke Signals* again, too, while you're at it.)

◆

Two days later we drove across town to my home town of Mahtomedi to see the premier of *The Girl from Birch Creek*, a documentary about Minnesota Supreme Court justice Rosalie Wahl. Her son Tim has been a very good friend of mine for a third of a century at least, and I've known Rosalie as a mom and friend for just as long. The film brought out aspects of her early life in Kansas that I'd never heard before, and though its one-hour length made it difficult to touch on every aspect of Rosalie's background and character, what did shine through was her simple decency, commitment to helping others, dedication to fairness...and also her poetic streak. It isn't often that you get to hear a Supreme Court justice sing a hymn a capella or recite a poem she's written.

◆

Thursday was Jazz-and-Pie Night. For several years we've been gathering once a month in Edina at the condo of Hilary's parents, Gene and Dorothy, to listen to cuts from our favorite jazz albums. Everyone brings a few tracks and gives a little speech about why they brought a particular number before putting it on; then we sit quietly and listen, interjecting an appreciative comment from time to time about the drummer, perhaps, or the tone of the reedman who's currently at the mike.

Gene often brings Big Band numbers or jazz vocals; Hilary's brother Paul is a fan of Happy Apple, Keith Jarrett, and Brad Mehldau; and brother Jeff has made an effort to introduce us to young Turks such as Gerald Clayton and William Smith III, though his selections range from Weather Report to the Wailin' Jennies. I sometimes throw a dash of flamenco into the mix. Yet each gathering produces quite a few surprises, and an added source of amusement is the habit we've gotten into of trying to devise a line of reasoning connecting the track that just came to an end with the one we're about to put on—even if there isn't one.

Thursday's playlist was a little skewed by the fact that Jeff couldn't make it and the CDs Paul brought wouldn't play because he'd burned them just that day and used the wrong pen to write the names on them; the lettering had somehow bled through to the other side. All the same, we ran through a very interesting set that included several numbers by songstress Anita O'Day, a rip-roaring live performance by Sonny Rollins of "You Are Too Beautiful," the Maria Schneider Orchestra doing "Over the Rainbow," a bouncy 1955 rendition of "Out of Nowhere" by Coleman Hawkins, baritone saxman Gerry Mulligan coursing through "Bweebida Bobida," Paul Desmond and Jim Hall performing "Bewitched, Bothered, and Bewildered," and Cannonball Adderley loping through a sweet version of one of my favorite songs, "I Can't Get Started (with You)."

Then we all went into the kitchen to sample Dorothy's incomparable pumpkin pie.

◆

Culture Week was brought to a fitting conclusion that Saturday night at the downtown Minneapolis Library where English essayist Geoff Dyer was interviewed by Fiona McCrae, publisher of Graywolf Press, which recently released a collection of Dyer's essays, *Otherwise Known as the Human Condition*.

Before the show we indulged in a plate of sashimi and some Happy Hour tempura at Origami, an intimate restaurant nestled in the shadows of the Federal Reserve Building a few blocks from the library. We arrived at the event—a fantastic building at night—and secured two seats in the mid-sized auditorium before rounding off our meal with a napkin-full of complimentary cookies from the table outside.

At that point I noticed that a party was underway down the hall, and in the best Dyeresque gate-crashing spirit we went down to see what we could see. As I had suspected, it was a pre-reading soiree sponsored by Graywolf Press. There was Geoff, of course, assuming a conversational pose in front of the water cooler just beyond the string duo as he listened to one of the Graywolf guests expound a theory of seemingly elaborate proportions. We got no further into the room, and hadn't intended to.

The conversation in the auditorium was top-flight. Geoff read one essay, in which he compares the world of *haute couture* to Amazonian fertility rites. (James Boswell touched on the same theme in 1768.) But mostly he talked about his approach to writing an essay, how America differs from England, and how he chooses his projects—or how they choose him. There were few surprises but plenty of well-fashioned sentences and off-the-cuff humor.

I started off the Q & A, remarking that I'd enjoyed his essay on W. S. Sebald and Thomas Bernhard. I went on to say that after reading it, I began to notice that Dyer himself sometimes uses the circular, repetitive, Bernhard style. "Do you actually like Bernhard? Do you consider him an influence?"

Dyer paused for a second, then replied sheepishly, "Guilty as charged." He extolled Bernhard's work, referred to the famous blurb about its affinities with Broch and Musil, and admitted that the opening passages of his book on D.H. Lawrence had been directly inspired by Bernhard's novel *Concrete*.

This strikes me as interesting because Dyer and Bernhard are temperamentally quite dissimilar. Bernhard is the ultimate crank, and no one will enjoy reading his work who fails to see that his extreme misanthropy is supposed to be funny—though he's being perfectly serious, too. Dyer, on the other hand, though also quite serious most of the time, in the end just wants to have fun. And share that fun with us.

At the age of twenty, Dyer conceived the ambition of emulating William Hazlitt, a man who had loitered his life away doing things he enjoyed and then writing essays about them. During the last quarter-century Dyer has succeeded pretty well in doing just that. The editor of an earlier, slimmer collection had urged him to organize his scattered pieces into some sort of theme, but Dyer was keen to emphasize how diverse and unrelated they were.

"If there was one thing I was proud of in my literary non-career it was the way that I had written so many different kinds of books: to assemble a collection of articles would be further proof of just how wayward my interests were."

I think it's fair to say, on the basis of the Graywolf collection, that Dyer's position as a contemporary "man of letters" is secure. Among the subjects under review are D. H. Lawrence; photographer Joel Sternfeld; Rebecca West's far-ranging travelogue about Yugoslavia, *Black Lamb, Gray Falcon*; Rilke and Rodin; jazz pianist Keith Jarrett's career; Albert Camus's Algeria; the Polish journalist-raconteur Rysard Kapuscinski; the literature produced about the invasion of Iraq; and an assortment of personal pieces about comic books, book-collecting, being an only child, getting married, and other such effluvia.

Dyer usually approaches his subjects in an engaged yet light-hearted, almost conversational way. His own restless personality can be felt throughout, though he usually steers clear of the flippant asides that make his shorter travel pieces (not included in this volume) so funny.

Is *Otherwise Known as the Human Condition* destined to become a classic of world literature? Perhaps not. Then again, how many essayists and reviewers have been granted ingress into that pantheon since Montaigne invented the genre? How many of us read Hazlitt nowadays?

I just now lifted my Centenary edition of *Hazlitt's Collected Essays* from the shelf (Nonesuch Press, 1930) and immediately notice that whereas Hazlitt's subjects are of a general nature— "Why Distant Objects Please," "On Hot and Cold"—Dyer's are almost invariably about particular writers or works of art. For now I'll take Dyer's collection. And I've found it far more mature and engaging than Martin Amis's *The War Against Cliché* (2001), for example. Dyer can't quite match the vast erudition to be found in Anthony Burgess's 600-page collection, *But Do Blonds Prefer Gentlemen?* (1986) Then again, who could? As Dyer remarks in another of his books: "That's one of the things about traveling, one of the things you learn: many people in the world, even educated ones, don't know much, and it doesn't actually matter at all."

Yet essayists need to know things. And Dyer knows his chosen subjects well—or well enough. When he doesn't know something that seems important, he might simply say, "I forget." Or "I should know that, but I don't." The approach is personal and candid, devoid of attempts to make definitive statements. Quite the contrary. In a recent interview he remarked, "I've always just been temperamentally disinclined from having this separation between 'stuff you live with in your actual life' and 'stuff you study'."

No doubt we'd learn more about European history and culture by reading Charles Rosen's recently-published anthology, *Freedom and the Arts: Essays on Music and Literature*, which has the same page-count as Dyer's collection. But I suspect it wouldn't be nearly as much fun.

This juxtaposition of "old" culture and "lived" culture leads me on to a second comparison. In a small way, Dyer's occasional writings might well be compared to Stendhal's diaries. Like Stendhal, Dyer is a great enthusiast who enjoys a good party though he's also prone to boredom and introspection. The observations are penetrating while the style occasionally teeters on the edge of "flighty." A buoyant clarity keeps everything moving ahead. Perhaps some Charles Rosen of the future might write an essay about him?

In any case, *Human Condition* would be a perfect choice to take to the cabin or the beach. If you grow tired of reading about the Indian vocalist Ramamani, flip a few pages and you're with Camus in Algeria, or revisiting John Coltrane's many reworkings of "My Favorite Things." What next?

The Absurd and the Impossible

"[Absurdity] is in fact an accurate and a productive way of understanding the world. Why should we be interested in a clearly impossible story? Because, as Gogol says, in fact the impossible is what happens all the time."

– William Kentridge

An old friend (now caring for her ailing mother in Nevada, if I'm not mistaken) sent me this quote not long ago via Facebook. Well, she didn't send it to me *personally*. Maria has 606 friends and no doubt she sometimes forgets who all is out there. But I'll bet she wouldn't be surprised to learn that the remark had piqued my interest.

I've been thinking about the absurd on and off for quite some time now. Ever since my college years, in fact, when *The Trial*, *Troubled Sleep*, *Nausea*, *Notes from Underground*, and other works in that vein were my daily reading habit. I got a charge out of reading such dismal stuff, don't ask me why—I was a mostly happy-go-lucky sort myself. Perhaps it was the combination of metaphysical speculation and novelistic detail as related by an assortment of hapless misanthropes living on the frenzied edge of nothingness—a common adolescent syndrome.

But there came a time—I think it was in 1972—I was wandering in the dark amid the grain elevators north of University Avenue and west of the KSTP tower, with the smell of malt in my nostrils, when it suddenly occurred to me that the universe could not be absurd. Why not? Because the word "absurd" can only have meaning in contrast to something that makes sense. If *nothing* makes sense, then neither "absurdity" nor "sense" hold their meaning.

218   *By the Way*

The word "absurd" does have meaning, but its point of reference is invariably narrow. Let me give you an example. Suppose I were to say: "Janine went to absurd lengths to make sure that the flowers on the table were fresh." What this means is, "Janine cares more about fresh flowers than I do." Or how about this one: "To argue that the earth is merely 4,000 years old is absurd." What this means is, "Anyone who can disregard the geological and astrophysical evidence available regarding the extraordinary age of the universe has really lost his or her senses—there's no point in pursuing ther argument."

In either case, an attitude appears absurd in contrast to another, more well-developed one. Yet between these two examples, the first is certainly less absurd than the second. Just because I don't happen to be much interested in fresh flowers doesn't mean that it's absurd to pay close special attention to them. In fact, in this instance it may be my focus that's narrow, not Janines's. While I'm fussing with cost-benefit analysis based on false equivalencies (plastic flowers) she sees the more brilliant, colorful world that erupts when fresh flowers are introduced to a room—and who, really, can say exactly how much that's worth?

Kentridge's remark refers to the fact that we don't really know what's possible and what's not, so it can be a mistake to set false limits by describing some alternatives as absurd.

The line separating what can and cannot happen gets especially murky in the outer reaches of time and space, beyond telescopes, on the far side of the River Styx. This may explain why religious thought is often sparked by tales and adages riddled with absurdity. The Zen koan may be taken as a case in point. And didn't Tertillian once remark,

> *The Son of God was born: there is no shame, because it is shameful. And the Son of God died: it is wholly credible, because it is unsound. And, buried, He rose again: it is certain, because impossible.*

This last line, which originally read *et sepultus resurrexit, certum est, quia impossibile* entered the lexicon of Western maxims in a bowdlerized form, *Credo quia absurdum*, "I believe, because it is absurd"—a remark that will throw a wet blanket on any discussion of religion, though it might help to explain the behavior of suicide bombers.

Poets and novelists have no qualms about combining images and events in ways that don't really make sense, and such concoctions are often refreshing: *Alcools* and *A Hundred Years of Solitude* come immediately to mind. Equally illuminating is are the absurdities we meet up with in *Don Quixote*, which spring from the mind of the protagonist rather than that of the author.

Nowadays poets are all but required to indulge in a little nonsense from time to time. Did it all start with Rimbaud?

Yet none of this strikes to the heart of Kentridge's (or Gogol's) remark, I think, which issues from a point of exasperation, if not despair. There are times when the world seems to be so far out of whack with our values and expectations that all we can do is throw up our hands with the cry, "How absurd!"

Flaubert remains the high priest of this attitude, though it seems to me his views are usually misinterpreted. We find it easy to note the disgust he feels in the face of bourgeois culture, but have developed a tin ear with regard to the deep affection underlying it. I picked up my copy of *Bouvard and Pecuchet* just now and was reconfirmed in that judgment. It's a very funny book, I really ought to read it again.

In the end, "the impossible" doesn't happen all the time. On the contrary, by definition, it never happens. And it may be worth pointing out that when words such as "crazy" and "absurd" and "impossible" enter a discuss, it means that thought is at an end. In the political sphere that's not a good terminal to arrive at. It certainly isn't a productive way of looking at the world, no matter what William Kentridge or Gogol says.

❦

FORD MADOX FORD

Those who knew him in London prior to the Great War, or in Paris during the Twenties, have given us a picture of Ford Madox Ford as an expansive, almost Falstaffian figure. His enthusiasm for romance in its courtly form and his undying infatuation with the long tradition of the printed word set him distinctly at odds from those young writers who were struggling to hammer out a new style suitable to the fractured character of the period. The fantastic, almost hallucinatory turn of his imagination and his propensity for stretching the truth with respect to the literary luminaries among whom he'd spent his early years merely confirmed the fact, in the eyes of all but a few of his young literary confreres, that Ford was a vain and fatuous has-been, if not, indeed, a never-was.

Depending on the source—and Ford's friends and associates over the years ranged from Henry James to Joseph Conrad, from Ernest Hemingway to Ezra Pound, from D. H. Lawrence to James Joyce, Steven Crane, and Jean Rhys—veins of affection *do* wind their way through the sketches that have been passed on to us. More typical, however, is the chapter devoted to Ford in Hemingway's *A Moveable Feast,* which may be the most widely known of the aspersions he received. Wyndham Lewis—never one to mince words—struck a similar blow when he described Ford as

> *...a flabby lemon and pink giant, who hung his mouth open as though he were an animal in the Zoo inviting buns—especially when ladies were present. Over the gaping mouth damply depended the ragged ends of a pale lemon mustache. This ex-collaborator with Joseph Conrad was himself, it always occurred to me, a typical figure out of a Conrad book—a caterer, or cornfactor, coming on board—blowing like a porpoise with the exertion—at some Eastern port.*

Evidently something about Ford rubbed people the wrong way.

Those who make Ford's acquaintance through his books will be left with a more favorable impression, I suspect, though it's important here to pick and choose. Ford wrote more than eighty books in all—poetry, historical romance, literary criticism, children's books, ruminations on civilization, travel books, art-biographies, political propaganda, culture studies of France, England, and the United States, science fiction, and personal reminiscences of the great men of the pre-Raphaelite circle in the midst of whom he spent his childhood and adolescence. Anyone who

picks up one of Ford's lesser works, many of which have been reprinted in recent decades, will catch echoes of the loneliness and the lack of confidence that plagued Ford throughout his gregarious life. This frame of mind manifests itself in a writing style that veers repeatedly toward the digressive, the repetitive, and the farfetched, so that reading Ford, we're often reminded of a little boy at school who stretches the truth because he's found it's the only way to get his chums to listen. There is no denying that Ford often wrote from within an incandescent haze of self-referential enthusiasm—a trait that led novelist Graham Greene to observe: "Mr. Ford has walked with kings and has indubitably lost the common touch—his style swings like ribboned glass."

Then again, Greene also remarked, "There is no novelist of this century more likely to live than Ford Madox Ford."

One or two of Ford's books will "live," no doubt. *The Good Soldier* is ensconced in Modern Library and Vintage paperback editions. Echoes of this landmark narrative can be heard in more than a few contempory novelists—Michael Ondadtje and Kazuo Ishiguro come immediately to mind. But *Parade's End*, Ford's World War I tetrology, is an altogether greater achievement, and it might well reach pop-culture status now that Benedict Cumberbatch has portrayed its central character in a five-part BBC production widely billed as "the thinking person's *Downton Abbey*." Then again, maybe not.

Written to a large degree from inside the heads of its protagonists, *Parade's End* is not altogether conducive to theatrical rendering, even at the hands of Tom Stoppard, the screen-writer for the BBC production. What Ford has done is to combine a fresh, "modernist" use of fragmentary imagery and a distinctly nineteenth-century emphasis on choosing the precise word to create the desired effect. In his early novels, Ford found it difficult to bring these elements together convincingly. It was his personal experience in the trenches during the First World War, along with a maturing perspective on his own untidy romantic life, that gave him the material required to fuse his literary and moral ideals into a single compelling whole.

Such a swashbuckling, stiff-upper-lip posture had become a rare thing by the time World War I came to an end. Perhaps it's rarer still in our times. Ford would not have fit comfortably within the rubric of a work like Sean O'Faolain's study of the modern English novel, *The Vanishing Hero*. In this monograph O'Faolain identifies the Twenties (the peak of Ford's career, during which *Parade's End* appeared), as a watershed in the novel's long history. He argues that the single common characteristic of novels written at that time, in English at any rate, is the virtual disappearance of "that focal character of the classical novel, the conceptual Hero." He examines the works of Hemingway, Greene, Woolf, Joyce, and several other novelists, presenting us with a fascinating critique of an age in which the search for a personal code was the most that could be expected of any character in a book—heroism of the traditional form was no longer an option, because there was simply no longer a *social* code the defense of which anyone could take seriously.

It's a complex and interesting study, and O'Faolain's point appears to be well-taken, at least with regard to the artists he's chosen to consider. Perhaps *Parade's End* is the exception that proves the rule.

Just consider the titles of the four novels involved: *Some Do Not...*(1924), *No More Parades* (1925), *A Man Could Stand Up* (1926), and *The Last Post* (1928.) In these works we follow the career of a towering and eternally beleaguered officer named Christopher Tietjens, "the last Tory," who strikes a blatantly heroic pose of precisely the type that O'Faolain finds absent from the literature of the times. It doesn't necessarily follow that Ford's novels are *good* novels, but it does alert us to the fact that his approach to contemporary issues is out of step with the times.

In may come as no surprise to us, therefore, that Ford's tetrology has been criticized on precisely those grounds. The English critic V. S. Pritchett, following this line of argument, suggests that by romanticizing the idea of the gentleman in the figure of Christopher Tietjens, Ford has rendered his work "tiresome and false to the modern reader." Pritchett elaborates on this point at some length, suggesting that in the character of Tietjens Ford "constructed an English gentleman as only something like German romanticism or idealism could see him." He finds Tietjens's willingness to suffer for the sake of others "inhuman."

"Ford's plain feudal Yorkshire squire," he writes, "with his love of the pre-industrial way of life, his scorn of the vulgar modern world, his dislike of ambition, his irritable abstention, his martyred sense of decency, looks today like a romancing not about a man but about a code."

I wonder what Pritchett, in his self-conscious "modernity," would make of the following passage:

> *I looked at his purplish hands, clutching the railing of the steps leading down from the garden to the bowling green. From here he had called on the youths of the village to go and fight and get killed in the war that was to have given back to Italy the towns of Trento and Trieste and brought perpetual peace to the world. His patriotism had not been the reason for his becoming the youngest mayor in Italy. The*

villagers had consistently voted for him because he was the largest landowner and a Jew, two things that made him more credible than others in matters of money. Villagers who had emigrated used to send him money to have mass said for their dead, trusting him more than the village priest. He had sold many tracts of land to his peasants with deferred payments and without interest. To those who suggested guarantors, he used to answer that the mouths to be fed in the buyers family were as good as any security. At that time he was loved, admired, and respected.

The details make it pretty obvious that this passage has not been taken from one of Ford's novels. It appears in *Memoirs of a Fortunate Jew*, a work of non-fiction written by the son of an Italian landowner living at the time during which *Parade's End* takes place. It's interesting to note, I think, that the values it espouses are essentially identical to those of Ford's fictional Tory landowner. Evidently there is nothing particularly British, or German, or fake, about *noblesse oblige*.

But the appeal of Ford's creation doesn't lie in the values of its protagonist per se. In lesser works Ford often wrote about "being a gentleman" to dreadul effect. If *Parade's End* works, it's because of the fireworks set off by the unlikely presence of such values in a world of mendacity, chaos, and destruction—things Ford knew about first-hand. He spent the first year of the war writing propaganda literature for the war office. The two resulting books, *When Blood is Their Argument* and *Between St. George and St. Denis*, though they can hardly be considered "mature" history, remain interesting and readable books, which Rebecca West, for one, referred to as "decisive" and "illuminating." Here we encounter, not a blueblood English point of view, but the hearty internationalism one might, perhaps, expect from a loyal Englishman of German descent who idealizes the French— which is what Ford was. When Ford enlisted, at the age of forty-one, in 1915, he was immediately commissioned and sent to France. He alone of the writers of his generation fought in the trenches, where he was gassed, suffered a concussion, damaged his teeth, and lost his memory entirely for three months. Whether the things we "moderns" have been through qualifies us to deflate the values that underlie Ford's vision thus becomes a dicey issue.

Tietjens himself, far from being a pompous story-book goody-goody, is well aware of, and frequently bemoans the disparity between his values and those of his contemporaries. He's an anachronism and he knows it. He frets about the ancestral estate, his Catholicism, and the traditions of a moribund hierarchical society, yet the impulse underlying these concerns is humane rather than exclusive. At the same time, the comic side of Tietjens absurd high-mindedness—not so outlandishly inane as that which feeds Cervantes' masterwork but similarly couched—should be evident to any reader. His tribulations are endless, yet the tone in which Ford describes them is consistently tinged with a kind of dreadful humor. And the fact that Teitjens's character is given to us largely through the medium of his own thoughts gives the grandiose and paranoiac aspects of his world-view a certain poignancy.

Ford undoubtedly sympathizes with his beleaguered hero, but his purpose in relating Teitjens adventures and predicaments has nothing to do with advancing a practical program for the betterment of society. Ford simply means to bring a robust and idiosyncratic figure to life—modeled largely on himself, no doubt, though he claimed to have drawn his inspiration from a civil servant named Arthur Marwood. To criticize it as naively idealistic or "romanticized" is to miss both the central irony and the abiding moral value of the work.

At one point in the narrative, Tietjens, in the midst of a sea of troubles, contemplates joining the French Foreign Legion as a means of escaping from his domestic difficulties—not, I think, what you'd expect from a typical English Tory younger son as conceived by a German idealist. His thought turns to the French, and his mind wanders:

The French he admired: for their tremendous efficiency, for their frugality of life, for the logic of their minds, for their admirable achievements in the arts, for their neglect of the industrial system, for their devotion, above all, to the eighteenth century. It would be restful to serve, if only as a slave, people who saw clearly, coldly, straight; not obliquely and with hypocrisy only such things as should deviously conduce to the standard of hogs and to lecheries winked at... He would rather sit for hours on a bench in a barrack-room polishing a badge in preparation for the cruelest of route marches of immense lengths under the Algerian sun.

This passage may give you some idea both of the absurdist element in Tietjens scheme of values and of the feverish streak in his imagination. French Foreign Legion? A slave polishing a badge on a bench? A long cruel march under the Algerian sun? Come on! Whether you like *Parade's End* or not will depend, I suspect, less on whether you find Tietjens's disinterested personal code of conduct believable, than on whether you can acclimatize yourself to the disjointed atmosphere of the extended interior monologues he submits us to.

Of course, Tietjens is not from being the only character whose voice we hear in *Parade's End*. A considerable section of the second volume comes to us from the point of view of his wife Sylvia, and much of the fourth volume is narrated by Teitjens's brother's housekeeper!

Which brings us to the matter of technique. If the moral tenor of Ford's fiction has received rather less attention than it deserves, then his sometimes vaunted technique has received rather more. Ford held strong views on how a novel ought to be shaped, how a scene ought to develop, how an event ought to be described, and more generally, on what posture the novelist ought to assume with respect to the story he or she is telling. These various concerns have usually been lumped together under the name "impressionism" and there is good reason, perhaps, to make use of this term in describing Ford's work. The long and the short of

FORD MADOX FORD 227

the impressionist theory is that the author should not in any way intrude on either the telling or the outcome of the tale he's telling. Events should come alive in front of us rather than being narrated, and the import of those events should impress itself upon us without the aid of didactic shading. The shape of the plot should carry the weight of inevitability and the magic of surprise, and we should be left with the satisfying feeling that life is terrible, but in a strangely beautiful just the same.

Ford's concern with such effects often led him away from the direct narrative approach toward nuances of suggestion, implication, and atmosphere, as events, reminiscences, and points of view. intersect. Such an approach is commonplace today. He developed these notions during his early years of collaboration with Joseph Conrad, but Ford took the process further.

We might, without going into the issue of their relative merit, compare this approach to those of two of Ford's illustrious contemporaries, Marcel Proust and James Joyce. Proust's world is highly reflective, highly meditative, and at the same time overflowing with social and narrative detail. No book could be further removed from the ideals of Flaubert than this one, in which the beauty and wisdom of the work is largely attributable to the thoughtfulness and sensitivity of its narrator. In Joyce's work, on the other hand, the flow of the narrative is continually being challenged and undermined by the wit and intellectual perversity of the author, who intrudes his cleverness in every way he can, with the result that our pleasure in reading is perhaps uncomfortably divided between the substance and the flavor of the text.

Ford's approach is more conventional than either of these, yet also, in some ways, more ambitious. He makes use of the extended interior reflective monologue, but without abandoning the broader third-person perspective—hence the repeated view-shifts that are a hallmark of his style. At the same time he attempts to establish an atmosphere "shot through with electricity"—a sort of "pointillisme," as he once described the technique to Pound. He extends this fractured approach to dialogue as well, on the grounds that in conversation remarks seldom relate to one another, because the interlocurors involved are too busy thinking of what they're going to say next to listen.

But above all else—and here is where he parts company with his more famous literary confreres—Ford held the belief that the author himself should never appear in the text.

These views were perhaps most succinctly expressed in *Conrad: a Personal Remembrance*, which Ford wrote on the death of his old friend in 1924. Here he discusses Conrad's views, which are his own as well, in the following terms:

> *We thought just simply of the reader. Would this passage grip him? If not it must go. Will this word make him pause and so slow down the story? If there is any danger of that, away with it. That is all that is meant by the dangerous word technique.*

Ford did not, as far as I know, ever utter a harsh word about Joyce's work. He and Joyce were friends, in fact, at least to the extent that Joyce stood as godfather to Ford's daughter Julie, and Ford published an excerpt of *Finnegan's Wake*, then called simply "Work in Progress," in his *transatlantic review*. Yet I wonder whether these remarks from his book about Conrad might have been directed toward his famously "modern" Irish colleague:

> *There are, of course, pieces of writing intended to convey the sense of the author's cleverness, knowledge of obsolete words or power of inventing similes: with such exercises Conrad and the writer never concerned themselves... we used to say that the first lesson that an author has to learn is that of humility. Blessed are the humble because they do not get in between the reader's legs. Before everything the author must learn to suppress himself; he must learn that the first thing he has to consider is his story and the last thing he has to consider is his story, and in between that he will consider his story.*

FORD MADOX FORD   229

But Ford was also enough of a writer to know that when one sits down to write, one simply writes. By the time he sat down to write *Some Do Not...*(1924) these techniques had become habitual:

> *...At least they weren't over there! They were prancing. The whole world round them was yelling and prancing round. They were the center of unending roaring circles. The man with the eye-glass had stuck a half-crown in his other eye. He was well-meaning. A brother. She had a brother with the V.C. All in the family.*
>
> *Tietjens was stretching out his two hands from the waist. It was incomprehensible. His right hand was behind her back, his left in her right hand. She was frightened. She was amazed. Did you ever! He was swaying slowly. The elephant! They were dancing! Aranjuez was hanging onto the tall woman like a kid on a telegraph pole. The officer who had said he had picked up a little ball of fluff...well he had! He had run out and fetched it. It wore white cotton gloves and a flowered hat. It said: Ow! Now!" There was a fellow with a most beautiful voice. He led: better than a gramophone. Better...*
>
> *Les petites marionettes, font! font! font!*
>
> *On an elephant. A dear, meal-sack elephant. She was setting out on...*

Taken out of context the passage may seem more obscure that it actually is, but it gives you an idea of the melange of thoughts, sounds, and images that Ford considered "good writing."

It seems to me that Ford's most obvious literary antecedent isn't Flaubert, as he himself often asserted, but Cervantes. On the surface we have the exaggerated romanticism, the outdated values, the effervescent absurdity of the central character surrounded by more sensible, but also "smaller" folk. Underneath it all, we find in both writers a deep familiarity with life and a well-developed capacity to describe and sympathize with a number of different points of view.

Among Ford's recent literary predecessors no one appears to have been fishing the same waters except Thackeray. A strange

230   BY THE WAY

comparison, perhaps. Yet the parallels between *Parade's End* and *Vanity Fair* are, I think, worth examining. One critic writes, "Thackeray was conscious of his Englishness as only an Englishman born in British India can be." Ford's consciousness of the English was, perhaps, that of a romantic expatriate whose father was half-German. Charlotte Bronte wrote of Thackeray's work:

> *There is a man in our own day whose words are not framed to tickle delicate ears; who, to my thinking, comes before the great ones of society much as the son of Imlah came before the throwned kings of Judah and Israel; and who speaks truth as deep, with a power as prophet-like and as vital—a mien as dauntless and as daring. Is the satirist of* Vanity Fair *admired in high places? I cannot tell; but I think if some of those amongst whom he hurls the Greek-fire of his sarcasm, and over whom he flashes the levin-brand of his denunciation, were to take his warnings in time—they or their seed might yet escape a fatal Ramoth-Gilead.*

Writing a century later, Ford's rendering of the decay of British society is less a prophesy than a requiem. Of his central figure one critic has written:

> *Tietjens is out of his time in a world where the laws have lost their reality, the system has collapsed and the synthesis of knowledge and belief has lost its validity; under his feet he feels the great landslip. England (his specific example) once had a defined and integrated culture, but during the Nineteenth century it had become a kind of pseudo-civilization marked for export. Like cheap trading-goods, imitations, her morals, manners, and religion were shipped to every part of the world. It was a process of weakening, dilution, and overextension in more than a physical sense.*

Thackeray's and Ford's work are both rich in social observation. Both carry a certain weight of ethico-political import. Yet both revolve around conventional romantic imbroglios involving gentlemen (Dobbin/ Teitjens) and rakes (Osborne/ Macmaster), sweethearts (Emily/ Valentine) and shrews (Becky Sharp/ Sylvia) all of them more or less sympathetically rendered.

Ford had few nice things to say about Thackeray, though he once conceded that *Vanity Fair* was a book fit to stand alongside his favorites, *Madame Bovary* and *The Sentimental Education*. He spoke with disdain of the casual way Thackeray went about establishing his "effects," and he hated the ease with which Thackeray assumed his place as a highly-esteemed member of the society he was pillorying. Yet Ford himself might well have assumed a similar position, given half a chance.

But the most distinctive parallel between the two is one of tone. Both Thackeray and Ford, their obvious differences in technique aside, give to their creations a sort of melancholy agitation. One middle-brow reviewer of *No More Parades*, the second part of the Tietjens saga, aptly described it as a work of "nervous and intellectual intensity." She also, with perhaps greater insight than Pritchett, expressed surprise that "Mr. Ford's novel is not a thoroughly English book—it is not permeated with English ideals and traditions; it has, in fact, a sort of unconscious anti-English feeling in it as if it were the work of one of those aliens in the British Empire, Celt or Semite, who in their souls resent what England stands for."

For all his emphasis on impressionist truth through disinterested imagery, the world Ford describes in *Parade's End* is steeped in exaggeration. Things are a little too excellent, or a little too sordid. A little too proper, or a little too out of control. Tietjens is, we're told, "the smartest man in England," while his wife Sylvia is "the most beautiful woman in England." Such phrases have less in common with the realistic descriptions of Flaubert than with the moral tales of Marguerite of Navarre. And for all of his expressed abhorrence of didacticism, I think Ford would have been flattered by the association.

And what of Ford's more famous, though far shorter novel, *The Good Soldier,* which he wrote at the age of forty, on the eve of the First World War? Martin Seymour-Smith, the polyglot author of the immense *New Guide to Modern World Literature*, writes: "No better novel in the realist mode has appeared in this century in any language." High praise indeed! Unlike the complex and sprawling *Parade's End*, *The Good Soldier* is a relatively brief first-person meditation, in which one member of a well-bred foursome describes the events that brought their polished world of elegance and propriety to disaster. The order in which our narrator chooses to relate specific events, while alluding to later, more calamitous ones in passing, gives his tale an aura of absurdity and dread from the very first sentence.

One feels the lurking presence of another of Ford's idols, the prolix Henry James, in these pages, although Ford's subtle exploitation of the narrator Dowell's phlegmatic naiveté gives the vagaries of the style added meaning. We know more than Dowell does, and some of what we know comes from our growing familiarity with aspects of his character of which he himself seems to be unaware.

Although Ford experienced commercial success during the Twenties with his war novels, the tenor of the times was shifting, as he himself was well aware. In 1924 he inaugurated a literary journal from Paris, *the transatlantic review,* in which he published exerpts from *Finnegan's Wake* and championed the works of young American writers like Hemingway and William Carlos Williams, whose blunt style struck him as possessing a vitality that English writing seemed to have largely lost. Meanwhile, strange as it may seem, Ford's own writing was becoming more repetitive, self-referential, and gassy. Having exhausted the emotional and imaginative heat of his war-time experiences, he returned to a prolix anecdotal style, reiterating tales of his illustrious childhood among the Pre-Raphaelite greats and expounding upon his favored themes of frugal living, vividly non-didactic art, and French food.

At the time there was widespread concern about the future of European civilization, which appeared to be teetering on the brink of collapse, although it was unclear whether a ruthless Capitalism or a fanatical Communism would be the agent to bring it down.

Eminent writers and artists of every stamp felt the need to address the issue. Their views covered a wide range of attitudes, from the occult vagaries of W. B. Yeats *A Vision* to the dry, closely-reasoned conservatism of T. S. Eliot's *Note Toward a Definition of Culture* and the crack-pot economic radicalism of Ezra Pound's Jeffersonianism.

By then sociologists and philosophers such as Vilfredo Patero, José Ortega y Gasset, and Karl Mannheim had been examining the issue of "elites" more systematically for some time. Are elites necessary? How might they best be maintained in the diseased social climate of post-war Europe? Pareto wrote in 1902, "The phenomenon of new elites which, through the incessant movement of circulation, rise up from the lower strata of society, mount up to the higher strata, flourish there, and then fall into decadence, are annihilated and disappear—this is one of the motive forces in history, and it is essential to give it its due weight if we are to understand great social movements." Thirty years later Adolf Hitler was to show the world how rapidly such a rise and fall could take place.

In the context of such weighty speculations Ford's vision may appear distinctly out of place. The ills of society would vanish overnight, he argues, (though, being a Papist, he is forbidden to be a perfectibilist and seldom expects to see things improve) if we would all a). limit ourselves to small-scale economic enterprises, preferably market gardening, crafts, or commercial dealings that allow us to interact with well-known clients regularly; b). cultivate and support the arts; c). treat our neighbors with kindness and generosity; d). eat our meals out-of-doors whenever possible; and e). make sure those meals are heavily spiced with garlic.

In some ways this simple formula for social regeneration anticipates the views of recent critics of industrial society. It might equally well be said to constitute a re-iteration of ideals advanced in Ford's youth by the followers of the Arts and Crafts movement. Ford himself was raised in what we would call a "counterculture" atmosphere, the seeds of his agrarianism and his devotion to craft—although not his interest in cooking—are to be found in the soil of late nineteenth century England. Yet Ford was more fully aware than many were then, or are today, how closely allied such views are with the traditional views of the Right. He claimed never to have taken an interest in party politics, although his distrust of democracy was personal: "I have always doubted my ability to interfere in the lot of my fellow-beings. So that if my one vote or voice could turn an election anywhere in the world I would employ neither, ever." His defense of traditional privilege was equally childish and idiosyncratic:

> *My own predilections have always been towards the Right. I like pomp, banners, divine rights, unreasonable ceremonies and ceremoniousness. It seems to me that when the world was a matter of small communities each under an arbitrary but responsible head then the world was at its best. If your community did not prosper you decapitated your chief. Till then he was possessed of divine rights. Presumably you cannot better the feudal system.*

These are the views of a man that can't bother himself to think deeply about politics. They betray the same excruciating spiritual generosity and confusion that drove the narrator of *The Good Soldier* to throw up his hands with a phlegmatic "What does anyone know about the human heart?" They bear no relation to modern political life, where arbitrary rulers are seldom responsible and where divinity has long ceased to be a meaningful concept. Nor do they suggest a deep-rooted familiarity with the particulars of that bundle of social, religious, and economic relations that historians refer to as the feudal system. The value of Ford's social program lies in its simple insistence that politics does not have the potential to solve mankind's problems. Beauty and Righteousness? Market-gardening and garlic? We may describe such rallying cries as politically irresponsible, but only if we admit at the same time that political life is brutally contentious and almost invariably oblivious to the crimes it commits in the name of justice, progress, or *reason d'état.*

There is no substitute, Ford is telling us, for authentic relations between human beings on a personal level. Art is the supreme manifestation of the human desire to glorify and share experience. Food, locally grown and eaten out-of-doors in the company of friends, is the ultimate manifestation of both the natural generosity of the earth and the warmth of the human heart. The conversation across the cafe- or dinner-table will, it is to be hoped, turn to art, or to gardening, or to politics or history, or to questions of love, or to anything at all in which those individuals present are genuinely interested.

Such an occurrence, in Ford's view, constitutes a sacrament of civilization, than which there is none higher. The spirit of the good life, of vegetable gardens and poetry and history and the sun of Ford's chosen Eden, bubble through *Provence* (1938), which may be the best of his later works. Although Ford will be doing all the talking, a place has been set at the table for us. We've been invited out to share a meal.

Ford's attitudes toward sex are also decidedly quaint. Yet here, too, it would be a mistake for us to dismiss them summarily. He is not interested in boldly depicting how bodies function in intimate situations, and he offers no metaphysical or psychological insight into the "roots" of the instincts that inspire us at such times. What interests Ford is the sexual tension that develops between men and women who love and/or hate one another—what it feels like, how it colors an individual's experience and oozes across the social space, how people ignore, live with, or respond to it, and what becomes of them as a result. The romantic elements of *Parade's End* might well have been lifted from one of Turgeynev's works. Yet no one has offered us a more *novel* rationale for sexual involvement, perhaps, than Ford did when his hero Tietjens reflects:

> You seduced a young woman in order to be able to finish your talks with her. You could not do that without living with her. You could not live with her without seducing her;

*but that was the by-product. The point is that you can't oth-
erwise talk. You can't finish talks at street corners; in museums; even in drawing-rooms. You mayn't be in the mood
when she is in the mood—for the intimate conversation that
means the final communion of your souls.*

Are we to characterize this attitude as naive? Unmodern? It
certainly confirms every remark ever made about Ford's habit of
patronizing others. After all, has the woman's interest in enduring
such talks been even momentarily considered? Perhaps she had
something entirely different in mind.

A remark made by Stella Bowen, the Australian painter who
was living with Ford during the period when he wrote *Parade's
End*, may shed some light on the issue. Bowen met Ford at a party
near the end of the First World War; they fell in love and not
long afterwards set up housekeeping in a little cottage in Sussex
so that Ford could forget about his combat experiences and get
back to earth and life and growth. They raised pigs.

*Ford, of course, knew a great deal more about human
relationships than I, but though his mind was skeptical
enough, the honest sentimentality of his heart had adopted
the idea of love-in-a-cottage with complete sincerity. It was
what he wanted, and when Ford wanted anything, he filled
the sky with an immense ache that had the awful simplicity
of a child's grief, and appeared to hold the same possibilities of assuagement. And in spite of discrepancies, or perhaps
because of them, I think our union was an excellent bargain
on both sides. Ford got his cottage, and he got the domestic
peace he needed, and eventually he got his baby daughter. He
was very happy, and so was I. What I got out of it, was a
remarkable and liberal education, administered in ideal cir-
cumstances. I got an emotional education too, of course, but
that was easier. One might get that from almost anyone! But
to have the run of a mind of that calibre, with all its incon-
sistencies, its generosity, its blind spots, its spaciousness, and*

*vision, and its great sense of form and style, was a privilege
for which I am still trying to say "thank you."*

A testimonial of this kind has no bearing on the aesthetic
value of *Parade's End*, of course, or any of Ford's other books, but
it ought to help us dispel the notion that he was trapped in an
atmosphere of delusional, antiquated romanticism. There were in
his time—and I'm sure there are still today—more than a few
individuals who valued life, art, love, and work, with the simplicity of a Provençal peasant or a medieval scholastic. Ford studied
it, promulgated it, and went to the front lines in defense of it. This,
too, may be described as a form of romanticism. But life—regardless of the age or era—is nothing if not romantic.

❦

NOVEMBER : POWERLESS

It's a funny feeling when you arrive home in the dark, flip
the switch in the kitchen…and nothing happens. You flip the
switch again, although you know perfectly well that's not how a
switch works. Then everything changes—inside your head.

Of course. The power is out.

You pull the flashlight from the drawer, dig some candles out
of the closet, find the matches (same drawer) and begin to illuminate the place. Getting a little classier, you find some taller bee's-
wax candles, put them in candleholders. Suddenly it occurs to
you that a mirror might be useful, though none are near at hand.

Hilary arrives home from yoga to find the living room bathed

238   *BY THE WAY*

in candlelight. How enchanting! You're such a dear.

The next morning, you look out the bedroom window to see that the cedar tree that has shielded the yard for thirty years is taking a siesta on the neighbor's garage. The temperature hasn't dropped much yet—it stands at 62 degrees—but it will.

The computer is down. (Duh!) It's impossible to get to your files, and you spend the day sitting beside the super-efficient Jøtul stove reading a Spanish novel—*The Wrong Blood* by Manuel de Lope. No music to listen to. Just the howl of the wind and the occasional snap of a wind-driven branch against the sliding doors that open out onto the deck.

By noon you've moved most of the food in the fridge into coolers that are sitting just outside that door. The spanikopita and pot pies in the freezer will get eaten tonight. Frozen cranberries? Might as well toss them, don't you think? There are now several power cords running across the street from neighbor to neighbor—they have power over on that side—although you haven't been included in any such arrangement. Well, you never asked.

A brief visit to the library with the laptop to check for urgent emails proves fruitless. (Let's face it, you're bored. You never get urgent emails.) Along the way you notice that you feel like an invalid when you're at home, but everything's suddenly fine the minute you leave the house. Your neighbor stops by at dusk to find out if your power is still out. His house is down to 40 degrees, he says.

Later that night, returning home from a heated racquetball match, you ponder the logistics of taking a shower in the dark. (Important meeting tommorrow, don't you know?) Will the water still be hot? But the lights at the end of the block are on, your next-door neighbor's light is on ... your lights are on!

Now what are we going to do about that tree?

Javier Marias / Penelope Fitzgerald

A few years ago I spent a dollar at a library bookstore to purchase a novel by the Spanish writer Javier Marias. I don't read much fiction any more but he's one of my favorites. When I got home I noticed it was volume two of a three-part series. My first thought was simply to toss it, but I eventually went online and discovered that there was a single copy of volume one available from a bookshop in Point Reyes, California, for $7.00. A dilemma. The novel might well be great, but at 1200-odd pages, would I ever read it? On the other hand, what if that's the only copy left in the entire country? Forever? Tossing good money after bad, I brought the book, and read both volumes with relish.

> *Let us hope that no one ever asks us for anything, or even inquires, nor advice or favor or loan, not even the loan of our attention, let us hope that others do not ask us to listen to them, to their wretched problems and painful predicaments so like our own...*

That's a strange way to open a twelve-hundred page novel in which the narrator never stops talking, don't you think?

But Marias is a thoughtful person, adept at generating those interior monologues that have won Proust such favor with readers.

He's less interested than Proust in manners and refinements in feeling, however, more interested in adventure, intrigue, duplicity, truth, courage, cowardice, and betrayal. It seems to me he might also have a better grasp than Proust of how memory actually works.

The best brief indication of the sophistication of Marias's approach that I know of appears in an interview he gave to BOMB magazine in 2000. At one point the interviewer asks Marias to define what he means by "literary thinking" and Marias replies, in part:

> *A character within a book can say two totally contradic-*
> *tory things, yet both can be true. Shakespeare does that all*
> *the time. You read Shakespeare and generally you understand*
> *everything easily. But when you stop and reread a bit, often*
> *you begin to ask, What's he saying? What is this? I give an*
> *example of this in my latest novel, or "false novel," as I have*
> *called it,* Dark Back of Time *(*Negra espalda del tiem-
> po*). It's the beginning of the famous monologue in Othello,*
> *in which Othello, before he kills Desdemona, says something*
> *like, "It is the cause, my soul, it is the cause. Let me not name*
> *it. You chased stars. It is the cause." You read that, you've*
> *listened to it a hundred times, you've seen it in films and*
> *generally you say, Okay. But then you stop and ask yourself,*
> *What's this? What does he mean? Which cause? What is the*
> *cause? You come upon things you apparently understood on*
> *first reading, but you haven't really—they are mysterious or*
> *even contradictory. That's literary thinking: something pro-*
> *ducing itself in flashes. It's less a form of knowledge than of*
> *recognition, at least in the kind of novel I like most, which*
> *would include Proust, Faulkner, and Conrad. Reading them,*
> *you recognize things you didn't know you knew. And some-*
> *times I try to create the same effect in my books.*

Eager to read volume three of the trilogy, which had not yet appeared in English, I secured a review copy from *Rain Taxi* magazine and finished the journey. The review I wrote went something like this:

In the last twenty years the Spanish novelist Javier Marías has produced a string of novels bearing a remarkable consistency in tone, all narrated by a solitary, ruminative observer who is obsessed by the untold histories of the people he encounters. This narrator works as a translator, has a wife named Luisa, from whom he's often estranged; he quotes Shakespeare and other writers more than occasionally—not to others, but to himself. He has a solid grasp of European history and a voyeuristic interest in what's happening outside the windows of his apartment. The similarities among the novels, and between the novels and the author's personal history, doesn't trouble Marías in the slightest. As he writes at the start of *Dark Back of Time* (1998):

> *I believe I've still never mistaken fiction for reality, though I have mixed them together more than once, as everyone does, not only novelists or writers but everyone who has recounted anything since the time we know began, and no one in that time has done anything but tell and tell, or prepare and ponder a tale, or plot one.*

This is a grandious statement with genuine anthropological import, and it's probably true, though we must remember that Marias didn't make it—the narrator of his novel did.

The three-part novel *Your Face Tomorrow* continues along the same path, echoing earlier works while offering new episodes in our narrator's story. It's longer than anything Marías has done before (roughly 1270 pages) and the fact that he succeeds in holding our attention throughout its course makes it arguably his most impressive achievement to date. The layers of intrigue it contains may be suggested by the fact that the narrator, one Jacques (or Jaime, or Jack) Deza, discovers a spot of blood in the home of a former Oxford don he's visiting on page 131 of the first volume, and we don't learn where that blood came from until a thousand pages later, as we near the end of volume three. But we're never allowed to forget that it exists, because Deza, who had tried to clean it up and found the outer edge impossible to remove, takes that persistent stain as a symbol of the dark deeds that are continually (though seldom completely) being washed away by time.

There are several dark deeds within the story itself, which involves the narrator's experiences working for MI5 or MI6 (he isn't sure which) as an interpreter, not of speech, but of character. He's been recruited by a man named Tupra on the recommendation of some Oxford friends who had once been involved in the same business and are impressed by his almost novelistic insights into character. He spends his days sitting behind a one-way mirror, listening in on interviews and then discussing with Tupra whether the man or woman in question is lying or trustworthy, would have courage in a dangerous situation, is "to what extent resentful or patient or dangerous or resolute."

Although it's all rather nefarious, he acts as if it's really none of his business. Yet near the end of the second volume he witnesses a scene of shocking violence initiated by his boss in a nightclub restroom (though he does almost nothing to stop it, to his later chagrin), and in volume three, he finds himself faced with the challenge of committing a similar act himself to protect his estranged wife Luisa.

Though the story is intriguing from beginning to end, the events themselves are few and far between. Much of the richness of *Your Face Tomorrow* is to be found in the narrator's private ruminations on those events and on the lives of his colleagues, several of whom did intelligence work during the Second World War. Their cryptic references to the past repeatedly bring to mind his father's experiences during and after the Spanish Civil War (which, not surprisingly, mirror those of Marías's own father Julien, a philosopher and protégé of Ortega y Gasset). During such moments of introspection, the narrator piles thought upon counter-thought, clause after clause, with mesmerizing beauty and clarity, into delicious sentences that can run to a page or more in length. To take a relatively brief example:

Everything that exists also doesn't exist or carries within itself its own past and future nonexistence, it doesn't last or endure, and even the gravest of events run that same risk and will end up visiting and traveling through one-eyed oblivion, which is no steadier or more stable or more capable of giving shelter. That's why all things seem to say 'I'm still here, therefore I must have been here before' while they are still alive and well and growing and have not yet ceased. Perhaps that's their way of clinging grimly to the present...and to stop other people saying 'No, this was never here, no one saw it or remembers it or ever touched it, it simply never was, it neither strode the world nor trod the earth, it didn't exist and never happened.'

Alongside this theme, which we might call historiographic, runs an ethical one initiated by Deza's boss, Tupra, who at one point comes close to murdering an ambassadorial lackey at an exclusive club. Deza, flabbergasted, sputteringly objects, and Turpa relies blandly, "*Why* can't one, according to you, go around beating people up and killing them? Why can't one, Jack?"

Such weighty issues provide a steady, gentle passacaglia beneath the narrator's acute yet unhurried observations of the life going on all around him in London and later Madrid, his problems with his wife, and his asides on Spanish and English culture, medieval history and literature, warfare, James Bond, Italian Fascist propoganda posters, hand-made German shoes, botox, and other subjects too numerous to mention. As he puts it, "Books speak in the middle of the night just as the river speaks, quietly and reluctantly, and their murmur, too, is tranquil or patient or languid—"

A reader new to Marías might be best off taking a look at one of the earlier novels, *A Heart So White* (voted one of the two best Spanish novels of the last quarter-century) or *Tomorrow in the Battle Think on Me*. But if *Your Face Tomorrow* lies close at hand, by all means take the plunge.

◆

My latest literary discovery is the British novelist Penelope Fitzgerald. (She's been around for decades, of course, but *I've* only recently discovered her.) When her books were being reissued in the 1990s I gave her a try, but found her a tough nut to crack. Recently I happened upon a book of her short stories, *Means of Escape*, which allowed me a point of ingress into her terse yet thoughtful idiom. And perhaps I'd matured a little myself during the interim.

Fitzgerald is actually a throwback, stylistically, to the era of the literary impressionists, of whom Joseph Conrad, Ford Madox Ford, and Stephen Crane are probably the chief exemplars in the English language. Gustav Flaubert is the godfather of the movement. Nowadays fledgling writers learn at MFA camps to "show, don't tell." The question remains to be answered: Show *what*?

Here is a passage from Fitzgerald's most highly acclaimed novel, *The Blue Flower*:

> By September carts were beginning to make their way into Jena from the pine-woods with logs for the coming winter. Branches from the tops of their loads scraped against the windows in the side-streets, which were littered with twigs like a rookery. Manholes opened suddenly in the pavements, and gratefully received the thundering rush of wood. At the same time, pickling had begun, and enormous barrels of vinegar began to trundle down the rungs into the reeking darkness of the cellars. Each house stood prepared according to its capacity, secreting its treasure of vinegar and firewood...

To my ear, this passage has everything—music in the prose, deep knowledge of the era in the details, and artless subtlety in creating a vivid multi-dimensional scene with relatively few words. I especially like the phrase "like a rookery," and "trundle down the rungs."

Fitzgerald has taken a route opposite to the one Marias travels on. Everything he describes is filtered through the mesmerizing consciousness of the narrator, handled, reconsidered, questioned, prodded and probed. Everything she describes stands complete, crisp and crackling dry, with the narrator's own persona nowhere in sight.

The effect would not be so powerful, except that the details Fitzgerald provides draw us almost immediately into the emotional nexus of her story. In *The Book Shop*, for example, we follow a few months in the life of a middle-aged woman named Florence who decides to open a bookshop in a small town in East Anglia. She meets up with subtle interferrence from the local blueblood, a petty woman who has other plans for the building in which Florence has located her shop. Our heroine hires a somewhat crass teenaged girl to help her run the place and gains the unexpected support of a reclusive grandee who has long despised the local woman who has become Florences's secret rival. Florence herself is a naive woman, perhaps, but also courageous, good-hearted, and genuinely devoted to literature and books.

The story plays out with all the cruelty of the foot operation Flaubert describes in *Madame Bovary*, but Fitzgerald's handling of the affair is more delicate. The last few pages contain a scene comparable to the final passages in Conrad's *Heart of Darkness*—but in reverse.

I found *The Blue Flower*, an imaginative recreation of a few years in the life of the German poet and philosopher Novalis, far more interesting than anything I've read by Novalis himself. But the book tells us less about Novalis, perhaps, than about the various women who surround him and influence his actions and emotions—his mother, his sister, the twelve-year-old girl he falls in love with in the space of a quarter of an hour, her older and much more worldly sister, and the daughter of the man he's lodging with, who would seem to be his soul-mate. He recognizes that fact and finds it uninteresting.

I'm describing the book as if it were a sort of romance, but there is very little romance in it. There is a lot of piety and strangeness and minerology and traveling back and forth across the countyside. There is friendship and social observance and the deep currents that tie siblings to one another in inexpressible ways.

Fitzgerald doesn't tell us anything about Novalis's later career. She presumes, perhaps, that we've read his "Hymn to the Night" or opened *Pollen*:

> – *The spirit always appears in strange, evanescent forms.*

> – *On the musical nature of all association and fellowship—Could musical relationships be the source of all delight and aversion?*

> – *The human world is the commonplace organ of God. Poetry conjoins us to God, as it conjoins us to one another.*

Fitzgerald started writing in her fifties, received a Booker prize in 1979 for her second book, *Off-Shore*, and continued to garner fulsome praise from the critics until her death in 2000. A.S. Byatt compares her to Jane Austen, hastening to add that she has Austen's precision and invention, but also qualities besides that are more "European and metaphysical." And it's true, Fitzgerald is utterly uninterested in who will eventually get married to whom. Yet almost every sentence in her work carries a tiny dose of judgement, of sympathetic irony, of penetration, of wisdom.

My dad, who's eighty-eight, took one look at *The Blue Flower* and remarked with a touch of good-natured distaste, "It reads as if it's been translated from a foreign language." It's true, Fitzgerald's prose doesn't sweep you along, but makes you pause and digest. She recognizes that a single, well-chosen word or phrase can make a scene "pop." She takes equal interest in the kindness, the madness, and the pettiness her characters exhibit, as if there were truths to be exposed, no matter what the moral valence. She also knows how to savor the feel and smell and look of things. The little things.

She quotes Novalis at the start of *The Blue Flower*: "Novels arise out of the shortcomings of history."

Quest for Firewood

Many things can be put off almost forever, but buying firewood isn't one of them. When you're out, you're out. I suppose you could do a *La Boheme* and rip apart your copy of *War and Peace* for kindling, or begin cruising the dumpsters of south Minneapolis for discarded furniture. But I'd rather not.

All the same, the task of buying firewood fills me with suspicion, frustration, and dread. The men (and occasionally women) who cut, split, age, and haul the stuff around are a breed apart, only one step higher, perhaps, on the ladder of atavistic trades, than the men who apply hot asphalt to warehouse roofs in the summertime. Yet I feel that I've got a lot in common with them. I love the woods, I love the trees, I've cut and split plenty of wood myself in my time, and feel an almost Hamsunesque attachment to individual trees, living and dead.

The chain saw and the power-splitter have no doubt changed the industry somewhat, but the men who come around to drop off the stuff don't seem to change much at all. I have found that dealing with these woodcutters can be a challenge. Suddenly you're back in a novel by Thomas Hardy, if not the Middle Ages, trying to get a square deal from an itinerant merchant who knows he'll probably never see you again and wouldn't mind pulling a fast one if he got the chance.

"Smells kinda green. Are you sure this wood was aged three years?"

"You betcha."

" Hey, that doesn't look like oak."

" Well, *most* of it's oak."

And so on.

I'm not a fanatic about it. I realize, for example, that a wood-cutter can make 20 or 25 percent more profit if most of his

248   *By the Way*

wood is twelve inches long rather than the advertised sixteen, but I don't care. On the other hand, I will not tolerate that log cabin stacking method which results in a lot more empty air and a lot less wood. And I've got a line marked on the wall in the garage, four feet up. That's where the wood is supposed to reach. It's a simple concept.

One morning a few weeks ago, when the grass was still vaguely green, I began the rigmarole of getting some firewood delivered. First, I called the number written in pencil next to the entry "firewood (good)" on the F page of our telephone directory. The voice on the answering machine identified itself as "Roger's Sheetrock and Taping" and suggested I leave a message. That didn't sound too promising. I next logged onto Craig's List and wrote down some numbers, made some calls, left some more messages. Before long I'd set up a delivery with a man from somewhere in the vicinity of Little Falls. His wood was a little bit cheaper, and you could order it in sizes, the biggest of which he described as "about the diameter of a one-gallon plastic milk bottle."

The day before he was scheduled to show he hadn't called to set up a time, so I called him again.

"Boy, am I glad you called," he said. "The guy who took the order never got your number! What did he quote you?"

The guy I was speaking with sounded like the same one I'd spoken with before, but I let it pass. "A hundred and five," I said. "Is that too high?"

"Too high? That's too low," he replied. Surprise, surprise.

He called the following afternoon at the appointed time.

"I've got good news and bad news. The good news is that I'm in Golden Valley. The bad news is that my brother is charging me more for the wood. I'll have to make it $115. Is there a problem with that?"

"Well, come on by and we'll take a look at it," I said finally.

A few minutes later Jeff was backing his pick-up truck into the driveway. I took a look. The wood looked smallish but reasonably dry.

QUEST FOR FIREWOOD   249

"This looks fine. But I gotta tell you, I do have a problem with that price," I said.

"OK, we'll make it $110," he said hurriedly. Big hairy deal. Five dollars. Fine.

Jeff was a short man of about fifty with a soft, rather shapeless face and a wispy four-day stubble. He had a kid of about fifteen with him, and once I showed him where the wood was supposed to go they got to work unloading it.

"Right here is the four-foot line," I pointed to a faded pencil mark on the Sheetrock.

"Well, that's your row, right there across the back," he replied, gesturing vaguely, not looking up.

I let that remark pass and asked, by way of conversation, "Is this your son here helping you?"

"No, that's my son's *friend*," he said. "My son is too lazy to get off his fat ass and work."

I felt we'd established some sort of rapport by that time and I blurted out good-naturedly, "I don't want you doing that chimney stack thing."

"The DNR *makes* you do it," he said. "They require it."

"That may be, but this isn't a state park, so if you don't mind, I'd like you to just stack the wood length-wise."

As Jeff and his helper unloaded the wood, stick by stick, into a wheel barrel and then back out of the wheel barrel onto the stack a few feet away, I told him my wife and I were heading up to the Leech Lake area for a few days, and inquired about the deer hunters.

"They're *everywhere*, and man, they're crazy," he replied knowingly. "This is the last weekend. They're desperate." Then he added with a child-like glisten in his eye. "I got my two already."

We talked about oak and ash. "You can't sell ash any more, they'll fine you five thousand!" As I watched the pile get higher and higher, Jeff told me about a customer earlier in the day who'd cursed and swore when he discovered he'd bought a fireplace cord rather than a real cord.

"I never said I was bringing a cord. Nobody gets a real cord for $110. That's ridiculous," he exclaimed, and I had to agree.

I was actually somewhat pleased with myself for giving in a little on the price. I wasn't the type who cursed and raged and gouged. Then again, I was also a little annoyed with myself—after all, a deal's a deal. Yet as we stood chatting, and I watched the pile rise higher against the wall of the garage, I couldn't help noticing that the wood left in "my" row in the back of the truck was never going to get it anywhere close to the line that defined a genuine fireplace cord.

"I gotta tell you," I said at last, "This seems to be falling well short of a fireplace cord. I'd say we've got maybe a $70 pile of wood here in front of us."

Jeff looked at me askance for a second, then he said, "O.K. Have it your way. Back in the truck." He said this more in faux-exasperation than in anger. Maybe he expected me to relent. I said nothing. After a moment of silence, he began to toss the pieces of wood that were sitting in the wheel barrel back into the truck.

"Here," I said, grabbing a stick of wood, "I'll help you."

◆

A few days later I arranged with a woman from Bloomington to bring around a fireplace cord. Once again, no one called to set up a time on the appointed day and I had to call her back. They were running late, she said. I have a racquetball match, I replied. An hour later I left a message informing her that the garage door wasn't locked. Just stack it against the wall on the right, I said.

When I got back a few hours later there was a heap of firewood sitting in the middle of the driveway. It was a handsome pile, as woodpiles usually are. The wood was generally small and a little short but it looked dry and good to me, and I enjoyed tossing the pieces one after the other into the garage and then stacking them in place. (I would have used a wheel barrel myself but mine has had a flat tire for about fifteen years.) When I was through, the stack was decent…only six inches short of the line.

Sheila called again later that day. "The battery died on my cell," she explained. "I didn't get your message until a few minutes ago. Did my boys drop that wood in your driveway?" She sounded upset.

"Not a problem," I replied. "I stacked it myself." Then I added, "It did come up a little short."

"Oh, they're on their way back right now. They'll top it up for you."

A few minutes later a pick-up came crawling up the street in the gloaming and two teenage boys climbed out.

"You guys must have been all over today," I said.

"Yeah! Tell us about it. Maple Grove, Crystal, Little Canada."

"Where's the wood from?"

"Everywhere."

They began to unload a few more sticks from the truck and I went inside.

I'd like to think the wood came from Remer or Bagley or Big Falls, but it's probably just blow-down material from right around the corner. It's a little on the short side, as I mentioned earlier, and I've already come upon a few chunks of cottonwood in the mix. The important thing is, the ordeal is over, and we're set once again for a year or two.

A few days later I got a call from someone at Roger's Sheetrock and Taping. "You want some wood?" the man said. "I can get some from my brother…"

◆

A a year later I got a call from Sheila. "We sold you some wood last year," she rasped. "How's it holding out?"

"I'm doing fine," I relied. "But thanks for calling." What I had it in mind to say was, "Actually, I'm almost out, because the "oak" you sold us last year was half cottonwood."

It was true. I was running out. I called a few numbers, including a guy in Stillwater that I spotted on Craig's List. "Golden Valley? That's too far." I called a number with a local area code for Ron's Tree Service and left a message. I called another number, it sounded good, but the woman told me she was out on the road. She'd call me back later, she said.

But Ron called me first. Not Ron, maybe his wife. A pleasant, articulate woman, at any rate. I'd made a few more calls by that time and had no recollection of who or what "Ron's" was, so I asked, "Where are you located?"

"We're in St. Cloud," she said.

"Where do you get the wood?"

"My husband buys it standing. We hire loggers to cut it and bring it in to the woodlot. We've got a big barn where we store some of it. We age it and send trucks down to deliver it in the Cities every day."

The price she quoted was 20 percent more than I'm used to paying. Then again, it was only half of what Paul's Fireplace Wood in Little Falls quoted me. And a little voice in the back of my head kept saying, "Maybe you wouldn't have so much trouble buying wood if you weren't so *cheap*."

The truck that showed up Tuesday morning was bigger than any wood-hauling truck I'd ever seen before, and it was full to the brim from front to back. Clearly I was the first stop. The smell of ammonia was in the air—a smell I associate with green oak—but the wood itself had that seasoned gray look, and it was expertly split into moderate-sized quarters.

Meanwhile, the two guys unloading it alleviated any disappointment I was feeling at the hitherto upscale and bourgeois nature of the deal. As usual, one of the unloaders was just a kid, while the other was a seasoned pro. "I'm actually a tree-trimmer," he told me with obvious pride. "I could bring down a cottonwood single-handed, though it's better to have someone around to hold the ropes…in case something goes wrong. They're paying me a lot of money to do this."

As he tossed the wood down into the rubberized wheel-barrel, he said, "Look at that. This stuff is dry. There's a layer of dust on it. Look at that bark fly off when it hits the wheel barrel. Ron is one of a dying breed. The production firewood operations have all the machines, but their wood doesn't look like this."

"I don't know what you mean by 'production' operation," I queried, keenly aware that I was about to learn something interesting.

Here the lad broke in. "You can get a unit. I think it costs $250,000. One guy sits there with a crane, brings in a log, then the machine cuts it. He sets up the pieces, also remotely, and the machine splits them. But half the time they don't line up right. Whatever comes out, that's what you get."

"Surely Ron uses a splitting machine, too," I exclaimed, glancing at the huge load of wood in the back of the truck.

"Yeah," the old pro replied. "But you load it by hand. And it runs by centrifugal force, not by hydraulics. Man is it fast. You release that handle and pow!"

I was trying to imagine where the centrifugal force might possibly come from, and why it would be better than hydraulic force. I suppose the "pow" is the sound of the splitting wood. Both of these men had a peculiar gleam in their eye as they described the process, as if they'd just emerged from a carnival tent. It must be some amazing machine. Pow!

The old pro gave me Ron's card as they were leaving. Also a refrigerator magnet, which seemed a little much.

"He has 1,500 people on his list," the man said as he climbed back into the truck. "He delivers to them every year…It's a business. But with a three-year aging process, it's a big investment, and it's tough to anticipate the market…When things slow down, he sells some of it to his brother."

MADAME BUFFALO

*...for in every one of us a mad rabbit thrashes
and a wolf pack howls, so that we are afraid it will be heard
by others....*

—Czeslaw Milosz

It would be easy to work up an essay on the theme, "We live in very unspiritual times." Just make a few references to mass culture, widespread chemical dependency, Grand Theft Auto, the knavery of political life, the perils of social media, and the deterioration of the nuclear family. The point being? Either that we must return to an earlier time, when such-and-such prevailed, or that we must hold true to our little cells of enlightenment or faith, weather the storm, and promulgate our message for the future, whatever it might happen to be.

It would also be pretty easy to devote an essay to the theme of how far we've come as a civilization, how alive with possibilities the present age is, and how truly transplendent things will soon be, once we get a few more of the wrinkles ironed out.

Just now I saw a swainson's thrush out in the garden in the midst of the drizzle. He's been out there all day. I've been watching him.

❧

The universe is interesting in the same way a campfire is interesting: it's active, ever-changing, dangerous, mysterious, and you can stare at it as long as you want to without worrying that it will start up a conversation, or turn away, or stare back. But a fire has advantages as a focus of reverie. You can stare into it from a comfortable position, either standing or sitting, without craning your neck. Its intricacies, though less dazzling, perhaps, are more absorbing, its alterations more rapid and musical—and to top it all off, there is the fact that you made it yourself.

And then there's the smoke.

◆

Gaspar de la Nuit is sometimes referred to as Maurice Ravel's pianistic tour de force. Extremely difficult to perform, it consists of scintillating waves of sound in a Listzian manner, designed to evoke the black magic described in the poems of an obscure French writer named Bertrand Louis (1807-1841) from which it draws both its name and its themes.

Have you ever tried to whistle the first movement?

That may sound like a facetious question, considering how diaphanous I've just described the music to be, but the melody that drifts through the middle of all those effects is simplicity itself. I sometimes find myself whistling it. I will be the first to admit that my version lacks something of the texture of Ravel's original. All the same, it's a nice tune, and I would hazard that if it hadn't been there, singing out, the piece would long ago have descended to the level of similarly complicated works by Scriabin, Messiean, and others that virtuosos strive to master, though few music-lovers choose to listen to them.

Ravel once remarked about the music of his compatriot Francis Poulenc, "What I like is his ability to invent popular tunes." Ravel's tunes don't sound like popular tunes. They're part and parcel of a rarefied harmonic palette, full of ninths and elevenths. But they do sing. The complexity sustains the atmosphere while the tunes remain simple, lyrical, even romantic. The two elements are deftly interwoven, in *Gaspar* and other works, so that we take them in whole. Well, I guess that's what music is all about, even the simplest.

In life, too, simplicity is a valuable quality. Yet without that background, that atmospheric charge, the simple life can become uninteresting and even deadening. There are times when we can't quite grasp the tune, and others when the the atmosphere doesn't seem to support it.

◆

Among the wise folk who were active during that golden zone of world consciousness when religions were being formed—Confucius, Buddha, Lao Tzu, Pythagoras, Moses and all the rest—the one who consistently receives short shrift is the Greek thinker Heraclitus. This may be because Heraclitus never founded a sect.

But perhaps that's the point. His views were not of the type that people become devoted to. Nor are they intentionally non-sensical, in the manner of a Zen koan. They're simply brief, enigmatic expressions of the way things are.

I made a broadside once, using cold type, of Heraclitus's twelve finest sayings. I don't know where that thing went, but I remember several of the one-liners I included:

The sun is the width of a man's foot.

It is difficult to hide our ignorance, especially when relaxing with friends over wine.

The fire, in its advance, will consume all things.

He who would be wise must acquaint himself with a great many particulars.

All things come to pass through the compulsion of strife.

Time is a game played beautifully by children.

One or another of these sayings returns to me from time to time, like a tune I heard long ago and subsequently forgot.

◆

The difference between the scientific and religious approaches to experience, in a nutshell, is this. Science has the proper tools at its disposal—reason, investigation, observation—to get at the truth, but it's constitutionally incapable of asking the Big Questions. Religion asks the Big Questions. It was created to satisfy our desire to know why we're here and how we should live, and it does a pretty good job by means of myth, tradition, ritual.

Metaphysics combines elements of both approaches. It makes use of reason and observation—the tools of thought—to answer the Big Questions. Yet all too often the answers metaphysicians arrive at don't satisfy us either. The results of metaphysicial inquiry are usually too prolix by half, and when answers do appear we may be surprised to see how closely they resemble folk wisdom.

◆

The Argentine poet Antonio Porchia (1886-1968) made a career out of wedding metaphysics and folk wisdom:

> *He who has made a thousand things and he who has made none, both feel the same desire: to make something.*
>
> *When I do not walk in the clouds I walk as though I were lost.*
>
> *The void terrifies you, and you open your eyes wider!*
>
> *It is a long time now since I have asked heaven for anything, and still my arms have not come down.*
>
> *I love you just the way you are, but do not tell me how that is.*
>
> *Striaght lines shorten distancs, and also life.*

◆

The single most important thing we can learn from metaphysics is to come to grips with contraries. A remark made by Aristotle, in his matter-of-fact way, may be to the point here.

> *It is plain, then, that [all thinkers] in one way or another identify the contraries with the first principles. And with good reason. For first principles must not be derived from one another nor from anything else, while everything has to be derived from them. But these conditions are fulfilled by the primary contraries, which are not derived from anything else because they are primary, nor from each other because they are contraries.*

But what are "the contraries"? We might take the One and the Many as an example. The One is unified, the Many are all over the place. Could anything be more obvious?

Yet we ought to go a little further and point out that if there had always and forever been only one thing, the idea of One-ness would never have arisen. The expression "unified" requires multiplicity. One-ness is the dream of the many, not the one.

The reverse is no less true, however. For the idea of the Many arises from an inkling of connectedness or movement toward a point of unity. In short, the concepts of the One and the Many, though opposed to one another, are also logically dependent on one another.

This kind of language drives most people up the wall but the thrust of the argument should be clear: Because the one and the many are logically inseparable concepts, neither unity nor individuality will serve us well as an ideal. On the other hand, a concept like Harmony offers a vision of order and proportion that can shape the dynamic opposition of the one and the many. In family life, art, politics, what we actually seek isn't unity but harmony.

◆

One defect of the monotheistic ideal is that it deprives the diety of conversation with equals. Lacking that source of stimulation, he becomes withdrawn, morose, and irritable. Maybe Hegel got it right after all: Monotheism of reason and the heart, polytheism of the imagination and of art.

◆

"The infinite qua infinite is unknowable," or so Aristotle says. On the other hand, Cioran observes—

> ...nihilism is neither a paradoxical nor a monstrous position, but rather a logical conclusion wrecking every mind that has lost intimate contact with mystery (mystery being a prudish term for the absolute.)

There is no contradiction here, however. Intimate contact with the absolute does not result in knowing it.

Children often meet up with the absolute at an early age, when they begin to ask themselves why there is something rather than nothing, or "Why am I me, and not you?" The frisson generated by such thoughts is powerful, and it's worthwhile for us to keep this pathway to the absolute open as we age, because it provides that invaluable point of perspective of which Cioran speaks, if I read him right. For the lucky few, this perspective becomes engrained, and every aspect of experience takes on the luminous shine of a miracle.

◆

And speaking of miracles, Pierre Mabille, in his classic surrealist text *Mirror of the Marvelous*, sets out a very useful contrast between the miraculous, the marvelous, and the magical. No need to elaborate it in detail, you can figure it out for yourself simply by analyzing what the words mean. But at one point he writes:

> *Despite the miracles it surrounds itself with, despite the fantastic elements it employs, a religion always begins as a reaction against an earlier paganism that it exposes as fantasmagorical and childish. It triumphs because of its rational usefulness. It tends to limit the field of the marvelous by providing answers to fears, security based on dogmatic assertions, and a more complete examination of the universe. The marvelous, on the other hand, proposes fewer solutions in favor of exploring unknown territory. The true believer ignores the unknown as soon as he possesses faith. Thus there's an equilibrium at work between the domains of the religious and the marvelous. The later never disappears entirely. Even during periods when orthodox mysticism is the most strict, popular stories survive.*

◆

I have long been a fan of fairy tales, and I often find myself tossing a volume into the suitcase when packing for a trip. My favorites from the Pantheon series are the French tales adapted from the work of Henri Pourrat (1887-1959), though many ethnologists find them too literary. I also like the Arab set translated and edited by Inea Bushnaq. The *Northern Tales* are OK, though I find both the Grimm set and the Swedish tales edited by the

Blechhers to be too cloddy and mean-spirited to enjoy fully. On the other hand, *Jewish Tales of the Supernatural* exhibits a fascinating blend of Old Testament didacticism, Eastern European ghetto atmosphere, and Caballistic magic. Calvino's book of Italian tales has many fine moments too, though the language can harbor an annoyingly feverish quality. It can be interesting to go back to the original from which Calvino drew much of his material, the *Pentamerone* of Giabattista Basile. This book, first published in 1674, has been called the oldest collection of European folktales in existence, and also the richest. It was written in a Neapolitan dialect, however, and remained outside the mainstream until Benedetto Croce translated it into Italian early in the twentieth century.

Whatever their source of origin—and very good African, South American, and Japanese volumes are also available, though I've never seen a Spanish one—fairy tales dispense with emotional nuances and sociological details to take us directly into the heart of things, where animals play important roles, fairies and genies upset the natural order, fools more than occasionally turn out to be wise, and naive but pure-hearted individuals triumph, in the end, over the deviousness and wickedness of their scheming relatives. You may observe that in "real life" animals don't talk, wishes aren't granted very often, and cleverness often wins out over sincerity. On the other hand, one of the most prominant, and dangerous myths of "real life" is the notion that we're in complete control of our destiny, everything happens "for a reason," and if things don't work out it's because we failed to discipline ourselves, calculate accurately, or explore our conscience in search of an explanation for why a tree just fell on the house. No, life is full of surprises, few of which have a reasonable explanation.

◆

Naiveté is a fine quality though it isn't one that we can cultivate. By definition, naiveté doesn't know itself. One thing we can do, I suppose, is avoid putting on airs, and be frank about the fact that we like grilled-cheese sandwiches and experience a child-like thrill every time we see a robin splashing around in the birdbath.

◆

Schiller writes, speaking of the appeal of nature, bird-songs, waves, stars, etc:

> *It is not these objects, it is an idea represented by them. We love in them the tacitly creative life, the serene spontaneity of their activity; existence in accordance with their own laws, the inner necessity, the eternal unity with themselves. They are what we were. They are what we should once again become.*

I suppose there is some truth to this remark, but reading it over it seems to me that Schiller doesn't quite get it. For, on the one hand, if we did once again enter into that unreflective "state of nature" we would not be able to recognize or appreciate the condition. In any case, this idea of nature of which Schiller speaks is entirely false. What is a bird call, after all, except a love call or a defense of territory? An expression of yearning, in other words, or of fear, defiance, or possessiveness. There is no unity to speak of here, no law. Nature is, in fact, just like us, and we are a part of it. We have our own territory, our own calls, of which we're perhaps hardly aware. Our love of nature—the dappled light, the cool air, the chattering squirrel at the birdfeeder and the mounds of purple clover on the highway embankment—is natural, instinctive, and also aesthetic. There are no ideas involved. Ideas are what stand in the way of that pleasant symbiosis.

As if to dig himself as deeply into error as possible, Schiller continues:

> *For what could a modest flower, a stream, a mossy stone, the chirping of birds, the humming of bees, etc. possess in themselves so pleasing to us? What could give them a claim even on our love?*

262   BY THE WAY

No, our satisfaction in nature, he contends, "is not aesthetic but moral; for it is mediated by an idea, not produced immediately by observation; nor is it in any way dependent upon beauty of form."

Yet it seems to me that what pleases us in nature is precisely the form. (In using the word "pleasing" Schiller ruins his argument. Ideas aren't pleasing; forms are pleasing.) Our response to nature is aesthetic—the form of a stream, a flower, a white pine, a heron. It's a matter of texture, diversity, proportion, a balance of shapes and weights and movements.

Yet although Schiller has made one misstep after another in his analysis, there is one aspect of it that's worth examining more fully. The mediating idea of which Schiller speaks is innocence or naiveté. Nature, he feels, is innocent—that's what makes it so appealling.

I think he's hit on something important here. Nature seems opaque to us. It seems not to have much of an inner life. The birds, the flowers, even the rocks—they do what they do, and nothing we can say or do has much of an effect on them. It's peaceful and relaxing to associate ourselves with complex, mute beings who have no interest in us. Furthermore, every crow we see could be the same crow—though we know it isn't—and this engenders an atemporal field of associations to which we grant a spiritual quality. It may be insulting to the crows that we think this way, but we don't really care.

Schiller refers to this quality of naiveté or innocence as a moral one, which is not quite the case. After all, when the grizzly mauls a camper we don't describe the act as moral. That's simply how a bear sometimes acts. When the ranger shoots the aggressive bear we accept the act as morally justifiable, perhaps, but at the same time something inside us cries out, "Mr. Grizzly didn't deserve that. He was only doing what he does, you know. Being himself." The moral realm is a human realm. A realm of weighing alternatives, of evaluating. As far as well know, the natural world largely lacks the interiority required to develop such concepts. At least we see little evidence of it, though animal mothers do care for their babies, etc. It's precisely this pre-moral naiveté that makes the natural world somehow meaningful, and even sacrosanct.

A good deal more could be said on this subject, but the long and the short of it is this: innocence is not quite the right word to describe what it is that we respond to in nature. Naiveté is a better word, though we must keep in mind that it derives from, and means hardly more than "native" or "natural." To say that nature is natural is not saying much—though Hume once observed that the natural can be opposed to the unnatural, the supernatural, and the artificial, in each case taking on different shades of meaning. It's not in the moral realm, in any case, but in the world of aesthetics that the roots of our marvelous association with our surroundings lie.

Yet here another obstacle immediately presents itself. We associate aesthetics with art, which is by definition artificial. A natural aesthetic must then involve affinities that take us beyond appearances into a deeper realm of shared being.

◆

Barbara Frederickson, a psychologist at the University of North Carolina at Chapel Hill, has written a book, *Love 2.0: How Our Supreme Emotion Affects Everything We Feel, Think, Do, and Become*. She argues that our ideas about love need to be overhauled. Love is neither a long-lasting, continually present emotion, nor a deep-rooted blood-tie of kinship. Rather, It's a "micro-moment of positivity resonance" that you can share with anyone you happen to come into connect with in the course of your day.

Part of Fredrickson's motive in advancing this unorthodox theory (according the article in the *Atlantic* where I heard about the book) is to remind lonely, love-starved people that the absence of a "significant other" in their lives doesn't mean they're incapable of loving or are leading a loveless existence. She writes: "Thinking of love purely as romance or commitment that you share with one special person—as it appears most on earth do—surely limits the health and happiness you derive" from love.

264   BY THE WAY

The point is well-taken—and it has often been made before. But Frederickson veers into error when she suggests that the myriads of single people who are looking for a partner are in the grip of a "worldwide collapse of imagination."

The fact is that Frederickson's definition of love—as a momentary thrill that we feel in spite of ourselves, which she and other biologists can no doubt write a chemical equation to describe—is a bit limiting itself. The most profound and satisfying thrill of love is, perhaps, a low murmur of heartbreaking affection for that special someone with whom we have shared many years of living.

Some would go further and take the argument into the theological realm—Richard of St. Victor, *Amare videre est*, and all of that. But we'll leave that train of thought for another time.

I suspect that individuals who experience the long-standing affection of a soulmate are also better able to tap into those micromoments of love that are all around us than those who lack a shared inner world. We love our spouse or significant other more than the clerk at Walgreens, not only because we know them far better and are tirelessly attracted and engaged by what we know, but also because we get far more in return. The ricochets of ongoing experience are the source of endless interest and more than occasional delight.

For myself, I love the snow on the trees, the music on the stereo, the article in the morning paper about tofu, and the pine siskins on the platform feeder outside the window. I love waving to the postal worker I see almost every day who returns my wave with an appreciative smile before returning to her plodding path around the block. But I love my wife Hilary a whole lot more. When she calls to tell me she'll be home from work early and expresses an interest in sharing a frozen pizza by candle-light while seated on the kitchen floor, that really sets me to chopping the onions and peppers.

This is not to say that Frederickson's researches are unimportant. She presents us with an entirely new meaning for the phrase "love triangle"—it involves mirror neurons, oxytocin, and vagal tone. And she offers compelling proof that love is connected to the heart—via the vagus nerve. Her research also lends credence to the power of Buddhist and Jewish teachings of loving kindness to strengthen vagal tone, thus helping people to become more loving, whatever their condition in life might be.

Her advice to single folk—to seek out little moments of connection—is sound, though I'm not sure where she stands on the subject of flirting. When she describes love as "a single act, performed by two brains," she touches upon a realization as old as the troubadours, though it's also possible to love something that doesn't have a brain—a pear, say, or a mountain, or a poem. In one of his lyrics the troubadour Bertrand de Ventadorn (1130-1190) sings:

Of course it's no wonder I sing
better than any other troubadour:
my heart draws me more toward love,
and I am better made for his command.
Heart body knowledge sense
strength and energy—I have set all on love,
The rein draws me straight toward love,
and I cannot turn toward anything else.

A man is really dead when he does not feel
some sweet taste of love in his heart;
and what is it worth to live without worth,
except to irritate everybody?
May the Lord God never hate me so
that I live another day, or even less than a day,
after I am guilty of being such a pest,
and I no longer have the will to love.

◆

Is it merely a coincidence that religions often come out of the desert? Probably. Yet there is something about clutter that tends to obscure the gravity and significance of things.

Is it merely a coincidence that we love the rustle of leaves, the sound of wind racing past our ears, the mesmeric lapping of waves against the shore? I don't know.

Majestic mountains, winding rivers, trees—these things are often pleasing to us because they exhibit harmonious forms. Scientists calculate the proportions of a seashell or the pattern of seeds on a sunflower to prove that Pythagoras was on to something with his "music of the spheres," but it may be more germain to observe that the interaction of wind and rock shapes mountains, that water gnawing at earth makes rivers. The clinging root and the grasping leaf give shape to the plants. When we stand in awe of a graceful island of sumac bushes that has spread itself across the side of a hill, we're admiring the harmony that's developed between elemental forces. There is nothing symbolic about it, and the math merely reinforces what we already feel and know.

◆

We compliment someone by saying "You were certainly in fine form today." But we criticise him or her by remarking "Your behavior was rather formal this afternoon." This contrast highlights the fact that form is of the essence of value—yet "pure form" is seldom interesting.

◆

When Pilate asked Jesus if he was King of the Jews, and Jesus replied, "So you say," was he exhibiting good form?

When Rollo the Norman kicked the king of France in the face and then observed that it was the customary greeting among his people, was he exhibiting good form?

I don't know the answer to these questions, though I suspect Rollo was simply being a jerk.

Discussions of form often center on the analysis of more or less static works of art—vases, statues, paintings. I bring up these episodes from history and folklore as a way of suggesting that form is an aspect of action. Tennis players, cellists, and talk-show hosts can be in good or bad form.

◆

It's difficult to sustain a discussion of "form" for long without resorting to gassy generalities because forms vary as do the materials of which they consist. All the same, everything we come upon in life displays marks of proportion, balance, fiber and texture, motion and incidental detail. Our familiarity with these things pleases, stimulates, and elevates us. In this way forms differ radically from norms. Norms underscore and promote mediocrity—that is to say, the middle. Forms underscore and promote excellence, excitement, inspiration—that is to say, the heights.

◆

...When an adventurer carries his gods with him into a remote and savage country, the colony he founds will, from the beginning, have graces, traditions, riches of the mind and spirit. Its history will shine with bright incidents, slight, perhaps, but precious, as in life itself, where the great matters are often as worthless as astronomical distances, and the trifles dear as the heart's blood.

These lines appear in *Shadows on the Rock*, a novel by Willa Cather set in the city of Quebec during the earliest days of the French regime. As I read them it occurred to me that we're all journeying to a remote and savage country—the future—and we all carry our gods with us, not quite knowing, sometimes, precisely who or what they are.

Do we, then, have graces, traditions, riches of the mind and spirit? I think so. Our traditions are as rich and expansive as civilization itself, and our practices range from taxing journeys through the wilderness to conversation with friends at a sidewalk cafe, with perhaps a visit to the library now and then in between.

Civilization is another concept we've been trained to be suspicious of, and narrowly conceived it can certainly become a instrument of oppression.

Our friend Cioran writes:

Each civilization believes that its way of life is the only right one and the only one conceivable—that it must convert the world to it or inflict it on the world; its way of life is equivalent to an explicit or camouflaged soteriology.

This isn't necessaily the case, however. Modern western civilization takes an interest in the wider world to a degree never before seen on this planet, and its genuine hunger for exposure to other forms of life is an inregral part of its dynamic nature.

You may find my take on the matter somewhat naive. Can I be unware of the imperialistic activities of capitalists looking for new markets, for example. Yet I see no reason to define modern lifeways exclusively in such terms. These are norms, after all, not forms. In fact, I find the soteriology—the theory of salvation—implicit in our civilization attractive, though it strikes me that curiosity, rather than conversion, is its proper tool. Yes, Christ refers occasionally to "the sword" and Heraclitus enigmatically asserts that "the fire in its advance will consume all things." Yet few of us, I think, believe that the Kingdom of Heaven, whether real or imagined, is anything other than civilized.

✺

THE MASTER CLASS: ANGELA HEWITT

A blustery November morning in downtown Minneapolis. Gray skies and gray concrete, a few cars on the road, a few panhandlers on the sidewalks. People are eating breakfast in the Keys Restaurant and shopping for household items in the flagship department store on the first floor of the Target corporate headquarters. The ice on the rink in Peavey Plaza is solid, but no one is skating this morning. You can examine the menu at Cafe Vincent in solitude, dreaming of pistachio-encrusted salmon, or wander into Brit's Pub to soak up the aroma of fried fish.

Orchestra Hall, sheathed in colorful heating ducts, looks dark and deserted, like a circus tanker that's run aground. There are no posters visible but the door is open, and eager young women carrying notebooks enter in pairs, followed by lanky, solitary, gloomy-looking, white-bearded men. Ushers are stationed here and there along the corridors—more of them than the guests, it seems—and as you enter the cavernous performance hall you'll notice rows of chairs set up on stage facing a big black grand piano, beneath a background of floating white acoustic cubes set at odd angles to one another. Many of the chairs on stage are already occupied, and there are people scattered across the first ten rows of the auditorium. It's a master class.

There is something quietly thrilling about such gatherings, I think. Their purpose is neither to dazzle nor to entertain, but simply to transmit information, to carry on a tradition, to sustain a guild. I may have been one of the few people in the audience who have no idea how to play the piano, and I must confess I was a little surprised to have received an invitation, but there could be no mistake about it. The blurb in the newspaper was crystal clear: "Public welcome, free admission." And so I went, expecting to learn a little something about the music and the performing tradition, and to watch the fascinating interplay between hallowed artist and aspiring apprentice, which can be affectionate, businesslike, haughty, or terrifying. I suppose I was also hoping to soak up a little of the luster of the truly great, who emit flashes of edgy brilliance in every casual gesture and remark to those in their immediate vicinity. In this I was not disappointed.

Angela Hewitt has been playing the piano since the age of three. She has been referred to as THE Bach interpreter for our times, and although this oft-quoted remark was probably made by the recording company she works for, it carries the ring of half-truth. Hewitt has also recorded Couperin on the piano, however, and Messiaen, and the complete Ravel. In fact, her teacher in Ottawa was French, and she studied in Paris for seven years. This familiarity with and love of French music may explain, in part, why her interpretations of Bach strike many ears as being charming and lyrical, while retaining a full measure of the clarity and precision for which Bach is well known. (Glenn Gould, the famous Canadian Bach-interpreter of the preceding generation, rather hated French technique and was not overly fond of Bach's French Suites either.)

After a brief introduction, the first of three privileged students adjusted the padded piano bench and sat down to play a brisk movement from one of Mozart's sonatas. The performance had polish, but there were clinkers in the fast runs and a vague feeling of "getting through it" rather than "bringing out the nuances." It was the type of performance that creates anxiety in the listener, in fact, and I found myself sighing every time she chose to do a repeat.

When the young woman had finished, Hewitt, a diminutive woman with a big smile, rose and strode purposefully over to the piano.

"Have you been working on this piece long?" she asked, a little nervously, forcing a smile.

"Actually, yes, " the young woman replied.

"Well, the first thing I would say is that whenever you play a piece, it shouldn't be all at the same level. You must decide which voices to bring out, which parts to play louder. Here, let me show you. I haven't played this since I was a child," and she proceeded to breath life and expression into a series of notes that were the same notes we'd just heard. After playing for perhaps forty-five seconds, she stopped and rose, and the student returned a little sheepishly to the bench, at which point they began to examine details in the score together, one by one.

"Here, in the left hand, if you pound out every note in the pattern it just sounds stupid. You must pick a thread to emphasize, like this." And Hewitt replayed the passage, which suddenly became musical. The student gave it a try, with a glimmer of success.

Much of the time it was difficult for those of us in the audience to hear exactly what Hewitt was saying because her head was turned away from us toward the keyboard, but snippets emerged from time to time. Some remarks were rather general: "With Mozart a note

THE MASTER CLASS 271

must always be *going* somewhere..." "Mozart is closer to the Baroque than we sometimes realize...." "Mozart is always imitating the human voice..." Others were technical, even banal: "...you really must work on strengthening four and five," "Oh dear! That fingering is just stupid." "...with an appoggiatura you must always emphasize the penultimate note."

As the session progressed, the student's play seemed to deteriorate a little, with more false starts, botched chords, and perhaps even less expressiveness than before, but nervous though she was, she retained her composure, making every effort to do what Hewitt was asking her to do. Finally the lesson came to an end. With a broad smile and perhaps a degree of relief, the Master graciously thanked the young woman for coming, and we all clapped as she sat down.

The second performer was a smiling, chubby young man, still in his teens perhaps, with a cheap suit and an unruly shock of red hair. He had chosen a more difficult Mozart movement, with several extended and tricky passages of hands-over-hands, and he played it with marked brio. When he'd finished Hewitt rose once again and returned to the front of the stage.

"I enjoyed listening to that," she said, "You played with feeling, with emphasis and dash." Then she looked over to the score sitting on the piano, and said "Oh dear! The Shirmer edition. That isn't the best edition. I see you've marked it up quite a bit. That's good," and turning to the audience she asked, "Does anyone happen to have the Urtext? No? Well, I guess it will have to do." And once again the bar-by-bar analysis began.

Here there was a degree of conversation, however; the student made an observation from time to time, and Hewitt listened, as if two colleagues were discussing how to interpret a score. She commented more than once on the youth's big hands (more power, but difficult to extract from between the black keys) and as he replayed this or that passage she would make comments: "Don't move your elbow like that. It requires plenty of energy simply to play the piece..." "This shouldn't be such a muddle. Chose the line you want and bring it out..." "..when you do that passage, it's better to concentrate on the arpeggios in the left hand and let the trill proceed on its own..."

Occasionally Hewitt would turn to look out at the audience on the floor, to reiterate or elaborate some point she felt was of general interest. "I always tell my students...."

And so it went with the third performer as well. She had prepared one of Bach's English Suites, which she performed with spirit, and when she'd finished Hewitt asked her if she'd been studying the piece for long, (not a good opening remark, I fear) and then observed "Bach is very close to the dance. Many of the movements are dance forms, of course—gigue, bourree, allemande—but even those that aren't specifically described as such should have a lilt. This is a nice 3/8 piece, but in the original manuscript every other bar-line is just a series of faint dots, as if Bach wanted the melodic lines to be longer and more flowing, and not quite so abrupt and mechanical..."

Then Hewitt began to work with the woman on the score. The two chatted, and even laughed on occasion. "First just play the chords. Get used to the hand movements playing the chords, and only when those movements become absolutely natural add the arpeggios..." "You can really sustain these notes more. If you wanted everything to be so crisp and even, you could play a harpsichord..." "...not so fast here. You really have more time than you think..." "This note is wrong in the text. It should actually be an E." "The ending should be strong. My mother always said that even if you botch a piece make sure the ending is strong. That's what people go away with. That's what they remember."

Once this pleasant and informative ordeal was over, Hewitt glanced at her watch. "I see we have a little time left," she remarked, and with that she walked to the front of the stage to entertain questions from the audience.

THE MASTER CLASS 273

For more than an hour Hewitt had been at the back of the stage, or at the piano with her back turned to us, or hunched over the student who was seated at the piano. Here at last she stood facing us, smiling freely, pointing with her yellow pencil to one raised hand or another. Clearly a fun-loving woman, but also severe and intense in her devotion to art, she was wearing a short woolly miniskirt marked with a crude green-and-orange pattern, black tights, and black, knee-length leather boots with high heels, almost like a New York beatnik from the fifties. She looked older, but also more interesting than her publicity photos suggest. As each question came, she considered it briefly in silence, and then spoke rapidly.

Someone in the audience asked her to comment on her recent foray into the music of Ravel, and she replied briskly, "Actually, I recorded the complete Ravel in 1987, so it isn't that recent. But I love Ravel, as with Bach, the combination of complexity and clarity, the color..." She went on to tell us that she'd studied not only piano, but also ballet, from the age of three, and it was very difficult when it came time to make a choice. "I was studying in Paris at the time, and most of my friends were dancers... but (here she laughed) music offered the prospect of a longer career. All the same, my dance studies have deeply influence my performance technique."

Many of the questions Hewitt fielded dealt with minor technical issues relating to trills and ornamentation. Someone asked her about memorization, and she spent a good deal of time describing her own methods, which were focused on committing a score to memory away from the piano. She told us that she once had a blind student who could effortlessly begin a piece at any point, having memorized it bar by bar through Braille, whereas many performers must start at the beginning of a movement or passage in order to recall the rest. "It's a lesson to us all," Hewitt said.

Did she ever memorize one hand at a time? Yes indeed, she replied, and began to hum the baseline from one of the *Goldberg*

Variations. "You must always approach Bach horizontally, voice by voice, and not vertically." Tension? "Play from the shoulder, not from the elbow. And if you're in pain, for God's sake stop playing immediately! Use ice, not pills. Pills never helped anyone. And sit up straight, not hunched over, so you can open yourself and communicate to the audience." Mastering a fast passage? "Play it slowly many, many times. And chose a tempo that you can manage from start to finish. Anyway, I know many professional pianists who often play far too quickly, and to no great musical effect."

One man had seen her perform the previous evening with the Minnesota Orchestra, and he'd noticed that she'd returned to the auditorium to watch the rest of the concert. He asked her to comment on that. "Well, I enjoy listening to orchestral music. And more than once. You imagine that the orchestra has everything down pat, but the performance changes from night to night, even if there has been no real discussion between musicians in the mean time." Then a hearty laugh erupted from her bird-like frame and she added, "Anyway, the conductor likes it if you take an interest in *his* work. Keep the conductor happy!"

Many of Hewitt's remarks were pedagogical commonplaces, I suppose, but no less worth repeating for that. The challenge lies in doing it all consistently, and doing it well. That added layer we call *expression*—the voicing, the tempo and dynamics, the touch— which transforms the material into genuine song, seems almost beyond the grasp of many performers, however, and one might well wonder why anyone continues to struggle with the peccadilloes of a composition that Horowitz, Rubinstein, Gould, or Hewitt herself has already elevated to unattainable heights. Yet it occurred to me, as I watched Hewitt penciling something in on a student's mass-produced copy of a score that was written 250 years ago, that I was witnessing a beautiful and even a hallowed process. However skilled or unskilled, however sensitive or dense, however GOOD or BAD they are, people continue to love making music for themselves. In so doing they enter into the flow of history, they share in

THE MASTER CLASS   275

the beauty, they sing along with Mozart, they *become* Bach.

I get the impression that Hewitt herself has never lost sight of that connection between composer and performer and audience, which ought really to be taken further back to whatever the sources of inspiration are that guide a composer's choices in the first place. There's a community of taste and feeling here that it's more than a pleasure to join by simply listening, whether we're capable of executing the music proficiently or not.

In a recent blog entry Hewitt wrote:

> *I am truly happy. And I don't say that lightly. I mean it. I have performed the complete* Art of Fugue *now in public. Last night in Florence was my first time with Contrapunctus XI-XIV and the 4 canons. And the first time I played Beethoven Op. 110 in about 15 years. Those two things together, along with the* Chromatic Fantasy and Fugue *by Bach (which was somehow different, even though I've played it for almost 40 years—I think it was influenced by the terrifying feel of D minor in the* Art of Fugue....). *What a programme—especially since most of it was "way-out-there" music and rather anti-virtuoso, anti-noise, anti-most things. The essentials of life pared down. Last works. At the very end I played "Vor deinem thron tret' ich hiermit," BWV 668—the chorale that Bach supposedly dictated on his deathbed and that was inserted on the final page of the first edition of the* Art of Fugue. *Applause after that seems misplaced. Never have I heard such silence in the audience in Florence as I heard throughout this recital. And to top it off, I played my own Fazioli which was absolutely amazing—especially for the Beethoven. Now for tonight in Rome (minus my own piano!).*

The fact that so few composers since the Second World War have endeared themselves to the music-loving public has driven more than one cultural critic to decry the decadent times we live in, and pine for those days when a more elevated standard of taste prevailed, etc. etc. It has been argued that "classical"

music was destroyed by the recording industry, or by the advent
of the electrical guitar, but in truth the matter is simpler than
that. That vein of music we call Western, mostly diatonic and
almost invariably regular in meter, has pretty well been exhausted in our times. Its life was extended considerably in the nineteenth and early twentieth century by the exploration of hitherto untapped folk traditions. The application of abstract and
aleatoric compositional techniques have been less successful.

But we'll leave that controversial subject for another time. It's
piano music that interests us at present, and the piano remains
the most expressive and versatile instrument ever created. Its
repertoire is unrivaled. From the pellucid charms of a Schubert
impromptu to the cosmic cacophony of a Scriabin sonata, from
the brooding lyricism of a Brahms intermezzo to the jangling
carnival exuberance of a piece by Milhaud, the piano touches an
astonishing range of moods and feelings. No doubt some feelings can be conveyed more effectively by the clarinet, say, or the
cello, or even the accordion, but the array of sounds generated by
the piano cover the breadth and depth of the human soul as well
as any single instrument can, I think. As the legendary German
virtuoso Wilhelm Kempff once put it, "No other instrument is as
wonderful as the piano. One is alone with the music."

On the other hand, it's difficult to fill a concert hall with a single piano, and we seldom get the opportunity to listen to a pianist
of international stature in an intimate setting. I recall one occasion
when Emanuel Ax was scheduled to perform a free mid-morning
recital in the student lounge of the West Bank Union at the University of Minnesota. I attended, along with twelve or thirteen
other students. Ax appeared in tie, tux, and thick-rimmed glasses,
his unruly shock of black hair sticking out at every angle, and sat
down to play, bristling with pent-up energy. I don't know whether
it was the condition of the piano, the meager attendance, or the
student in the front row of folding chairs (there were two rows
in all) who was just then eating a bag of potato chips, but after
a few stormy bars of the *Waldstein Sonata* Ax stood up and said

THE MASTER CLASS   277

to no one in particular, "I cannot continue," and strode haughtily out of the room.

In the end, what captivates most lovers of piano music, I think, is the quest for the perfect interpretation of a piece—or the exploration of different but equally engaging interpretations. The rising popularity of CDs created a great divide in the lives of many music-lovers, because the versions that were first made available in that format were seldom the same as the ones they'd grown up with. Yet the lure of a new, digitally recorded performance, even by the same artist whose vinyl version we already knew and loved, was difficult to resist. Many controversies ensued over whether the sound quality of a new recording adequately compensated for a decline in an artist's vision or technique.

At times we may be driven to buy a new interpretation as much by our love of the one we already have as by our dissatisfaction with it. I have enjoyed the piano music of Ravel, for example, since I purchased my first recording of *Le Tombeau de Couperin*, performed by Beveridge Webster on the Dover label. From there it was but a short step to the Odyssey box set of Ravel's complete piano works by Robert Casadasus. In the CD format Thibaudet's complete Ravel, Nojima's *Gaspar de la Nuit* and *Miroir*, and Cecile Ousset's equally fine interpretations, have been jostled but not ousted by the addition of Hewitt's versions.

With Debussy it's been quite the opposite. I have had difficulty finding a recording of his piano music that I like. Most interpreters accentuate the dreamy touches that strike me as frivolous or sentimental. Maybe the trouble is that I simply don't like Debussy much—though Michael Beroff does his best to bring out the composer's metaphysical side.

Many pianists have recorded Satie, and you can take your pick between somnabulantly hypnotic, unpleasantly peevish, and musically straightforward approaches. Satie's pieces are almost invariably short, and they range in tone from the playfully martial to the pleasingly oneiric, so that the flavor of most recordings is dictated as much by the selection of the pieces as by the performance itself. Back in the days of vinyl, Aldo Ciccolini was considered the master among Satie interpreters, but his recordings of the complete piano works were marred by their inclusiveness. And while we're on the subject of French piano music, I ought to mention that Rogé's two-CD set of Poulenc's solo piano works is a genuine classic. Likewise William Bolcom's handling of Milhaud's piano work.

The Catalan composer Federico Mompou may deserve a note in this context. He composed almost exclusively for the piano, exploring spare modernist landscapes of sound within which the echo of childhood songs can often be heard—the perfect soundtrack music for a disquieting de Chirico cityscape. He studied in Paris but spent most of his adult life in Barcelona, performing occasionally for friends and publishing a new set of haunting, crystalline, meditative compositions from time to time. Even today his work in not well-known, though it offers an interesting contrast—simpler, more strange, and more consistently lyrical in some ways—to the better-known compositions of his contemporaries north of the Pyrenees.

Gonzalo Soriano and Carmen Bravo recorded a representative sampling of Mompou's work for EMI in 1958; in 1992 Alicia de Larrocha produced a digital recording of his *Songs and Dances*—it may be the best single CD available. In 1995 the German modernist pianist Herbert Henck recorded selections from the fourth book of Mompou's *Musica Callada* for ECM. Like a fine wine that's lost its fruit but retains a degree of structure, these late pieces are unusually distended and spare. And for the die hard Mompou aficionado, we have the complete piano works in a four-CD set by Josep Colom.

But when we think of piano interpretations, it isn't the modern French repertoire that's likely to come first to mind. Rather, our thought roams across the rugged hills and green valleys of the nineteenth-century German and Central European literature, guided by the towering twentieth-century pianists who recorded it, some of them one-time students of teachers who had studied with the composers themselves. Beethoven, Schubert, Chopin, Listz, Brahms, Schumann. There is so much *rubato* here, so much *legato*, so much potential for *romantic expression*, that individuality counts for a great deal, and there are a hundred and one ways to get things right. I return repeatedly to Brendel's recording of Schubert's last sonatas, to Pollini's Beethoven.

With Mozart the situation is different. His sonatas have never been numbered among his most significant works, though it would be a mistake to dismiss them entirely. As the scholar Alfred Einstein once observed, "even the apparently simplest clavier pieces by Mozart are difficult."

The way I see it—I, a novice, an amateur, sitting here on the couch with the poems of Novalis in my hands, the K. 332 playing on the stereo, and snow falling outside the window—the professional performer faces several dangers. The natural temptation would be to exaggerate the drama, to "Beethovenize" the material. On the other hand, attempts to bring out the Baroque lightness and precision of Mozart's keyboard works are likely to emphasize how texturally thin they are. Horowitz himself noted on one occasion, "Mozart was a virtuoso composer just like Chopin or Liszt, but his virtuosity in expressed in fewer notes, and every note is equally important. Because of the spare textures, Mozart's piano music needs more color, not less, than so-called Romantic music in which color is already an integral part of the composition."

Many of the great performers have recorded Mozart sonatas, of course, and I've been tempted to investigate how Brendel or Ax approached K. 457 or K. 329. I was raised on Glenn Gould's Mozart, which would be considered a shame by most experts. Gould was not keen on the sonata form itself, and the tempi at which he performed Mozart's allegros are often feverish to the point of derisiveness. On the other hand, the passion and restraint he brings to the andantes is, I think, remarkable.

I haven't heard the Gould versions since I packed away my

turntable years ago. I had high hopes for Mitsuko Uchida's Mozart recordings of the 1980s, and they're unquestionably fine works, but they lack something—edge, or depth, or heft? The interpretations Horowitz recorded in the mid-1980s, on the other hand, are well-nigh perfect—brilliant, thoughtful, and yes, colorful.

The same issue confronts us when we turn to Bach, of whom Gould was at one time the universally acknowledged master. I was tempted to ask Hewitt to comment on the obvious contrast between her work and Gould's, but was deterred by the thought that the issue was too obvious not to have been dealt with many times before, and I couldn't bear the thought of a disdainful reply along the lines of "Oh, no. Not that again."

Hewitt and Gould are both Canadian and they've both recorded most of Bach's keyboard music on the piano. There the similarities end. After an attenuated career as a concert performer Gould retreated to the studio forever, convinced that touring was a thing of the past. Aside from her stellar concert career, Hewitt has participated in a program to bring classical music to communities that might not otherwise experience live performances, an effort she feels is essential to ensure the health of the discipline. Yet to his credit, Gould appeared regularly for many years on a radio program and he also wrote a good deal of entertaining musical criticism. The desire to communicate widely and to advance the medium was strongly felt by both musicians; it simply manifested itself in different ways.

The more dramatic contrast is in temperament. Gould was a legendary neurotic, larger than life in his intellectual intensity. To see what I mean, rent the film *32 Short Films About Glenn Gould*, or *Genius Within, the Inner Life of Glenn Gould*. Where Hewitt records Ravel and Chambrier, Gould records Hindemith and Schoenberg.

Fortunately we don't have to choose between the two. We might be in a Gould/Bach mood, or a Hewitt/Bach mood. We might be in the mood for a dose of harpsicord/Bach, or we might be entirely bored ourselves with the sewing-machine aspect of the idiom, and turn to the sobrieties of Swelinck or Frescobaldi or a refreshingly *galante* recording of Couperin. Whatever the mood, some piece of piano music is likely to match it. The instrument's almost fathomless intricacies are admirably suited not only to the dexterity of the human fingers but also to the cosmic range of human thought and the subtle shadings of the human heart.

Advent Reflections

So much is contained in a single word—a single letter. Thus, "Celebrating the birth of God" carries a different connotation from "Celebrating the birth of *a* god." Maybe the phrase "Celebrating birth" says it all.

My Greek is a little rusty after all these years, but as I recall, the prefix "gen-" carries a range of inference that spans race, kind, line of descent, origin, creation, sexual relations, and reproduction. Just think of the modern equivalents: generation, genius, generator, genuine, and genesis. But we must also include such words as genus, genealogy, generic, and general.

Clearly that simple prefix can take us in two different directions. On the one hand, it calls up a series of concepts having to do with novelty, creativity, authenticity, and uniqueness. On the other, it refers to concepts that lump things together into groups on the basis of their type or ancestry. We hold no one in higher esteem than the "genius" yet reserve our most withering distain for the merely "generic."

These two aspects of the expression will never be fully reconciled, but it would be a mistake to imagine that they're altogether opposed to one another. We meet up with both at every family gathering: the idiosyncrasies, the differences between family members that stimulate and nourish us (though they can sometimes annoy us, too) and the veins of affection that run ever-deeper, and constitute the reality (rather than merely the pedigree) of the clan.

Praise be to whoever cooked up a universe replete with affinities, both elective and congenital. May we become ever more generous and genial in our efforts to expand the reach of such ties.

When we were young, Christmas meant time off from school, a tree in the house with lots of "stuff" under it, sweet things to eat, and better-than-average hymns in church. There was plenty of magic involved, though it seemed to dissipate in an instant, and the classic conversation with friends on the day after Christmas invariably opened with a question: "Whaja get?"

We eventually made the discovery that Christmas wasn't the only holiday celebrated at the end of December. This could hardly be a coincidence. Some of us arrived eventually at the conclusion that Christmas was merely a veneer that had been applied to a much older, earthier, and deeper strain of religious feeling tied in with the fact that the sun had reached its lowest point on the horizon and was beginning to rise higher in the sky again.

In time that position began to ring hollow, too. We know with mathematical exactitude just when and to what degree the sun will begin to climb in the sky again, and there's little reason for us to celebrate the inevitable. Yes, spending time outdoors at night is always a good idea. So is gathering around a bonfire with friends. But our relations with solitude and earth and community and darkness can be cultivated at any time of the year. No one is really *worried* any more about whether or not the sun will climb in the sky again, and everlasting life is an entirely different kettle of fish in any case.

Christmas celebrations have always suffered from the fact that we have no idea whether the promise of salvation they extend will ever be fulfilled. The "hopes and fears" we share at that time aren't much different from the ones people were sharing two millennia ago, which gives the season added resonance. Any way you look at it, there's an element of mystery involved.

Not that we have to choose between the two traditions. Many of the elements of Christmas that please us are pagan—the star in the east, the Christmas tree, the Yule Log, and the manger scene itself. Meanwhile, pagan ceremonies associated with the return of the sun also have the effect, matters of astronomy aside, of focusing our awareness, in the midst of abject darkness, on that kernel of liveliness within ourselves that shares some affinities with the blazing firmament.

I have noticed that for a few days each winter, the morning sun shines into the house through the window behind the piano and strikes a narrow strip of wall between two doors in a hallway thirty feet away. It doesn't mean much, but there it is. I haven't been waiting for this event to take place; quite the contrary, I've forgotten all about it. But I get a certain pleasure every year when I see it again—as if for the first time.

B ack in the days when astronomical events were mysterious and therefore important, the sky *was* the calendar. The question wasn't so much *if* the sun would return, I suspect, but *when*. Yet the evidence suggests that the staggering effort put forth in pre-historic times to mark the seasons accurately went beyond merely practical considerations.

For example, many of the ancients ruins of the American Southwest have been shown to have an astronomical orientation. Among the more remote and intriguing of these is Chimney Rock, which rises above the pines of Southwest Colorado like a towering knobby ridge. Archeologists had long been puzzled by the sophisticated core-and-veneer masonry at the top of the ridge, typical of the sophisticated structures at Chaco, a hundred miles to the southwest. The mystery was compounded when scientists who surveyed the site in 1988 discovered that the buildings up on the ridge rested on solid bedrock. This meant that not only the stone and timbers, but also the soil and water for making the bricks, had been laboriously carried by hand up the 1,200 foot escarpment from the river valley below. Why?

Archeologists excavating the site discerned by chance that someone standing in the courtyard of the loftiest and most elaborate pueblo on the ridge could, on certain nights of the year, watch the moon rise directly between the two "chimneys" that stand further to the east. Could Chimney Rock have been a lunar observatory? Perhaps. But there was a hitch. The moon rises at a slightly different point on the horizon every month. Its position also changes from year to year, moving from north to south and back again following an 18.6 year cycle. At each end of its path it pauses for two years before beginning its return journey. Astronomers call this pause the "lunar standstill."

The archeologists studying the site in 1988 happened to witness the moonrise during just such a "standstill." This meant that the moon would soon begin to rise further south along the horizon, and it would then be sixteen years before the dramatic sightings became possible again.

The infrequency of the event—a two-year window once every sixteen years—was clearly a mark against the theory that Chimney Rock had been used by the Anasazi as a lunar observatory. But archeologist J. McKim Malville of the University of Colorado determined, by analyzing the tree rings of the beams used to construct the buildings, that the site had been active first in 1076, and then again in 1093, sixteen years later. Could it be mere coincidence that the northerly lunar standstills of the late eleventh century began in 1075 and 1094? Probably not.

The bigger question is, Why would the Anasazi care to track the moon so precisely in the first place? Yes, humans have been dazzled for millennia by the night sky and fascinated by the interplay of fixed stars and roving planets. Modern observances of Easter, Passover, and Ramadan are all dictated by lunar cycles. But the sixteen-year wobble in the moon's orbit can be of no practical use to anyone. So why haul heavy beams and tons of dirt and water up a mountainside just to keep track of it?

We'll never know for sure what part the moon played in the lives of the ancestral Pueblan people—they lacked a written language—but the effort they took to establish an observatory and a ceremonial center at the top of a towering ridge of inhospitable rock, many day's walk from the bustle of civilized Anasazi life, strikes me as remarkable testimony to their love of the heavens. To them, the heavenly orbs were gods. Beautiful, yes. Regular in their course, sometimes. Worthy of reverence? No doubt about it.

The moon is often visible from the heights of the ridge, but the last time it appeared in the gap was in 2004. The U.S. Forest Service, which manages Chimney Rock, arranged a series of night-hikes at that time to give visitors a chance to witness the event. I didn't make it down to see the show, alas.

See you there in 2022?

Watching the heavens has been a rigorous intellectual exercise since well before Babylonian times, of course. The discovery of a "sky disc" near the town of Nebra, Germany, in 1999, is a classic case in point. The disc, made of a rich, green-blue piece of copper thirty centimeters across, is riddled with stars, orbs, and crescent moons. It's been dated back to 1,600 B.C.E. and was originally thought to be a sort of portable Stonehenge. But German scientists determined in 2006 that  the function of the disc was more sophisticated than anyone had previously imagined. The disc helped "wise men" of those remote times determine when it was necessary to add the thirteenth lunar month to the solar year, bringing the two systems back into rough alignment. (A lunar year is eleven days shorter than the solar year, so the two systems are always going out of whack.)

No one can say for sure when star-gazers pushed astronomy and astrology to a deeper level—one in which the connections between inner and cosmic life began to come into sharper focus. We don't see those connections clearly, even today! A beautiful rendition of the times when such things were inextricably mixed can be found in the early minutes of Ermanno Olmi's film *Cammina Cammina* (*Keep Walking, Keep Walking*). The film chronicles the pilgrimage of a ragtag bunch of peasants, guided by their intrepid "holy man" and a Roman centurion who's been put out to pasture, as they follow a bright light that has streamed across the sky, fulfilling the prophesies. In the film's opening scenes we see Mel (short for Melchoir) prepare to sacrifice a little lamb to expiate the sins of a young woman who's come to him for help. That evening we watch as he uses some astronomical instruments to add a star to his canvas star chart—a deer hide draped across a couple of shrubs just beyond the campfire. When a huge white star rumbles across the heavens, everyone knows the event they've been waiting for has come to pass. For some, it will be the last star they take an interest in.

Olmi's original five-hour version, made for Italian television, has been lost, but the 171 minutes that remain are available on Netflix. They have more than enough stunning winter landscapes, crusty and humorous farmers and shepherds, lovely young maids, lavishly adorned magi, and learned, serious-minded youths to hold our interest. Olmi is a past master of the casual crowd scene, as anyone familiar with *Tree of the Wooden Clogs* will attest. In *Keep Walking* he binds these crowds to the landscape with its pastures, thickets, night skies, storms, river-crossings, and mountain paths. He also succeeds in individualizing quite a few of the pilgrims by a quirk, an episode, or a telling aside.

For the most part, these are poor, simple folk, downtrodden and eager to make contact, not with greater wealth or leisure, but with righteousness. The "holy man," Mel, wears the same

ADVENT REFLECTIONS   287

sheepskin rags as all the rest, though he's studied the heavens in great detail and knows the scriptures intimately. His little sidekick Ruppo finds the sacrifice of lambs distasteful and decides fairly early in the film that he doesn't want to be a priest after all, but he continues to dutifully haul out the huge book of Psalms, almost bigger than he is, whenever Mel wants to impress someone.

When the film was released in 1983, the *New York Times* described it as handsomely photographed but "almost intolerably solemn and tedious." Yet I've seen it twice, now, and each time found it astonishingly brilliant and subtle. It's not terribly Christian—Well, there were no Christians in those days—but it's not too Jewish, either. There are currents of energy, confusion, tenderness, conviction, and a vague reverence for it knows not what running all through it.

I probably don't need to tell you that the ragtag caravan ultimately finds the blessed manger. Yet the film remains focused on the pilgrims rather than the holy child. In fact, guided by a dream, Mel steals away from Bethlehem in the night, accompanied by his followers, and is later berated by one of them as a coward. He defends himself vehemently: "We shall build temples to celebrate the coming of God to earth."

His accuser replies scornfully, "Above all, you shall celebrate his death."

There is something uncannily thoughtful about the entire enterprise, and it's hard to imagine it was made for Italian TV. The film is dubbed (in Italian) which gives unusual richness to the voices, and makes them seem dignified and disembodied, like the voices in the Hercules films we used to watch on TV when we were kids.

In the course of a long career in the book business, John Toren has edited and designed scores of books, reviewed many, and written three or four. His articles have appeared in a range of publications including The *History Channel Magazine, Minnesota Monthly,* the *Minneapolis Star-Tribune,* the *Milwaukee Sentinel, Twin Cities Magazine,* and the *Minneapolis Observer.* He holds degrees in history and anthropology from the University of Minnesota and occasionally teaches a course in geography in its LearningLife program. He also writes and publishes his own quarterly magazine, *Macaroni*—now in its 104th issue. It received an Utne Independent Press Award for General Excellence in 2007.

You can visit John online at *macaronic-john.blogspot.com.*